CREATE A THRIVING
WORKSPACE

CREATE A
THRIVING WORKSPACE

---

7 essential design principles
for positive high-performance
physical work environments

ANETTA PIZAG

Published in Australia by Anetta Pizag
+61 414 085 408
www.pizag.com.au
anetta@pizag.com.au

First published in 2015

© Anetta Pizag 2015

www.createathrivingworkspace.com
info@createathrivingworkspace.com

All right reserved. Without limiting the rights under copyright above, no part of this publication may be reproduced, stored in a retrieval system, or transmitted in any form, or by any means (electronic, mechanical, photocopying, recording or otherwise) without the prior written permission of the publisher.

Author:	Pizag, Anetta
Title:	Create a Thriving Workspace: 7 essential design principles for positive high-performance physical work environments / Anetta Pizag.
ISBN:	978-0-9943013-0-7 (paperback)
Subjects:	Commercial buildings, Interior design, Success in business

Author photo by Julie Renouf (julierenouf.com.au)
Cover and internal design by Bo and Jelena Acimovic (jennyinforest.com)
Edited by Tamara Protassow (tamaraprotassow.com)
Editorial assistance by Erik Teichmann

Disclaimer
The material in this publication is of the nature of general comment only, and does not represent professional advice. It is not intended to provide specific guidance for particular circumstances and it should not be relied on as the basis for any decision to take action or not take action on any matter which it covers. Readers should obtain professional advice where appropriate, before making any such decision. To the maximum extent permitted by law, the author and publisher disclaim all responsibility and liability to any person, arising directly or indirectly from any person taking or not taking action based on the information in this publication.

I dedicate this book to:

This book is dedicated to everyone who is eager to make a difference in this world, and wants to be the best version of themselves both at work and in life.

This book is also for those who believe that work should be a fulfilling and meaningful part of life, and who want to give themselves and those around them the best chance to achieve this.

Table of Contents

Let's Begin 11
  The space is important 11
  Where it all started 12
  Let's speak the same language 14
  Work is changing 15
  Workspaces are lagging behind 17
  Where is the evidence? 20
  It's easy to get lost in the jungle 22
  The way forward 23
  What makes a high-performance workplace 24

Principle 1: Create Space for a VISIONARY Business 27
  The big picture 29
  Key design strategies 34
    Strategy 1: Invite people on an exciting journey 34
    Strategy 2: Let your company's values shine 38
    Strategy 3: Make your workspace a part of your brand 41
    Strategy 4: Stay in harmony with the environment 46
  Putting things into practice 57

Principle 2: Create Space for a SMART Business 63
  Why should we be smart? 65
  Key design strategies 73
    Strategy 1: Promote the use of the right work tools 73
    Strategy 2: Put your data in the right place 77

Strategy 3: Create a well-functioning floor layout	80
Strategy 4: Support flexible ways of working	84
Strategy 5: Make the most of Activity-Based Working	89
Strategy 6: Create 'neighbourhoods'	92
Putting things into practice	96

Principle 3: Create Space for a PRODUCTIVE Business — 103

Productivity matters	105
Key design strategies	112
Strategy 1: Provide clean, fresh air	112
Strategy 2: Make people feel comfortable	115
Strategy 3: Provide good quality lighting	119
Strategy 4: Minimise distractions and interruptions	126
Strategy 5: Reduce sources of negative thoughts and feelings	129
Strategy 6: Promote good posture, movement and exercise	135
Strategy 7: Encourage productive habits	140
Strategy 8: Provide opportunities for quality breaks	142
Putting things into practice	146

Principle 4: Create Space for a DIVERSIFIED Business — 151

Why do we need diversity	153
Key design strategies	160
Strategy 1: Press people's 'genius' button	160
Strategy 2: Allow people get into the right 'work mode'	163
Strategy 3: Promote the right sort of thinking	167
Strategy 4: Support different types of interaction	175
Strategy 5: Accommodate different personalities	180
Strategy 6: Accommodate different work styles	183
Putting things into practice	188

Principle 5: Create Space for a CARING Business — 195

- Why should we care? — 197
- Key design strategies — 205
  - Strategy 1: Create a healthy workplace — 205
  - Strategy 2: Create a pleasant and harmonious space — 210
  - Strategy 3: Boost positive emotions and happiness — 213
  - Strategy 4: Help people to connect with the space — 218
  - Strategy 5: Promote caring relationships — 222
  - Strategy 6: Create a positive overall experience — 224
- Putting things into practice — 227

Principle 6: Create Space for an ENGAGING Business — 235

- Why should we engage? — 237
- Key design strategies — 244
  - Strategy 1: Set the foundations for a strong community — 244
  - Strategy 2: Make the workplace open and transparent — 249
  - Strategy 3: Provide a sense of ownership and influence — 252
  - Strategy 4: Let your team play and have fun — 258
  - Strategy 5: Integrate work and life — 262
  - Strategy 6: Smooth out cultural differences — 266
- Putting things into practice — 271

Principle 7: Create Space for an EVOLVING Business — 279

- Why should we evolve? — 281
- Key design strategies — 288
  - Strategy 1: Bring your people on board — 288
  - Strategy 2: Create spaces that are easy to change — 294
  - Strategy 3: Test, evaluate and refine the design as you go — 300

Strategy 4: Consider people working remotely	305
Strategy 5: Get ready for coworking	310
Putting things into practice	318

Putting the Pieces Together — 321

Working like an orchestra	321
You have many resources	323
Bridging the gap	324
Your investment	329
The future	330
Related Readings	333
Acknowledgements	349
About Anetta Pizag	350
Keep in touch	351

LET'S BEGIN

Creating a high-performance workplace can be a daunting task, but it doesn't need to be. If you know where you are going, and have the roadmap to get there, not only are you more likely to find your destination, but you will enjoy the journey more. You have now made the first step.

The space is important

The spaces we inhabit greatly influence our lives and who we are. They can enhance our life experiences and form a part of our identity, as we often feel a special connection to particular spaces. At their best, they provide us with inspiration, energy, and support to do what we aim to do.

What we see, hear, smell and touch around us, whether in nature or in the built environment, influences how we think, feel and act. As Winston Churchill famously said, 'we shape our buildings and afterwards our buildings shape us'.

Many wonderful pieces of art wouldn't have been produced and many scientific breakthroughs wouldn't have happened if their creators weren't in the right place to experience some sort of inspiration or epiphany. (A famous example is the doctor Jonas Salk, inventor of the polio vaccine, who experienced the key insights that led to the creation of the vaccine while taking a break from work in an Italian monastery.)

We also know from personal experience that we are different people in different places. Just think about where you go to recharge, to connect with friends, or to develop a deeper connection with yourself. Places can mean so much to us that we are willing to invest a great deal of money and time to visit or to live there. Many of us work hard for years or decades to buy that dream house, or reward ourselves with holidays to special destinations.

To be at our best, it's important for us to be in the right space, and this is also the case for workspaces. A well-designed or well-chosen space helps us to be in the right frame of mind, and to perform to the best of our abilities. Of course, no place can guarantee that things will always work out the way we want, but a space with the right features can make it much more likely that they will.

Where it all started

My best childhood memories take me back to places I loved: meadows, lakesides, special streets, buildings and rooms. The places I grew up in played an important role in who I became. Even today, when I find myself in places resembling those in my childhood, cherished memories instantly resurface.

As I grew older, I became fascinated by the possibility of creating amazing places through the marriage of art and science, places where people might have similarly powerful, memorable experiences. I studied architecture in Hungary, driven by a dream of creating beautiful, sustainable, high quality spaces. However, it wasn't yet clear for me what 'quality space' really meant, so I spent my studies and much of my career uncovering the answers to this question.

I then worked in architectural practices in the Netherlands, New Zealand and Australia. While I had valuable experiences and worked with the most inspiring people, the traditional architectural viewpoint about space design – seeing the building as a means to an end, a functional piece of art – left me with a void. I sensed that there was more to know about creating quality environments, so I decided to explore other disciplines.

For a few years I worked as an environmental consultant, advising other architects about designing environmentally efficient buildings. However, both as a consultant and as an architect, I saw how often the quality of a building was compromised, because members of design teams pursued different agendas, followed rigid processes, and made ill-considered decisions. (I've seen several buildings, for example, that turned out to be engineering masterpieces but were rather unpleasant places to be in.)

I love learning. Throughout my career I've studied a wide range of subjects to better understand the relationship between people, places and performance. I've learnt, for example, about how buildings can make people sick, how the environment can help people to learn better, and how we can design high-performance, people-centred spaces with the aid of science. I've also studied leadership skills, and what makes businesses succeed.

Studying neuro-linguistic programming (NLP), a form of psychology, was a turning point for me. As I learnt about the important role of people's thoughts and emotions in what they can achieve, I started to look at space design differently, kind of inside out. I realised that the purpose of a building was not only to be visually attractive, functional and environmentally efficient, but most importantly, it was to help the people who use it have an experience in the space that works for them.

Understanding people's relationship with their work environment was particularly intriguing for me. I have spent a large part of my work life in corporate offices, many of which made it difficult for me to think and work at my best. I also visited many other offices, and realised what dysfunctional, unpleasant, or even depressing places many people work, and in fact spend most of their lives in.

I became dedicated to doing something about this, creating workplaces that people actually love to go to and where they can truly thrive. I knew that if I succeeded, it would be a win-win-win for all involved: the people using the space, the organisation and the broader environment. This is when a new chapter in my career began, and when the idea for this book took root.

Let's speak the same language

In *Create a Thriving Workspace*, I intend to show you how you can enhance the performance of your business by creating an environment that supports your people's best work. But before getting into detail, let me clarify a few fundamental terms I'll use throughout this book:

- **Thriving:** This is a wonderful word which marries two powerful concepts – *feeling* and *performing* brilliantly – emphasising that the two go hand-in-hand. A thriving person lives up to their potential while having an amazing time. A thriving business enjoys great success while maintaining a positive, vibrant atmosphere. And a thriving workspace is a place that helps all these things happen.

- **People:** Despite this book being about workplaces and their occupants, you'll notice that I rarely mention the words *employee, staff* or *workforce*. Instead, I refer to them as *team members, workers* or simply *your people*. In my opinion these terms sound more respectful and better acknowledge people as individuals. But most importantly, workplace occupants also include members of non-hierarchical organisations, as well as coworkers, leaders, managers, and anyone else using the workplace.

- **Workplace:** I won't mention the word *office* a lot either. For many people, *office* means an institutional-looking and dispiriting place that is more designed around the perceived needs of the business than the needs of people. Furthermore, this book looks at workplaces in a much broader sense than just offices, recognising that knowledge work can take place in a wide variety of places.

- **Business performance:** Well, it means different things for different businesses, so it's up to you to define. What's most important for your business? Generating higher profits? Growing your brand? Attracting and retaining top talent? Providing an outstanding quality service? Solving a problem that previously seemed insoluble? Dealing with happy clients? Changing lives? Attracting exciting new opportunities? Being surrounded by a dedicated and passionate team? Or perhaps all of these?

- **Work performance:** What do your people need to achieve to make these things happen? What skills do they need to master? How do they need to think and behave in order to propel your business forward?

- **Knowledge workers:** If you're reading this book, it's extremely likely you're one of us: a person whose job is to solve non-routine problems, and whose greatest assets – your ideas, experience and knowledge – lie in your head. You are one of the people I wrote this book for and about.

Let me make it clear upfront: there's no point in me telling you how to create a space where people can complete routine tasks quicker and more accurately. And I'm certainly not going to talk about how to fit the largest number of people into the smallest possible space to save on rent (and wreck productivity into the bargain), because – despite some business owners and accountants thinking otherwise – that's a shockingly ineffective approach.

What you'll read about in this book is the ins and outs of creating a space where knowledge workers can turn their thoughts into results – whether developing or delivering products or services – in the most effective way, while enjoying what they do.

Work is changing

If a person from the year 2000 was suddenly transported to one of today's typical workspaces, they might not notice radical changes just by looking at the space, but they would certainly be astounded to see how differently people actually work now.

Business and work are changing

The advancement of information sharing has transformed the way we work. Using web-based and mobile technologies, most of us can now work pretty much anywhere and anytime, while staying connected to our organisation. New business models are emerging as online networking opportunities, outsourcing and remote working have transformed how teams are formed and work together.

New generations are reaching the workforce, bringing their own set of expectations and habits; they seek fun and freedom of choice, demand transparency, and want to be treated as equals. Boundaries between work and life are becoming blurred; people are looking to integrate work with their personal lives, and to be surrounded by friends at work. They strive for meaningful and enjoyable work, expect their organisations to demonstrate environmental and social responsibility, and are rarely willing to stay in an unsatisfying job for long.

Work is becoming more collaborative, and we can see a shift in emphasis from analytical to creative work. Play is becoming an integral activity in many organisations; games are used to enhance learning, problem solving and innovation.

Living up to new challenges

Instant communication and easy access to information impose new demands on us. Work is getting increasingly complex and requires constant learning. We need to deal with information overload, interruptions, and more time pressure than ever before.

To work well, we need to be able to focus amidst distractions, plan and manage our time and tasks effectively, and prioritise and delegate well. We also need to master a new set of skills and adopt new attitudes. Some of the most highly valued skills in today's business are non-technical, such as creativity, decision making and resourcefulness, along with empathy, networking, developing relationships, and working well in teams. And the most favoured attitudes include passion, motivation and confidence, as well as authenticity, flexibility, resilience, and commitment to the organisation's mission.

Organisations need to keep up

In order to deal with constant change and to remain competitive, organisations need to be lean, agile, and able to manage teams that are diverse in terms of age, background and skill-set. To attract and retain ideal candidates and to retain high performers, leaders need to accommodate these people's expectations. Common expectations include, for example, reducing hierarchy, practising open communication, keeping up-to-date with technology, and offering flexible work arrangements.

The workspace needs to change too

Workspace design needs to respond to these changes and challenges, and support team members in all positions to meet the demands of modern work.

The way we use the workplace is also shifting. Many are now geared towards promoting social interaction and providing inspiration for workers, since in our technology-dominated world people tend to be hungry for personal connection and emotional support. Furthermore, more and more workplaces are turning into 'hybrid' spaces, also accommodating retail, education or hospitality facilities.

As leaders recognise that the physical space can enhance the profile of the business, and thus attract the loyalty of workers and customers, the best workplaces are now designed to communicate key messages – such as the organisation's culture and mission – to anyone coming through the door.

Workspaces are lagging behind

As leaders start to recognise the potential of the physical space, more and more workplaces are being built or upgraded to provide a better environment to workers. But there is a long way to go, and sadly, inadequate, old-style offices are still the norm. The workspaces that served organisations relatively well over the past several decades are becoming increasingly unfit to support new ways of working, and even hinder both workers and businesses from reaching their full potential.

Typically, more effort is being put into making workspaces 'functional' than into supporting people's needs, and as a result, many office dwellers find themselves having to work in unpleasant and unhealthy conditions. (When people ask me what I do, and I tell them that I help create workplaces where people can work better and feel happier, they often reply, 'That's radical!' or, 'Good luck!'.) This is particularly alarming, if you consider that most people spend more time at work than in any other place, including their own living room.

Substandard working conditions disengage people and undermine their performance[1], and businesses pay a high price for this, including losing talent, opportunities, and reputation. As someone I know put it, 'You give someone a junk environment, you're going to get junk performance.'

Common mistakes

We all want to work in better environments. How come there's such a gap between our intentions and the reality?

Most workers have been conditioned that the workplace is not for them but for the 'organisation', so until recently, it didn't occur to them to strive for better work environments. (It's puzzling to see how much effort some people put into keeping their gadgets up to date, but are ready to settle for last-century workplaces.)

Designers and decision makers often set the wrong priorities. They tend to put more attention into reducing accommodation costs than into supporting workers' performance, despite the fact that accommodation costs are only a small fraction of what an average company pays for wages. They waste people's precious talent – the force that could propel the business forward – rather than pay a bit more for the space. (If you had a Ferrari, would you want to pull it with horses to save on petrol?)

Some business owners, on the other hand, have the right intentions, but don't quite know what they want. Astonishingly, many are ready to part with a large sum of money without having any idea of the results they are after. When asked the question, 'How will you know that your investment has been successful?' they seem lost. Also, they often choose ineffective design strategies: doing what they have always done, doing what has worked for other organisations, or falling for the hottest trend – all without considering the broader consequences of their decisions.

---

1 Here are a couple of devastating performance statistics about issues that could be greatly improved through better workspace design: Australians rank second last among their peers on the 2013 Global Innovation Index. The average worker loses over two productive hours a day due to unnecessary distractions. Most organisations operate at around 55-60% of their potential.

Misconceptions

There are a number of misconceptions floating around that lead to misguided decisions, such as:

- Work performance is a management issue; the space doesn't make much difference.

- Creating a high-performance workplace must be expensive, and is unlikely to be worth the investment.

- We probably have to rip out our current fitout and start things from scratch.

- We are already doing the right thing; we have a breakout space with a fish tank and bean bags, a ping-pong table, and a centralised utility room.

- Spending money on making things nice for people is a luxury.

And I also hear unfounded objections that stop people from doing the work on their space, for example:

- We have too many limitations; there are many things we can't change.

- There is not enough information about which design solutions work.

- You cannot plan people's behaviour, so how could you make them work better?

- Designing a great workplace is just common sense; there's no need to think too much about it.

- We are not Google; we don't have their budget, nor do we want to work in a theme park.

Do any of these sound familiar? I trust that after reading this book you will feel clearer and more confident about what you can actually achieve with the resources you have, and understand your opportunities to make a real difference.

Where is the evidence?

- A vast amount of research information is available for us to better understand the relationship between the physical space and high performance. Modern science confirms what we already know from personal experience: that the qualities of our environment do matter; our emotions, thoughts and actions are not only shaped by our personality, relationships, history and other personal circumstances, but also by our surroundings.

- But most importantly, research provides a valuable resource for designing better work environments. Here is an example:

💡 Zoo design is showing the way

To explore what a space needs to be like in order to make people feel well, researchers have looked at the design of zoos. Zoos have dramatically transformed over the past decades. You may remember visiting some as a child, and seeing sad animals locked in tiny cages. Today, more and more zoos make the effort to place their animals into a setting as close as possible to their natural habitat. The enclosures are now much larger and more diversified, giving the animals control over their behaviour. They can choose to be within sight or hide; they can forage, play or rest, just like they would do in nature. And in some places, it's the visitors who are enclosed, and the animals roam free.

What led to this change in zoo design? It was the realisation that an animal might stay alive in a barren cage, but it won't flourish. Scientists now know that animals can only thrive in environments that are natural to them, and which allows them to feel well – physically, mentally and socially.[2] Are zoo designers ahead of the game? Well, there's certainly a lot we can learn from them.

---

2 'Biologist Stephen Boyden (1971) defines the optimum healthy environment as "the conditions which tend to promote or permit an animal optimal physiological, mental, and social performance in its natural or 'evolutionary' environment."' – as stated on the website of Whole Building Design Guide.

We have a lot of similarities to animals, in that we can only realise our potential in spaces that suit our evolutionary needs. Our environment not only needs to be habitable – being healthy, having clean air, and providing opportunity to rest – but it also needs to help us to feel well, find fulfilment and pursue a high quality life.

After studying what sort of environmental conditions are required for animals and people to feel well, environmental psychologists and biologists have identified a set of criteria that buildings should aim to fulfil. These include[3]:

- Providing opportunities for spontaneous social encounters
- Providing opportunities for us to rest, physically and mentally
- Allowing us to find privacy, and to be alone or mix with others as desired
- Offering connection to nature
- Providing opportunities for movement and exercise
- Having sound levels that are neither too high nor too low
- Being aesthetic, interesting and diverse environments, engaging our senses
- Providing us with a sense of social equality
- Allowing us to stay comfortable
- Making it easy to find our way around

---

3 As outlined on the website of Whole Building Design Guide. (See Related Readings at the end of this book.)

It's easy to get lost in the jungle

People often ask me, **'So what's the Magic Pill? What is the one thing that makes workplaces work?'** My answer is rarely what they expect; it's not about taking a side in one of the hot debates (such as whether open-plan offices are better than private offices), or picking a favourite trend (like using standing desks).

As every business and every team is unique, you can't expect to find universal design solutions for your specific needs. For me, the magic pill is: asking the right questions, talking to the right people, learning from the best resources, and considering everything that's important for the business and everyone associated with it. **In short, for your workspace design project to succeed, you need to make well-informed decisions.**

However, if you are ready to get started, you might find it challenging to find trusted advice and answers to your questions. Chances are that you are also unsure about how far your budget can take you, and what sort of results and returns you can anticipate. **To navigate through the complexity of a workspace design project, it's best to follow a framework or some sort of expert guidance.**

The difficulty is that currently there is no well-established design model for creating high-performance work environments. When you look at publications or search online, what you find is lots of scattered ideas, many of which are contradictory, fashion-driven, biased, or only suitable for specific types of businesses. There's an abundance of exciting theoretical ideas, but few practical solutions.

High quality, reliable information is hard to find, as it is mostly published in academic literature. These publications also tend to be hard to digest, written by and for designers and scholars, in their own jargon.

You might assume that the architects or interior designers you work with should be able to provide the answers and guidance you need; however, they are rarely the right people for this role (even though many of them would disagree). This is not so surprising if you consider that designing an attractive-looking, functional and buildable fitout requires a whole different skill-set from providing advice on how your workspace could make your team members feel, think and work better, in alignment with the strategy and culture of your business.

Some architectural and workplace consulting firms do offer expert Workplace Strategy advice, but this service can be extremely costly and time consuming, as the process usually involves extensive project-specific research conducted by a large team of consultants. Only big businesses can afford such fees, and so smaller ones miss out on this service.

In short, there are no easy resources showing business owners, in a structured manner, what they need to know about creating a well-designed, tailored workspace. The intention of this book is to fill this gap.

The way forward

This book offers a comprehensive range of practical and powerful strategies for creating thriving physical work environments. We will look at aspects of performance and productivity that are most relevant to today's businesses – such as innovation, collaboration, and trusting relationships – and explore the key principles that make workspaces, as well as businesses, highly successful.

Create a Thriving Workspace is neither a book of inspirational ideas, nor a book about management or psychology; however, it ventures into these fields and presents design strategies in context. The strategies outlined in this book can benefit new building and interior projects, as well as upgrades and relocations. Furthermore, you will learn to make better choices about where and how you and your teams work, and thus improve your results without even changing your physical space. Finally, this book will prepare you to effectively collaborate with consultants and contractors involved in your workspace project.

Why do you need to know about this?

'Shouldn't I just leave all this to the specialists?' you may ask. Going down the traditional path – leaving the design to the 'experts' and staying out of their way – is likely to lead to disappointment. And if they are true professionals, they might even refuse to work with you under such conditions.

Even if you engage the best professionals, your active participation in the design process is imperative. You are the expert on your own business, so the knowledge you share with your consulting team will form the foundation of the design. You will also need to take responsibility for your decisions; designers can give you suggestions, but at the end of the day, you and your decision-making team will sign off on the plans.

What makes a high-performance workplace

When looking at the most successful, consistently high-performing businesses, including how their workplaces are designed and how their people work there, we can find some recurring patterns. These organisations all possess the seven qualities described below, which are also reflected in and supported by the way their work environments are designed:

1. VISIONARY – They pursue a powerful vision for the business, follow a clear set of values, and have a strong brand. Their workspaces send inspiring messages about the organisation – who they are and what they stand for – which helps motivate their people, align their teams, and attract the right talent and business opportunities.

2. SMART – They have effective systems, processes and technology in place to optimise communication and delivery of work. Their workspaces are designed to make it easy for people to access all the resources they need – including other people, information, work tools and technology – so that they can communicate better, collaborate better, and work more intelligently.

3. PRODUCTIVE – They give their people the best support to be able to work efficiently. Their workplaces are comfortable and minimise negative influences such as distractions and stress, providing people with the best conditions to focus and think clearly.

4. DIVERSIFIED – They nurture diverse teams, knowing that diversity fuels problem solving and innovation, and promotes a culture of respect. Their workplaces allow everyone to work effectively, using different skills and engaging in different activities, regardless of their age, personality or preferred work style.

5. CARING – They genuinely care about their team members and customers, and in turn, their people care about the company more and are happy to work harder. Their work environments are healthy and attractive, and promote a positive work experience; they are places people actually want to go, and where they find it easier to excel.

6. ENGAGING – They nurture a vibrant culture where people feel they belong, and are simply great places to work. Their workspaces assist people in building trusting relationships, allow them to have fun, and serve as a home for a flourishing work community of highly engaged and proactive team members who work brilliantly together and also deliver an outstanding customer experience.

7. EVOLVING – They not only keep up with, but thrive on change. And as they never see their business strategies as 'finished', they don't see their workplaces as finished either. They operate in flexible, frequently-changing environments that make it easy for people to constantly evolve the way they work in response to new opportunities and challenges.

These companies reap the fruit of their efforts on many levels, showing us what a thriving workplace can achieve. Their people are more productive, have more breakthrough ideas, and solve problems better. They work in better spirits, are more loyal and committed, and are happy to go the extra mile. Team members trust each other more, support each other better, and communicate and collaborate more effectively. The company improves its reputation and market position as a result of providing a higher quality service and improved client experience. Costs are reduced and profits are increased through major improvements in work efficiency, attracting and retaining top talent, and making more and better sales. Work becomes more enjoyable and rewarding for anyone associated with the business.

Here's the recipe

The way I see it, **these seven qualities are benchmarks of excellence in workplace design.** If you compare the workspaces of, say, a booming tech-development company like Google and a successful bank like NAB, you'll find that they look vastly different. However, both of them do a wonderful job in demonstrating these qualities – in their own ways.

By considering these seven qualities whenever you have a decision to make about your workspace, you can ensure that by the end of the day, every single aspect of the physical space – e.g. colours, textures, materials, lights, sounds, room layouts, furniture, technology and media – will work towards the flourishing of your business.

I'm about to show you exactly how to do it.

PRINCIPLE 1

VISIONARY

CREATE SPACE FOR A VISIONARY BUSINESS

Creating a workspace that embodies the DNA of your organisation

Who are we? Why are we here? What is important to us? What difference are we making? ... Creating a 'Visionary' workspace is about asking these big questions and then translating the answers into timber and steel, furniture and paint – the physical environment. A space that embodies the essence and purpose of your business not only unifies people and makes them a stronger team, but keeps everyone on track on the company's journey towards creating a better future for its clients, members and stakeholders.

The big picture

The 'visionary' workplace

By looking at the place where a person lives, we can find out a lot about them: Are they shy or outgoing? Rebellious or conforming? Adventurous or creatures of habit? Loners or team players? What are their interests and hobbies? Do they make their own path or follow others? Are they pursuing clear goals or just drifting around? ... And we get a sense of how well we would probably get along.

Similarly, when looking around a workplace, we tend to draw conclusions about the organisation: who their members are, what is important to them, how they aim to improve people's lives, and what sort of experience they create for their own teams as well as their clients through their products, services, and the way they do business.

In a 'visionary' workplace these messages reflect the truth and highlight the best of the business. The space embodies the organisation's purpose, values and brand. Everything people see and feel in the space aligns with, and even enhances, what they already know about the business.

Why is this important?

Both as workers and as customers, we don't just want to make transactions; we want to engage with organisations that stand for something bigger than themselves – a worthwhile cause. We want to feel that through our work or purchase we contribute to a happier, fairer, more inspiring world. We want to be on a journey with those who are on our side, who share our standards, beliefs and passions.

To attract committed people, your businesses needs to present itself clearly and consistently across all communication platforms, including the work environment; it needs to demonstrate the values, beliefs and personalities you seek to attract. This will make it easier for your clients to get to know and trust you, and for your team members to commit to your vision. Imagine dealing with people who just know they are in the right place as soon as they come through the door, whether for the first time or for the thousandth time.

Miscommunication happens

Relatively few organisations operate in workspaces that speak the same 'language' as they do. The question I often ask of leaders, 'What messages do you aim to communicate through the space to your teams, clients and the market?' usually remains unanswered.

It's a common misconception that people don't need constant reinforcement of what the business aims to achieve; it's assumed that those who are in touch with the business should already be clear about that.

Many leaders believe that in order to articulate who they are as a business, all they need to do is market their business well, engage in conversations with their stakeholders, and offer products or services that speak for themselves. These are of course important. However, those leaders fail to recognise that the workplace also has its role in this process – that it essentially acts as a 'message board', speaking either for or against them.

Some organisations don't have clearly defined goals, values and brands, so they simply don't have much of an identity to portray. In contrast, others have solid ideas about who they are, but are confused about how to capture certain elements of their identity through building and interior design. (For example, some people seem to be convinced that the only way to present a clean-cut image[1] is to create a sterile-looking environment, or that the only way to incorporate the brand is to use the company's corporate colours throughout the space, regardless how those colours influence people's psychology.)

---

1   It's not uncommon that presenting a respectable, authoritative, clean-cut image is the main driver for designing buildings with their facades fully clad with unshaded glass. While recent energy efficiency regulations make it very difficult for such building designs to obtain a permit in Australia, some business owners and developers are still aiming to create buildings that look as close to a shiny glass box as possible.

Misleading workspaces

As a result, most workplaces express messages which are incongruent with the organisation's purpose, values and brand. Even if leaders communicate the most powerful messages through words, this lack of congruence can weaken their meaning!

For example, I know organisations that care about the resolution of environmental issues, but their workspaces waste resources such as energy and water, and send mixed messages about sustainable living and working practices. (I worked for a company in the environmental sector that encouraged its employees to cycle to work, but we were not allowed to store our bikes in the office, because that would look unprofessional.)

I have seen the workplaces of promising start-ups where confidence and belief in the company's success were among the most appreciated personal attributes of the team. However, their office suggested that the organisation didn't believe in itself. (The interior showed no sign of planning; every element was thrown together as a quick reaction to urgent needs of accommodating extra staff or equipment. The space communicated scarcity; it was only fitted with the bare essentials, as if spending even a little time and money on making the office nice was something the company couldn't afford.)

And when you see all those workplaces that look alike, with no character, you just can't get a sense of the people who work there. These spaces leave us with a feeling of void – a bit like talking to a machine instead of a real person when making a phone call.

These workplaces can erode relationships with anyone coming in. Workers may get inconsistent messages about the vision of the business, and about what sort of behaviour and attitude is expected from them. This can lead to a lack of direction, conflict and indifference – all enemies of high performance. And clients or prospects may get mixed messages about what the business really stands for and struggle to build a connection with the brand.

In such environments, businesses often struggle to attract the right people (staff, clients and business partners) and opportunities, or keep attracting the wrong ones. Clients are more likely to see the business as a commodity, so it is forced to compete on price. The space can even undermine the reputation of the business, and raise questions about its integrity.

> ### 💡 Saying 'no' to my heroes
>
> I've never in the past applied for a job without researching the employer and checking out if their vision and values aligned with mine. It was always important for me that the company I worked for was committed to creating healthy, aesthetic, green environments. I was competitive; I got an offer after most of my interviews. However, I stopped counting how many times I needed to say 'no' to employers that I had previously seen as heroes, because their workplaces didn't at all reflect the values they claimed to have. While they took pride in creating high quality architecture, they worked in dark, stuffy, uninspiring offices.
>
> Some may perceive this attitude as superficial judgement, or maybe even arrogance. But would you trust working with building professionals whose own workspace was clearly a low priority for them? And how enthusiastic would you be about joining their teams?

Following our calling, finding our fellows

We all strive to make a difference in our lives, to make this world a better place somehow. But the extent to which are we able to fulfil our purpose through work varies. We view our work either as a 'job', a 'career', or a 'mission' / 'calling'. Those with a 'job' only work to make a living, and they look forward to being somewhere else after work where real life happens. Those who pursue a 'career' are motivated to learn, and they want to improve their skills and succeed. But only those who see their work as a 'mission' or 'calling' find their work truly fulfilling, knowing that they are contributing to something meaningful.

We all know that developing a compelling business vision and a powerful brand identity require effort; so does setting up a work environment that reflects all of these. But the payback is huge, as shown by the results of companies like LEGO or Pixar, whose workplaces are extensions of the company's vision.

Visionary leaders know that a workplace that embodies the DNA of the organisation is better at attracting the kind of people and opportunities that will advance the business, and contributes to a positive customer experience.

Team members are more motivated, know their direction, and set better priorities, with the result that they need less management. They work in greater synergy and with a stronger sense of purpose. What's more, they tend to be more involved in maintaining a dynamic and inspiring environment. With the space and the people mutually supporting each other, the business has the potential to gain unprecedented momentum.

You not only need a clear vision and goals for your business, but also for creating your workplace. Designing a building or a new fitout can be a complex process with unexpected twists and turns. It requires coordination between many parties (users, consultants, suppliers, contractors, authorities, etc.), and even if everything is carefully planned, you often come across unforeseen issues to deal with. You often need to work under time pressure and make quick decisions. Developing a set of specific goals and guidelines for your design project right at the beginning will help you make better choices throughout this process, and create a workspace that you and your teams can be really proud of.

> ### 💡 And then saying 'yes'
>
> Eventually I got an offer from a company I was happy to say 'yes' to. As soon as I entered the office, I got the impression that this environmental consultancy walked the talk, and it cemented my trust in it. The space had plenty of daylight, lots of indoor plants, design features to improve energy efficiency, and an elaborate waste recycling system. Most of the materials and products were recycled or reused, but their creative use made the space look attractive and fresh. It was a green workplace with an honest and easy-going atmosphere. After settling into this environment, I wasn't surprised to find myself in a team of diverse but like-minded people, all living an active and environmentally conscious lifestyle (both at work and at home) as second nature. I had finally found a team where I belonged.

Key design strategies

Key design strategies for creating a 'visionary' environment:

1. Invite people on an exciting journey
2. Let your company's values shine
3. Make your workspace a part of your brand
4. Stay in harmony with the environment

By adopting these strategies, your workspace will become a powerful communication tool as well as a source of inspiration for your team members and clients. In your new space, you will find it easier to attract well-aligned people and exciting opportunities. Your teams will become more motivated and cohesive, and will work with greater focus towards a shared vision.

To progress well towards this vision on a day-to-day basis, your people will need to be able to communicate seamlessly and organise their work efficiently. The associated strategies will be introduced in the following chapter, Principle 2: Smart.

Strategy 1:
Invite people on an exciting journey

Breaking the mould

'Doing good can help improve your prospects, your profits and your business; and it can change the world.' – says Richard Branson, founder of Virgin Group, in his book *Screw Business as Usual*.

Branson is known for an uninhibited and rebellious nature that some find controversial. But what he stands for is magnetic: revolutionising how business is done by shifting the focus from short-term financial goals towards repairing the damage to the environment, elevating humanity and enriching the life of everyone affected by the business. He believes – and his enterprises testify – that pursuing these goals will naturally improve the profitability of a business, and that the best way to get there is by pushing boundaries, focusing on the best in people and having fun.

Virgin constantly raises the bar of customer experience. Their facilities – from airport terminals to gyms, from retail outlets to offices – are all shining examples of what Virgin stands for. They are welcoming, friendly, innovative spaces that stand out from the crowd, designed to operate efficiently and to invite people to do business 'the Virgin way'. (Some of the messages you can read on the walls in Virgin's offices include: 'I can see you workin' good', 'Life's too short for boring', and 'Your journey into space starts here'.)

Virgin is a business with a clear purpose which you can see and feel in their facilities.

Meaningful work boosts performance

But what exactly is the purpose of a business? Purpose is the impact it aims to create beyond making profit, the way it wants to enhance people's lives. This is the primary reason why you and your colleagues started or got involved in the business in the first place, and a big part of why you want to go to work each day. This is the answer to the questions: What's the ultimate goal you're all striving towards? How do you make a difference? What are you and your teams most passionate about?

Purpose is a key part of your business and workplace strategy. Don't move on before you find answers that touch something deep inside you and your team members. Once you've nailed it, you'll be ready to create a space that sends the right messages to everyone who walks in.

Communicating your business purpose clearly and consistently – including how your workplace looks and feels – will certainly strike a chord with those whose personal mission or calling aligns with your organisation's objectives. When we work with meaning and a strong sense of purpose, we are more driven to live up to our potential and thus perform better. We work with passion and pride, and are willing to go the extra mile. We are still affected by challenges, as everyone is, but are better equipped to deal with them.

We don't need to be superheroes to qualify for the badge of pursuing a mission or calling. When our team works towards an inspiring goal, and we understand how our contribution moves things forward, even a simple job can be fulfilling.²

💡 Let's have some scary goals!

Love, fear and high performance was a keynote speech I attended given by Michael Rennie, Managing Partner of McKinsey & Company.

Rennie talked about how he had been trying to understand the drivers of human performance throughout his career. The answer he found is very simple and consistent across cultures: there needs to be a big, scary, almost impossible, meaningful goal, as well as a supportive, trusting, caring team environment. If the goal is not exciting enough it just doesn't bring out the best in the team.

He also asked the audience, 'If you think back on your career, think of a time that you describe as a peak performance experience, what was there more of or less of? What was different about it?' Interestingly, the answers coming back from the room matched his experience, as well as with the findings of 10 years' and $30m worth of research.

When these two things – 'love' and 'fear' – line up, the performance increase is substantial. A lot of research shows that productivity of labour in factories nearly doubles, and in knowledge-based jobs it increases by 5 to 8 times!

---

2 This is well illustrated by the popular urban legend: 'President John F. Kennedy was visiting NASA headquarters for the first time, in 1961. While touring the facility, he introduced himself to a janitor who was mopping the floor and asked him what he did at NASA. The janitor replied, "I'm helping put a man on the moon!"'

The role of the workplace

A well-designed workspace helps people develop a stronger sense of purpose at work. The best workplaces embody what their users stand for and reflect their enthusiasm. When we walk into a workplace like this, we're immediately reminded of why we are there, and the difference our work makes. Furthermore, these spaces strengthen our belief that we can in fact hit those 'scary big' goals, and help us develop a sense of camaraderie by reinforcing that we are all on the same journey. Beyond inspiring us to perform better, these spaces attract new talent, clients and business partners who want to be part of the same vision.

Design suggestions

- Express your business vision and mission throughout the space. Decorate your walls with images, graphics and statements that showcase your enthusiasm and illustrate how your organisation makes this world a better place. These might be, for example, simple words (perhaps presented as wall art), photos of those who benefit from your contribution, and display boards of completed as well as future projects, along with inspiring examples to follow.

- If your niche allows, integrate your products or services into the fitout, or create opportunities for visitors to get a taster of what you do when they come in. (For example, The office of the Automotive Aftermarket Industry Association in Maryland, US, has created a car-themed office with a 1955 Nash Metropolitan automobile serving as the reception desk, and with artworks built from car parts. The whole office has a vintage automotive feel.)

- Create opportunities for your people to share their passion. You might allocate rooms or wall surfaces where everyone is welcome to display their own artefacts and put up messages. (I have worked in offices where the walls were covered by photographs and inspiring pieces of art made by those who worked there.)

- What's the ultimate purpose of your business? To create memorable experiences? To make life safe, pain-free and happy? To bring out the best in people and help them live their dreams? To establish better harmony between people and the Earth? Whatever it may be, **create a mini version of your ideal world in your workplace.** Read on, and hopefully you'll find the ideas you need to do this successfully.

Strategy 2:
Let your company's values shine

An inspiring business vision is hugely powerful in attracting team members who are striving towards the same goals as you do, and in getting them to jump into work with focus and enthusiasm. But this can only be maintained when they feel they are on the right path to turn that vision into reality, and when they are actually able to work well together and agree on the steps to take.

Your set of business values is the compass that helps your team members stay on track towards the desired destination. They are guiding principles that shape your people's behaviour, and assist them in setting priorities and making decisions in everyday practice. (While your purpose is the answer to the question WHY, your values are answers to the question HOW.)

Aligned values make relationships stronger, whether in business or in other areas of life. Therefore, we are more attracted to working in organisations that share our personal values, and collaborate better with them. Knowing that we all stand on common ground makes us more flexible, empathic and tolerant. We need less management and supervision, we know how to act in certain situations, and we make better decisions to move the business forward.

Values are often the main deciding factors (for all parties) in recruitment, as well as in establishing partnerships. Furthermore, the values embraced by the business are also an essential part of the customer experience, and often drive customers' decisions about who to engage.

Shared values go a long way

I have heard of a large company where management decided to consolidate all employees' personal values into a set of company values. This ensured that everyone could come to work being true to themselves, instead of checking their personal values at the door and conforming to standards imposed on them (as so many workers do). This gave a huge boost to their engagement and teamwork, and it became nearly impossible to get a job at that company, since almost no-one left.

Values and the physical space

When the physical space embodies the core values of the organisation, workers relate to those values better and live up to them more. They become an integral part of the work experience.

Unfortunately, many leaders communicate one thing with their words and another with their work environment. (This can be just as confusing as talking to a person whose words don't match their body language. They might say what we want to hear, but their whole presentation suggests deceit.)

For example, leaders who claim to stand for the highest quality in everything they do often provide sub-standard conditions for their people to work in. And businesses that claim to be innovative, flexible, and ready to take risks have workplaces that seem stuck in the last century. This incongruence not only affects workers, but can undermine the reputation of the organisation.

Design strategies

So how can your workspace speak your values?

You often see words and images that represent the organisation's values stuck up on office walls. This might be a good start, but we are only skimming the surface. If the workspace as a whole does not embody these values, these displays will probably be met with rolling eyes.

The formula for creating a values-aligned work environment is simple: **use the same philosophies to guide your design decisions as you use for your business decisions.** If *ABC* is one of your values, create a workplace that either does or promotes *ABC*. Here are a few examples:

- Innovation – Use innovative features, and make your workplace conducive to lateral thinking.

- Transparency – Minimise barriers; make it easy for people to see, hear and talk to each other.

- Authenticity – Create a workplace with a genuine feel, and which invites people to be themselves.

- Environmental sustainability – Minimise the negative environmental impact of your workplace.

- Putting people first – Create a comfortable, pleasant and empowering environment.

- Fun – Create a positive environment, employ humour, and provide opportunities for fun and play.

- Flexibility – Create a flexible and adaptable work environment that can be suited to different ways of working.

Do these sound trivial? Yes, of course they do. But you'll find that making these distinctions at the beginning of your design project will really help you create a space that feels like your second skin.

(The following chapters will provide specific strategies that support each of these objectives.)

Case study: IT Success Recruitment Services

When Graeme Isaacs, director of IT Success Recruitment Services, engaged me to help him design his company's new office fitout, he knew exactly what set his business apart from the competition. Their core values included *authenticity, honesty, transparency* and *dynamism*. IT Success had no hidden agenda; it served its candidates' best interests and opened up amazing new opportunities to them. Graeme also took special care of his staff; he worked hard to ensure that they came to work with a smile on their face each day, and that they loved to be in the office.

Graeme wanted to create a space that reflected the company's values – which helped visiting candidates feel more trusting and open and which was an energising and nurturing environment to work in.

The space we created had no visual barriers between the visitors and staff areas – it was all open, which was unprecedented in the recruitment industry. To further emphasise transparency, we chose workstation desks without dividing screens. The space had bright uplifting colours and beautiful artworks throughout, along with domestic-style furniture. At the centre of the office was a lounge area which was tastefully decorated with personal artefacts, some of which reflected Graeme's spiritual views.

Graeme's original objectives have all been achieved. Beyond that, his office has proven to be successful in encouraging a free flow of ideas and maximising the energy and productivity of staff. (While Graeme originally planned to put his company values on the walls as word graphics, he found later on that this wasn't necessary.)

Strategy 3:
Make your workspace a part of your brand

Learning from retail

When we walk into a shop, we quickly get a glimpse of the type of products we can find there (e.g. style, quality, price) and the level of service we can expect. In other words, we get a sense of whether we are in the right place to find what we need, just from the look and the vibe of the shop fitout. Apple shops are excellent examples; you can walk into any of them and immediately recognise that the qualities of the space are similar to the qualities of the products you can buy there, such as sleek design and easy navigation.

This is because shop designers tend to put great effort into creating spaces that reflect the brand they're working with. They know that the retail space serves as a marketing tool, and if it sends the right messages to customers, sales go up.

How does it work?

People are emotional beings whose purchase decisions are strongly guided by their moods and gut feelings. They want to get a sense that the new product or service will fit neatly into their world and make it a better place. Before committing to it, they need to feel some personal connection to it and trust that it will deliver on its promise.

And that's where brand comes into play. When the customer sees the business as a good friend who they can trust and appreciate, emotional attachment occurs more naturally. But for that friendship to form, your business needs to have a unique and visible personality, just like flesh-and-blood friends do, with your own interests, values, attitudes, passions, opinions, etc. As Tim Reid, host of *The Small Business Big Marketing Show*, says: 'People can copy what you do, but not who you are. And the *who you are* is all about that emotional connection you make with your prospects and customers. It's your BRAND.'

The brand needs to be communicated consistently across all platforms, including the subliminal messages sent by the physical environment, otherwise it's not believable.

Branding in the workplace

The same principles apply to workplaces; if your environment embodies the personality of your business, it's easier for your prospects, clients and team members to develop a close relationship with it. In the past, this design philosophy was rarely pursued beyond the retail and hospitality sectors. But today, leaders in many industries see their workspace as a part of their brand, a tool for deepening relationships with anyone who comes in the door.

Enticing customers – building greater engagement and loyalty, generating more sales – is just one part of the benefits. A workplace that reflects the brand also speaks to team members: 'This is who we are'. It reminds them of the experience the organisation aims to deliver to its customers, and reinforces the work ethic, attitudes and behaviours expected from them.

Misguided attempts

Before looking at how to translate your brand into interior design features such as room layouts, furniture and decor, let's make it clear how not to.

Companies often use their corporate colours as feature colours of their workplaces and leave it at that. Furniture and wall colours tell little about the essence of the organisation, and can even have adverse psychological effects. For example, a red logo or a green font type have completely different meanings and trigger different emotions compared to a red carpet or a green wall. The business owners who decorate their walls with marketing imagery, in the name of creating brand presence, are also missing the point.

 The man in the hard hat

> Once I worked at a building engineering firm that went through a merger with a large multidisciplinary group which also serviced several other industry sectors (including road building, mining and water management). As a result, our organisation went through a re-branding process. To remind us of our new identity, a set of banners, each representing an industry sector that the group worked with, were placed strategically in the boardroom. From that day, every time I attended a meeting in that room and saw those banners I noticed my mind wandering with thoughts like: 'I am an architect and consultant, employed to help create green buildings. And here is this man in a hard hat helping to put an enormous concrete ring into the ground. He represents the organisation! I must be in the wrong place!' Such self-talk is often not logical, but is powerful nevertheless.

Your space as a person

A much better approach is to capture the essence of your brand in the design, focusing on the experience you want to provide for your people and the impression you want to give about your company.

One excellent strategy is to treat the space as if it was a person. As a starting point, create a detailed picture of who your company would be (or should be) if it was an individual. What would they be like? What would be their unique attributes? What would set them apart from your competitors? What impression would they make on those coming in contact with them?

Let this picture guide your design decisions. It might be hard to envisage how to give your workplace a personality, but let me assure you, this is not rocket science once you've got your message right. And it can be real fun. (It's a bit like shopping for clothes that highlight your personality, or for artwork for your home.)

💡 'This is who we are – design around this'

A great example of a workplace that has been designed around the brand is the South Melbourne office of CO2, an Australian environmental services company. Andrew Grant, managing director at the time, explained the revolutionary process they had followed to create an environment that's just the right fit for the organisation.

At first, they worked with Tim Reid, marketing expert, to develop a solid brand identity for the company. As a part of this process, they did an exercise to imagine what CO2 Australia would be like if it was a person. They described 'his' core values, personality traits, and the people he would associate with. They also identified the type of car he would have, and his favourite music, food, colour, etc.

As another exercise, their team also explored other products and brands they admire (e.g. Apple, Rip Curl, Macquarie Bank), along with the qualities and benchmarks they set for themselves (e.g. the qualities embodied by WWF and by German engineering). Finally, they formulated what they do and how they make people feel special.

Then they gave this brief to the graphic designers who developed their marketing imagery, website, corporate stationery and other collateral. And when CO2 moved into their new location, they also gave this briefing document to the designers and said, 'This is who we are; design around this'. The designers loved working with such a meaningful brief, and created a work environment that deeply resonated with CO2 Australia's people.

(See the full case study in Principle 5: Caring.)

Case study: JobAdder

JobAdder is a Sydney-based software company with the brand and slogan: simplicity. In our interview, CEO Brett Iredale talked about how their brand values directly tied into the design of the office:

> 'We design recruitment software that's easy to use, clean and simple. The user interface is white, spacious and clean, because people like to use products like that. And our office also looks like that. Our competitors' offices, processes, sales – the whole experience – are cluttered and confusing. So we distinguish ourselves in the market just by being simple, easy, clean.'

Software and infrastructure were also set up in the spirit of simplicity. They decided to use only cloud-based software as well as file-sharing and phone systems. There is no server or network, which is really unusual in a software company. This has not only defined the way they work, but also made an amazing difference to the look and character of the office. Without server rooms, network cables, desk phones and piles of papers, the space is kept free of clutter.

The office space has essentially become a marketing tool.

> 'Before moving here, we used to go out to our clients, but now we insist that they come to us. Our office tells them a story about who we are, and the philosophy of the company.'

The responses are overwhelmingly positive; when customers come in, they want to be associated with JobAdder, partly because of the space. Put simply, the space helps them acquire new customers.

And the space also helps recruit the right staff. It's a very nice office which people generally find an attractive place to be in. But most importantly:

> 'When people come in for an interview, and our office has a huge impact on them, I know straightaway that they are on the same page. I don't need to tell them how to fit in. And they can see what we have here, and ask for a job.'

(See the second part of JobAdder's case study in Principle 6: Engaging.)

Strategy 4:
Stay in harmony with the environment

For many companies, their take on environmental issues is an important aspect of their purpose and identity. Now, I'm not here to tell you how green your workplace should be. But I encourage you to review the environmental objectives of your business, and to set up your workspace in alignment with that.

'Sustainable', 'green', 'conscious', 'responsible', 'small footprint', 'efficient' – these are just a few of the many common phrases referring to roughly similar concepts. Unfortunately, these words are often misused, and their exact meanings are debated. In this book, I use these words for describing products, activities and mindsets which support our most harmonious relationship with nature.

Mixed emotions

The topic of sustainability triggers negative associations in many of us. It is often mentioned in relation to global warming, pollution, depletion of natural resources, endangered wildlife, and a grim future for the whole of humanity. Many of us feel pressure and guilt, knowing that the changes we are currently making to minimise the negative impact of our activities and to restore nature's balance are not sufficient.

Most of us are also unsure of the way forward. We are regularly bombarded by token advice that promotes models of good behaviour, such as 'Use recyclable shopping bags!' or 'Take four minute showers!', through various media. We hear endless debate, much of it people arguing why they should *not* consider the environment in their actions. We see some sort of a 'green' label attached to almost every product and service we come across. These experiences only create a distance between us and the environment, and suggest that all it takes to live with a small footprint is to tick some boxes and follow what others tell us to do.

In this culture, it's probably no surprise that many people expect the solution to come from governments and environmental authorities. They can provide rules and guidance, but cannot make us act with conviction.

What is your motivation?

When it comes to creating a green workplace, many organisations only want to do what they have to: complying with legislative requirements and meeting the expectations of the market. Others pursue green practices due to ethical reasons as they feel a sense of responsibility. And some believe that creating a work environment which is respectful of nature can lead to a win-win-win situation that benefits the business, the people and the planet. For them, going green is an attractive opportunity. Not surprisingly, this third group has the best results.

To create an environmentally efficient workplace that excels on all fronts, you need to:

1. Consider both environmental and human interests
2. Follow the right frameworks
3. Adopt smart design solutions
4. Create an environmentally aware culture

1. Consider both environmental and human interests

A building's environmental performance has a strong influence on how the organisation and its people think and perform, and vice versa. Ample research shows that green buildings increase the productivity of workers (while saving on operational costs), and also, that highly engaged, environmentally minded workers make their buildings operate more efficiently.

The problem is that building and organisational matters are usually addressed separately. Engineers, whose job it is to design the 'guts' of the building, rarely look into what needs to happen inside the human body and mind for people to work well. On the other hand, managers rarely discuss the efficiency of building systems in the context of organisational performance. Creating an efficient ecosystem while dealing with these issues in isolation is not easy. So I encourage you to develop the environmental and business objectives for your new workplace in sync, with the involvement of all key members of your project team.

Finding balance – avoiding the pitfalls

Unfortunately, designers often perceive that serving the people, the business and the environment are conflicting goals, and feel they need to make major compromises. However, an abundance of case studies testify that with well-considered, intelligent design solutions it's possible to achieve great results in all three areas.

Of course, making small trade-offs is inevitable. Therefore, to get the best overall results, it's important to strike a good balance between the different objectives. This is not always easy.

In the past decades, we've seen many workplaces that were attractive-looking but wasteful, for example, using large amounts of materials that damage the environment in their production, and wasting power due to inadequate thermal insulation and inefficient air-conditioning systems. Thankfully, the environmental qualities of buildings, in general, have been steadily improving over recent years.

However, today we can also see workplaces that favour the environment at the cost of people's wellbeing and productivity. For example, some are so under-lit – with the aim of reducing lighting power consumption – that they feel like a gloomy cave and make you drowsy. Others have unfinished concrete walls and exposed service pipes all around, designed to save on finishing materials. While these features work well in certain situations, they can also make the space feel stark and unfriendly. And in some cases such a large part of the budget is allocated to environmental features and procedures that not much is left for enhancing users' work experience.

The way I see it, compromising human performance for environmental objectives can rarely be justified. People's entire existence relies on natural resources (such as power and materials that go into food, transport, clothing, accommodation, etc.), and in exchange, they bring value to this world through their efforts and talent, in part, in the workspaces provided for them. If a workspace wastes people's potential, no matter what its environmental credentials are, it cannot be called efficient. And it doesn't make financial sense either, if you do the maths.

> ### 💡 'One hit wonder'
>
> I remember when I first visited one of Australia's iconic green office buildings, which has rightfully earned much acknowledgment for its highly efficient and innovative engineering solutions. As one of the mastermind engineers guided our small group around, explaining the environmental features of the building, I was amazed at how intelligent the design was, and how each piece of the building worked together like clockwork to create the most effective, integrated system.
>
> But once we were shown through the workstation areas, I was really disappointed to see how dull and lifeless the workspace was, with rows of identical workstations, grey surfaces all around, no unobstructed views to the street, and absolutely no eye-catching interior features. (I know I was not the only one left disappointed … Later on I saw this building listed among the 'world's ugliest'.)
>
> I'm not sure why, but this building – Australia's most 'sustainable' building – remained unoccupied for many years.

Remember, the building is only a vehicle. It is only a tool to help people do what they need to do and be who they need to be.

2. Follow the right frameworks

Setting appropriate environmental targets (e.g. for power consumption, water consumption, qualities of materials used) and then ensuring that every element of the design supports these targets are challenging tasks, even for seasoned design professionals. However, pre-set design guidelines can help you set reasonable goals and can also offer a plan to follow.

Environmental rating schemes

To create a workplace with higher than average standards, it can be worthwhile to follow the design suggestions of one of the environmental rating systems applicable for commercial buildings and interiors[3]. (In many cases, this is even mandatory.) Most organisations that administer such schemes also offer education and guidance for making environmentally informed design decisions, which can be helpful even if you don't pursue formal recognition.

Before choosing a scheme to follow – ideally before the start of the design, or even before the selection of the site or tenancy – you should carefully evaluate the pros and cons of the different options. Not all of them are suitable or beneficial for all building types or sizes[4].

Also, they all have their own focus. Some will only help you minimise the power consumption of your new space. Others will assist you, for example, to install efficient water and waste management systems, to choose low-impact materials and products, and to provide facilities that encourage sustainable means of transport (such as bike riding). And the most holistic schemes also promote such human objectives as happiness, beauty, or supporting a fair world.

You might also consider obtaining a formal third-party recognition for creating a green workplace. Beyond the improved environmental, human and financial outcomes resulting from this process, obtaining a prestigious certification has multiple benefits: It communicates the building's environmental credentials to the building users and the public in a credible way. It demonstrates the business's integrity and improves its reputation. It raises the profile of the development and may increase the value of the real estate. And it attracts people who want to be associated with green thinking.

Be prepared, though, as obtaining formal certification can be a complex, time consuming and expensive process. You will need to include a set of environmental features in line with the given guideline, ensure that all

---

[3] Some of these schemes are: National Australian Built Environment Rating System (NABERS) administered by the NSW Government, Green Star Office and Green Star Office Interiors administered by the Green Building Council Australia, Living Building Challenge administered by the Living Future Institute, One Planet Living administered by Bioregional, and Sustainable Design Scorecard (SDS) administered by the City of Port Phillip.

[4] If your project is small, the costs of pursuing a prestigious certification scheme could take up a significant part of your budget. Instead of spending on administrative and consulting fees, it might make more sense to use that money on features that directly benefit your teams – for example, to enhance the functionality and appeal of the interiors.

building consultants support you in this goal, and deal with sometimes excessive amounts of paperwork. (Specialist environmental consultants can guide you through the process, help you make the right decisions, and do much of this work for you.)

Best practice standards

Alternatively, you may consider pursuing best practice environmental standards such as 'carbon neutral', 'closed loop waste management', 'zero energy balance', 'zero water balance', 'low environmental footprint', 'passive house', or 'cradle to cradle design'. These are widely recognised standards and design frameworks – each with a different focus, as their names suggest.

Just like pursuing third-party certification, creating a building or a fitout that meets any of these standards usually requires the involvement of specialist consultants.

Going your own way

While following a suitable framework will certainly improve the environmental qualities of your workspace, none of the pre-set guidelines can give you all the answers you need for creating an environmentally efficient workplace that's just right for your business[5]. To get the best results, you will always need to pursue some objectives not addressed by any guidelines.

So whether you follow a framework, or choose to create a green workplace your own way, you and your team will need to be prepared to make your own informed choices.

---

5   Most design frameworks only focus on design attributes that are easy to measure and quantify, such as the amount of energy and water used in the building, the amount of construction waste produced that goes into landfill, or the toxin content of materials. Only very few consider such 'abstract' qualities as how inspiring and functional the space is, and how it influences people's thinking and behaviour – even though these also have major environmental implications. Designing a building to an environmental rating scheme or best practice standard is very often a numbers game.

3. Adopt smart design solutions

A few rules of thumb to consider

For the best overall results, your design team will need to work through the different aspects of your workspace in the right order. Each step will reduce the amount of resources your building will consume in operation, and at the same time, will make it easier and more cost-effective to implement the subsequent steps:

1. Start with the **layout and orientation**. Make sure that the floor space is used efficiently so that there are no 'dead' areas, and that the sun works for you, not against you (i.e. you have warmth and daylight in the right places, at the right times).

2. The **building fabric** should be highly weatherproof, which includes well-insulated facades, roofs and floors, as well as high quality, appropriately shaded windows. Ideally, the building should allow for the harvesting of renewable resources (such as solar power and rainwater).

3. The building's systems (air-conditioning, water heating, equipment, water fittings, etc.) should all **operate efficiently**.

4. Promote and expect environmentally **conscious behaviour** from building users (such as switching off lights and air-conditioning in empty rooms, recycling waste, etc.), and design the building around that.

5. Supply as much of the building's resources as possible from **renewable sources** (solar power, wind power, rainwater, sustainably sourced timber, etc.).

Consider the whole life cycle of the building in every design decision you make. Ask questions like:

- Where are the materials **sourced** from? How were they manufactured and transported?

- What resources are used for **construction**, and what are the impacts (e.g. waste, pollution)?

- What impact does the building create during **operation** (e.g. power used, water used, waste produced, wastewater produced, etc.)?

- What is involved in the **maintenance** of the interiors? How, and how often, are the various elements going to be cleaned and replaced?

- What is the estimated **lifespan** of the building, the fitout, and its components? What will happen to all of these at the **end of their lives** (e.g. will they be disposed of, reused or recycled)?

Wherever possible, choose durable, long-life products and materials which have been produced with low impact, e.g. derived from sustainable sources, or fully or partly recycled. There are several credible green product certification schemes to help you make the right choices.[6]

Remember, you don't need to have a brand new building to make a great difference; refurbished buildings also have huge potential. (Many of the greenest buildings in Australia are refurbishments.)

Designing, building and operating a green workplace is a huge topic, so this list of advice is far from comprehensive. However, the design strategies in this book all support efficiency and stand on ethical foundations.

Costs and benefits

Serving the business, the people and the environment go hand in hand beautifully. The vast majority of the most sustainable workplaces are also exceptionally attractive and healthy environments that house thriving businesses. Case studies show that there is clearly a business case for sustainability. Beyond having a smaller footprint, green workplaces enhance the organisation's profile, provide a healthier and more pleasant environment for work, substantially enhance work performance, and have lower operating costs, thus yielding higher returns on investment.

It's a common misconception that creating an efficient workplace must be expensive. Some green products and systems are now either the same price or even cheaper than other alternatives. Research shows that a good level of

---

[6] These include: Good Environmental Choice Australia (GECA), Green Tag, Forest Stewardship Council (FSC), and Australian Forestry Standard (AFS)

environmental performance can be achieved at no increased cost compared to constructing a building with average environmental standards, and that a significant improvement can be achieved at an average 5-10% increase in construction costs.

However, it is essential to make critical decisions early. Integrating environmentally efficient solutions into the design is significantly cheaper and more effective than attaching 'green' features as add-ons later on.

4. Create an environmentally aware culture

Ideally, sustainability should not be an added layer of design but a way of thinking. When we honour our intricate connection with the broader environment, we have better awareness of the consequences of our decisions, set better priorities, and think more creatively about doing things efficiently and with low impact, both as members of the project team, and as building users.

A building cannot perform independently of its users. If they don't care, even the most brilliantly designed building won't perform. But if they do care, they will make the most of the opportunities in any workplace.

Perhaps many would disagree, but in my experience, real change starts with people who find personal fulfilment in connecting with nature, restoring its balance, and contributing to the well-being of this planet's citizens. They make conscious choices each day to achieve this through their work and lifestyle.

Workplaces with the highest environmental standards tend to attract and inspire these sorts of change-makers, and to support them in their commitment to make a difference far beyond the boundaries of work and the workplace.

Case study: Bullitt Center

The Bullitt Foundation is a non-profit group with a mission 'to safeguard the natural environment by promoting responsible human activities and sustainable communities'. The foundation's new office building in Seattle (opened in 2013), the Bullitt Center, is the result of a visionary effort.

It has been designed to be the greenest commercial building in the world, and to receive a Living Building Status by meeting the requirements of the Living Building Challenge – the most ambitious environmental certification system in the world.

Vision

The Bullitt Foundation advocates that built environments should be designed to be healthy, useful and beautiful, without excessively burdening the planet. Further to that, they 'should also be a source of joy, well-being and inspiration'. Denis Hayes, President of The Bullitt Foundation, states:

> '... architects should never have to choose among aesthetics, functionality and performance. If faced with such a trade-off, architects need to probe more deeply into their designs to solve for all three ends simultaneously.'

Hayes suggests that nature is a rich resource of knowledge, since it has been solving similar problems for billions of years through optimising the use of limited resources. Studying nature can help us find breakthrough ideas in design, and also teach us about creating beauty. He states:

> 'Buildings that seamlessly blend beauty, efficiency and functionality are almost always inspired by something Mother Nature invented millions of years ago.'

Building

The six-storey building is pushing the boundaries of environmental performance in all possible ways, and aims to advance what a green building can achieve by a quantum leap. Here are some of the building's credentials:

- It was designed for a 250-year lifespan.
- It was designed to be energy- and carbon-neutral. (This was achieved through the combination of using efficient solar panels and implementing energy conservation measures that cut the building's energy consumption to less than one fourth of a typical office building of similar size.)

- It was constructed from as many local and non-toxic building materials as was possible (hundreds of commonly used hazardous substances were replaced with healthier alternatives).

- It harvests all the water its residents use and processes all sewage on site (through the use of rainwater harvesting and an innovative wastewater management system).

- It handles all of its waste on site.

- It provides fresh air and daylight to each worker.

- It is a beautiful, healthy, human environment that is more pleasant and more supportive of productivity than most commercial buildings.

Approach

I've seen Jason McLennan – creator of the Living Building Challenge – explaining the thought process that set this project apart from common practice. Designers traditionally approach a building project by asking first, 'What amount of resources will the new building need to use?', and then, 'What amount of these resources can we source from the site we have?'. The Bullitt Center's design team did the opposite: they asked first, 'What amount of resources can the site provide?', and then, 'How can we meet our needs with what we have? How big a building can these resources sustain?'.

Seattle is known for its gloomy weather, and is seen as a less than ideal place for harvesting solar energy, let alone providing enough energy for a whole commercial building. Overcoming seemingly impossible challenges like this, and creating a cutting edge design (with an unprecedented ecological performance) required a number of technical, legal, and social innovations. This could only have been achieved through the collaboration of the tenants, architects, engineers, contractors, university researchers and environmental certification bodies, all sharing the same vision.[7]

---

7   The process also involved negotiations with authorities and suppliers who, inspired by the project's vision, were ready to rethink their rules and practices in order to find common ground.

Putting things into practice

A non-traditional workplace: The Royal Children's Hospital

Melbourne's new Royal Children's Hospital opened in 2011 to replace its almost 50-year-old predecessor, a typical, institutional-looking hospital which belonged to a past era. The new building, designed by Billard Leece Partnership and Bates Smart Architects, provides a radically different, positive and engaging hospital experience to children.

Here you won't need to walk through plain corridors, sit in sterile-looking waiting rooms, stare at pale green walls, or smell the odours of chemicals. The building doesn't look or feel like a 'hospital'. **It doesn't communicate sickness – it's all about life.**

The designers took into account how an injured or sick child might feel, and expressed empowering messages through forms and textures, lights and sounds, furniture, artwork, internal layout, and signage for navigation. The building speaks children's language, **making them feel relaxed, happy and safe,** while also engaging everyone else involved in the care of a sick child, both families and staff.

'We are in nature'

Children are fascinated by nature, and this inspired the designers to create an environment in which nature is present everywhere you look. The building is airy and filled with natural light. There are views to a nearby park or to internal landscaped courtyards from most spaces in the building, from circulation areas and sitting bays to patient rooms and operating theatres.

Graphics, illustrating animals and landscapes of Victoria, are placed on almost every conceivable wall surface. Each floor has a theme. When you arrive at the basement car park, you see drawings of friendly earthworms, and as you're moving up, you encounter sea life, forest life, mountain life, and birds in the sky. The names of inpatient units also follow these themes; for example, Dolphin Ward is 'Underwater' (Lower Ground), while Koala Ward is in 'Tree Tops' (Level 3).

'Let's have fun'

This hospital is a fun place to be; it offers plenty of opportunities for discovery, and for engaging, magical experiences for children. (And also for grown-ups. When visiting the hospital, I could feel my inner child waking up.)

In front of the entry you can't miss the two-storey cylindrical fish tank. This makes taking the stairs to the emergency department a real adventure, giving you the opportunity to see the fish tank in its full height. The hospital is also famous for its meerkat enclosure.

The foyer has several large scale artworks, including a multi-coloured sculpture called 'Creature', and a series of floating leaf-like canopies called 'Sky Garden'. The information counter is also an impressive piece of art. (My interpretation would be a UFO.) The seats don't look like seats either; they have interesting shapes and textures, reminding you more of boulders, creatures and elements of a landscape.

In the context of hospital design for children, science calls these features 'distractions'. However, their role is more than what this term suggests; they invite children to focus on what they enjoy, instead of leaving them alone with their health condition in an unstimulating environment. If the building could speak, it would say something like: 'Let's have fun, healing doesn't need to be scary. We are here to help you enjoy life.'

'This is a safe place'

These striking features also assist with easy navigation through this enormous building, which is crucial for making children – and adults – feel relaxed and safe.[8] In addition, the signage uses simple words that children

---

8 Richard Duerden, whose company, Diadem, was involved in implementing the wayfinding signage and environmental graphics for the hospital (for the builder), said something really interesting about wayfinding. It can often be really difficult to explain to a child how to get from point A

understand. (For example, instead of the intimidating medical term 'Ophthalmology', the sign says 'Eye care'.)

Several other features contribute to making this hospital feel safe. There are no off-putting service roads around the building; the surrounding landscaped garden and the intriguing design of the main facade make entering the hospital a pleasant experience. Although the building is vast, it is broken down to human scale, so it's not at all dominating. And there are soft edges all around; walls, furniture and ceiling edges are all rounded.

'Our purpose is healing'

The Royal Children's Hospital is a healthcare facility that actually looks and feels healthy. And by advocating for health in the right way, it achieves way more than just providing a pleasant experience. Directing children's focus to the external world and away from their sickness, helping them connect with nature, making them feel safe and engaged – these are all design strategies that actually improve health outcomes in hospitals, as shown by science[9]. Design can heal people, and even save lives!

---

to point B in a huge complex. But when you can tell them something like, 'Go straight ahead to the beach image, and then go up the stairs to the level with the forest', they will get it. An environment like this not only helps children navigate more easily and makes them feel better; it assists with healing, and also takes a huge load off staff, since they need to deal with fewer queries.

9   These are all fundamental principles of evidence-based healthcare design, supported by a large body of research spanning several decades.

❓ Questions to consider

- What is the purpose of your business? What difference does it make?

- How do your services or products change people's lives?

- What gets you and your team members jumping out of bed each morning, full of enthusiasm for the work day ahead?

- What are your most important business goals?

- Once you have achieved these goals, what will the results look like? And what will be the rewards?

- What core values drive your organisation and its people?

- Who are your ideal team members? What inspires them? What is important to them?

- What sorts of clients would you like to attract?

- What impression do you want people to get when they come through your door?

- What messages do you aim to communicate to your teams and customers?

- If your business was a person, what would he or she be like?

- What is that common ground that holds your teams together?

PRINCIPLE

2

SMART

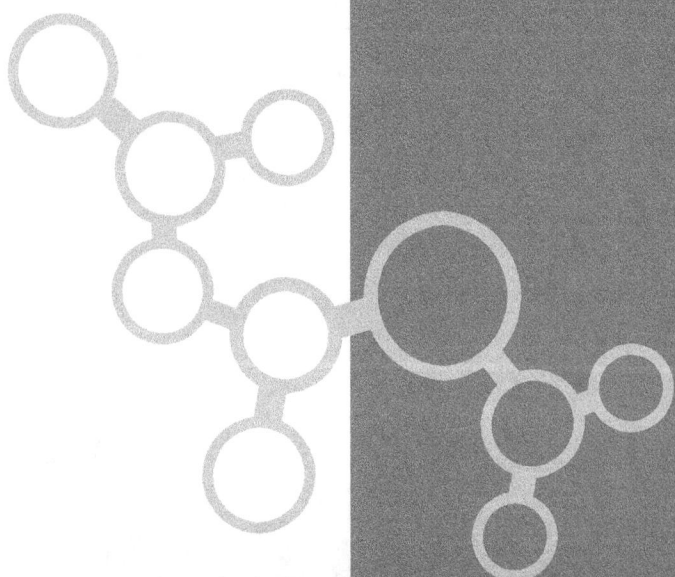

CREATE SPACE FOR A SMART BUSINESS

Creating a workplace where we can easily access all the resources we need – including other people, information, work tools and technologies

The most important resource of a knowledge business is its people's thoughts. The work tools and media we use at work, the systems for managing knowledge and data, and the interiors of the workplace that guide how we think and interact with others are there to provide a pathway for our thoughts to turn into products and services that customers value. A smart workplace is one that lays down the all the stepping stones for this to happen as efficiently as possible.

Why should we be smart?

Easy access to information

Over recent years, the advances in communication technology and easy access to information have completely transformed our lives. And from our new information-driven and globally connected culture several trends have emerged which are revolutionising how knowledge-based businesses operate.

Technology has liberated work from the physical space, since it enables us to stay connected to our teams and our company's data network from any place with network coverage. This opportunity jump-started the models of flexible working (people regularly shifting location within the office) and mobile working (people working outside the office), both of which are now leading workplace trends.

Collaboration has become more open and community-centric, often spanning across different disciplines and industries. Business teams are becoming borderless and more dynamic. Organisations are becoming less hierarchical and more transparent, and many of them are now part of the sharing economy.

These trends impact all levels of business activity, prompting leaders to rethink their business models along with all aspects of how they work. To keep up with competition as well as expectations from staff and clients, organisations also need to be tech-savvy and seamlessly integrate technology into work, ensuring that it improves everyone's way of working and experience of work.

Knowledge is power

Efficient communication has always been an important element of productivity in organisations. But today, with more communication channels to choose from than ever, and with more open, transitory and geographically dispersed teams, a fluid exchange of information and knowledge is critical to fruitful teamwork and thus business success.

Knowledge is becoming one of the most valued assets of organisations, as leaders are recognising that the competitive advantages gained through technology are transient, while knowledge is longer lasting. And the emphasis is on knowledge, as opposed to information. Information is some sort of a message in a shareable format, typically digitised, while knowledge lives in people's minds.

An abundance of quality information is available for free or low cost, so more and more organisations can only charge for knowledge-based services. However, when team members fail to share their full knowledge, and perhaps even leave, much of this remains unrealised. So organisations not only need to manage (i.e. create, transfer and store) information well, but also harness their people's latent knowledge in order to achieve lasting success.

Technology and workplace design

Technology is like the fourth dimension of the workplace; it drives how the workplace functions and what it looks like, and can even guide the design process – as I'm about to explain.

A range of business activities can be conducted remotely. It's often not essential to go to the office to do focused work or to meet people we could talk to online. We can hold meetings on the go and collaborate with team members who might even be on a different continent, for example by using cloud-based video conferencing services. As a result, **the function of the workplace is shifting;** one of the main reasons people go to the office today is to meet others in person, and to be in a motivating environment where it's easy to connect with their work. (This will be further explored in Principle 7: Evolving.)

Companies are increasingly under pressure to adopt **Bring Your Own Device (BYOD) strategies.** It's a real challenge for organisations to keep up with changes in technology[1], and at the same time, workers have increasing expectations – especially Millennials who are now starting to dominate

---

1   As Martec's Law states: 'Technology changes exponentially, organizations change logarithmically.' What this means in practice is that change in technology is faster than what organisations are able to absorb. While this is only a theory, it seems to describe what's actually happening quite accurately.

the workforce. They tend to be tech-savvy, mobile-centric workers owning more current devices than what many IT departments are able to provide. The technology they use is an important part of how they experience work, and they want to have the same quality experience they have at home.

BYOD has pros and cons: it increases workers' satisfaction and productivity while providing cost savings for the organisation, but on the other hand it raises issues around practical implementation and security. Regardless, BYOD, and the use of mobile devices in general, completely transform the look of the workplace. They allow for the most flexible ways of working, and call for a different floor layout and furnishings than working with desktop computers.

A range of software tools are available to help us **navigate in and make the best use of the workplace.** These include applications for finding and booking vacant meeting rooms or desk spaces in flexible workplaces, and space utilisation measuring tools which provide valuable information for creating more efficient floor layouts (meaning, reducing floor area without creating congestion). With these tools, flexible working becomes a more attractive and viable option for organisations.

Wearable devices can measure people's habits, and provide information about how these habits influence their productivity, health and wellbeing. These insights can then inform the design of better workplaces. For example, it is possible to track and analyse how workers move around the office and who they talk to.[2] This data, recorded through tiny wearable electronic sensing devices, can tell us a lot about the relationship between the space design, how people interact and how they perform, and help us create more collaborative environments. Other devices measure people's posture and body movements (e.g. while typing or handling the mouse), along with the physical strain put on their bodies during work. These data then can support the design of more ergonomic work settings.

---

2 These studies should be conducted with the greatest respect to worker's privacy. Ideally, participation should be voluntary, and the data evaluated should be randomised.

When to keep technology at arm's length

Many of us are habitually plugged into our devices round the clock. The opportunities and demands arising from easy access to information can whirl us into a hyperactive life in which we are constantly hooked onto scattered bits of information, and if we are not careful, we could end up burnt out. Many people now realise that **we need a new set of rules and habits** to protect our minds and our relationships. We need to learn to consume the right information at the right time, and to draw some boundaries.[3]

This applies to work too. Workplaces need to offer the opportunity for people to get offline and be present, to work with non-digital media or just to relax, so that they can stay switched on and maintain high performance over time.

Putting aside digital devices and **using low-tech tools** instead can also **help us achieve better results** in certain tasks. The work tools we use are not just the means to execute work, but actually guide how we think and approach our tasks. For example, pen and paper tend to be more inviting for doodling a half idea than sophisticated software. This means that even in the most technologically advanced workplace, certain things should be low-tech.

Designing for knowledge management

The limitations of technology

Sharing information is now easier than ever. On the down side, with much of our communication being digital, we talk to each other less. We need to watch out, as face-to-face interaction has a very important role in learning and skill-building, along with developing trusting relationships, which is the foundation of knowledge exchange.

Geyer, an Australian design and research practice, has conducted a study to understand which attributes of a workplace can assist with the effective harnessing of knowledge. The results highlighted the limitations of relying

---

3   Interestingly, Millennials, who are perceived by older generations as having their lives taken over by technology, are the very generation which have learnt to switch it off, as they want to maintain balance in their lives. They are beginning to master technology, so that it works for them not against them.

on technology; for transferring and storing data respondents did use technology, but for sharing knowledge the vast majority preferred face-to-face interaction.[4]

Other studies, employing wearable sensors for observing the behaviour of thousands of employees, have revealed: 'face-to-face interactions are by far the most important activity in an office' – as reported by HBR. And a new coworking space in Las Vegas involving Zappos' employees, designed to maximise mobility and collisions, had such convincing results after just six months – a '78% increase in participant-generated proposals to solve specific problems, and an 84% increase in the number of new leaders' – that they decided to adopt a new metric for measuring the efficiency of the workplace: 'collisionable hours' (the number of unplanned interactions) per acre, as opposed to the old-school cost-per-square-metre measure.

These results are understandable, considering that experience and tacit knowledge are the most valued forms of knowledge in organisations, and these are best shared through social interactions.[5] (These include unplanned conversations and mentoring catch-ups, and people overhearing what their colleagues say.)

Chatting with our colleagues allows us to express subtle messages, such as emotions, through our body language and to get instant feedback. In contrast, technology-driven communication is less subtle and responsive, and so some of the meaning gets lost in translation.

Proximity matters

Getting people to talk to each other is not as easy as it may sound, and the physical distance between them strongly influences how often they talk.

A decade-long study at Massachusetts Institute of Technology, concluded in the 70's, observed how engineers communicate, and found that the frequency of communication dropped exponentially as the distance between people

---

[4] Geyer's research also showed that in small companies people tend to talk more in person, while in larger companies people tend to follow documented procedures, and so communication is largely driven by technology. As the researchers state: 'large companies share information, whereas small companies share knowledge'.

[5] Studies suggest that somewhere between 70 and 95% of what people know about their work is learnt through informal interactions with their colleagues, not through formal trainings.

increased. For example, people working 6 feet apart were four times more likely to talk to each other than those working 60 feet away. And people who were more than 75 feet apart almost never talked. Though this is old research, the core findings still accurately describe how people communicate in the modern corporate environment – as confirmed by more recent studies.

Recent studies, conducted by Sociometric Solutions (specialists in wearable sensing technologies), found that proximity also boosts digital communication. As reported by FastCompany: 'In one [study], engineers who shared space were 20% more likely to communicate digitally and emailed four times more frequently when collaborating on a project. The result: their projects were finished 32% faster than those from staff working in different places.'

The path from thought to result

Space plays an important role in creating and managing information and knowledge, and might be one of the most potent tools organisations have for turning what's in their people's heads into tangible results. To make value creation seamless, your workplace should support every stage of this process.

- **Provide access to the right sort of work tools and technology,** and limit access to those that may not support efficient work. Using physical or digital media that don't suit our task, or that we are not good at using, causes frustration, wastes time and can lead to major miscommunication. (For example, most of us know too well how using the wrong teleconferencing application can quickly turn a meeting into a complete mess.) Choosing the right tools for any task takes skill, and your workplace could be an excellent education ground for that.

- **Plan for the efficient management of data,** so that your people can easily find and access the information they need. Wasting people's effort by double-handling can cost a lot in money and morale. Furthermore, poor decisions about data management can hijack major business decisions, for example, about office locations or workplace arrangements. Conversely, in a workplace where data, information and communication technologies as well as the physical space all align, technology becomes 'invisible'. Content becomes the focus of work, and business decisions can be driven by real opportunities instead of arbitrary constraints.

- **Support the different stages of developing knowledge.** Professional work is complex, involving a range of individual and team activities. We can only work well collectively if we are able to develop our own contributions without interference, and share our ideas and results with others. When any of the components of our work suffer, it impacts on the whole. To maximise team performance, the space should enable people to immerse themselves in different types of work activities – whether data crunching or brainstorming – without imposing on each other.

- **Give your people the freedom to organise how they work.** Let them move around, occupy a space that best suits their task and mood, and work in close proximity to those they need to talk to regularly – so that they can learn from each other and collaborate better. Make sure you provide the right amount of flexibility. Pushing people into a work style that is alien to them can be more daunting than liberating, resulting in resistance and a decline in overall performance. When you adopt flexible work practices, make sure your new strategy suits your organisation's work style and culture, and is carefully implemented.

- **Once you choose to adopt flexible working, make the most of it.** Flexible working can be done badly, well or spectacularly well. Make sure that your workplace is tailored to enhance all elements of work, and is designed for optimal communication between individuals and teams. Offer a wide range of different work settings for individuals and teams, organised strategically for optimal workflow. Let these spaces evolve as your teams' work styles change, and as you learn about what sort of spaces produce excellent results and where you need improvements.

- **Help people feel safe and trusting.** Working in an environment that offers too many options, and where things are constantly in motion, can be disorienting, exhausting, and sometimes alienating. To feel safe, people need to know they have a familiar place they can always go back to which is their own. On another note, connected, trusting relationships are essential for knowledge exchange; however, trust is hard to build in an environment where relationships are casual, short-term and often virtual.[6] To encourage your people to share openly, you need to create a workplace that supports clear communication and real relationships. Allowing close-knit groups to create their own 'homes' within the workplace will support both of these goals, helping people feel comfortable to fully open up.

---

6 Research shows that employees with fixed desks have at least as much trust as those who work in flexible workplaces. Flexible working alone does not enhance trust.

Key design strategies

Key design strategies to create a smart workspace:

- Promote the use of the right work tools
- Put your data in the right place
- Create a well-functioning floor layout
- Support flexible ways of working
- Make the most of Activity-Based Working
- Create 'neighbourhoods'

By getting these strategies right, your people will be able to work smarter and more intelligently, communicate and collaborate better, and develop in their jobs faster. All these will lead to better organisational efficiency and significant savings on cost.

Creating an environment that provides optimal comfort conditions and minimises distraction and stress will further enhance work efficiency. These strategies will be explored in the following chapter, Principle 3: Productive.

Strategy 1:
Promote the use of the right work tools

We are introduced to new technologies and applications almost every day, and the number of choices can be overwhelming when it comes to choosing the right tool for our task – whether it be organising data, documenting new ideas, designing a product or service, or communicating with our peers.

Our attention is heavily biased towards digital media, since that's where the innovation happens. There is not much exciting news on the non-digital front – imagine the headline: 'breakthrough chalkboard technology to revolutionise our work'. And so we often forget about non-digital media such as working with pen and paper, crafting models and using role-playing props, or we tend to see these as old-school and inefficient.

In my experience, we tend to choose work tools mostly based on their ease of use and their capability of capturing, sharing and archiving our thoughts, and not so much based on their capacity to improve work outcomes. For example, it's much easier to type up a quick email and send it to our team (knowing that it's automatically documented), than to talk to everyone in person. So we often default to email even when those conversations would be more fruitful.

Which is the right work tool?

The tools and channels of communication we use, whether a sophisticated piece of software or a beermat, have a much broader role than just conveying our thoughts; they also guide how we think[7]. Have you ever noticed how different, and probably more authentic, your words are when you speak to someone as opposed to writing a report? And how different your ideas are when you develop them on paper or a whiteboard, as opposed to using some sort of design application? Many architects swear by pen and paper for developing their early design concepts because that gives them more creative freedom and helps them create more original and soulful buildings than using drafting software. Other designers find it more natural to use digital media.

All types of work tools and media offer some form of freedom, and also impose some limitations. For example, on the computer it's easy to be slick and precise, or to come up with hundreds of variations on a theme. On the other hand, it's difficult to capture rough ideas, or to choose the right direction from a plethora of choices. To get the best results, our choice of tools should suit the nature of our task.

The tools we use also influence the way we engage with others and our tasks. Scientific studies have explored how effectively team members contribute towards the team's goal while using different methods of self-expression

---

7   At training events I always take handwritten notes. In a crowd of tablet users, this might make me look behind the times. But freehand writing helps me remember what I've just learnt better, which is more important for me than being able to file my notes with ease or looking trendy.

(such as text, speech and body gesture), both in online and face-to face situations. It's been found that in face-to-face teamwork members tend to be more actively involved and more creative compared to interacting through digital media, in which case they are more likely to adopt critical thinking or absorb knowledge passively rather than contribute to it. Studies also suggest that having the opportunity to express personality and emotions during teamwork is likely to increase engagement and performance.

The type of media we are most comfortable using also depends on our age, history and education. In general, younger generations are better at using audio, images, videos and interactive elements in multimedia environments.

Media intelligence and the workspace

To perform effectively in our media-rich environment, we need to acquire 'media intelligence' – the ability to chose our tools wisely – but we also need an environment that offers the right choices.

The space we work in should support the use of the right sorts of tools, and restrict the use of those which might be familiar to us and easy to use, but not really effective in the broader context of our work.

First, you need to get clear about what results you want from the different activities you're creating a space for, and how people should feel and think in order to do well. The next step is to identify the optimal digital and non-digital work tools, along with those that should be avoided.

You may consider questions like: Is this tool reliable and efficient? Does it allow for capturing, documenting and sharing ideas? Does it promote the right sort of thinking? Does it promote engagement and participation? Does it help team members communicate clearly and connect with each other on a personal level? Does it enable people to express both emotional and rational aspects of their messages? Are people able to use this tool, express themselves authentically, and make sense of the messages they receive?

Here is an example:

💡 Slides or scribble?

When preparing for giving an in-person presentation, you might consider using PowerPoint, or a whiteboard or a flip-chart for adding visual content. These are all useful tools, but each creates a very different learning experience.

PowerPoint makes it possible to include complex data and interesting visual elements in the presentation, and to easily replicate the content. However, you will need to darken the room (to make the slides easy to see), and this can make it difficult for the audience to make handwritten notes and to ask questions – as they can't easily make eye contact with you. Also, using PowerPoint tempts you to focus more on the content and less on engaging the audience. (You need to use this tool very skillfully, otherwise the presentation can become disengaging – there's a reason why 'death by PowerPoint' has became a catchphrase.)

If this is the sort of presentation you are aiming to deliver, it's probably best to use a room that is set up for a speaker/audience type of interaction – with you facing your audience, and the audience facing the screen. This will allow you and your slides to be the centre of attention.

Whiteboards or flip-charts are great tools for making a presentation more informal, and for drawing in the audience. However, you can only scribble simple messages on these, and it takes some time and effort to do that during a presentation.

If this is the type of experience you are trying to create, you have more freedom around how to set up the space. For example, you could use a more casual café-style room with a non-hierarchical layout in which participants feel more encouraged to stand up and contribute.

Design suggestions

- Provide the right balance of spaces for face-to-face and remote meetings, or set up your meeting rooms to support both.

- Provide access to a range of communication tools, so that your people can express both the rational and the emotional aspects of their messages. For example, create rooms equipped with audiovisual equipment, whiteboards or chalkboards, and storage space for props, allowing people to write, draw, talk, make gestures, and use external files and objects in any combination.

- Create space for using traditional, non-digital work tools, for example, a workshop-type space where people can build things and make a mess. The qualities of this space should not suggest that working with old-fashioned tools is not serious or important work; make this space just as attractive and comfortable as the rest of your workplace.

Strategy 2:
Put your data in the right place

Going paperless

More and more offices are going paperless – either partially or fully – as the barriers to electronic data-handling are diminishing, and as leaders are realising the benefits for work and organisational efficiency.

In a paperless office you need less desk space (since there is less stuff for workers to spread out on their desks[8]) and less storage space. Electronic data-handling reduces the use of paper and the amount of waste produced, so it's also good for the environment. There is less mess and clutter, along with less mental clutter, since people don't need to stare at piles of files all the time.

---

8   One of the main reasons workers feel they need a large desk is because they have a lot of paper to spread out on it, and they haven't yet figured out another way of storing files and accessing information. Of course, storing paper is not the purpose of a desk, but once the space is there, people are inclined to fill it.

When paper is not blocking the business, documentation and information-sharing become more efficient; double-handling is minimised, and people spend less time finding the information they need. This practice makes the business more nimble by enabling people to work in a more flexible manner; they are no longer anchored to a single location – the space where paper with key information happens to be stored. Switching to paperless also triggers a shift in mindset; it helps people think more openly about new ways of working, and encourages them to push boundaries

The risks

Paperless practices also have their downsides, as they invite us to develop the routine of sitting down in front of a screen for almost any sort of task.

- This increases the amount of sedentary work we do, which has many negative implications on work and health (discussed later in this book).

- It tempts us to communicate with our team mates through electronic means, even when face-to-face communication is a viable and better option.

- Working with computers most of the time also limits access to our talent – the part of our intelligence which only comes alive through physically engaging activities like walking, acting, writing or drawing freehand, or building models.

- Some tasks are simply more difficult to do on the screen than on paper, like sketching out unrefined ideas or reviewing large drawings.

For these reasons, I firmly believe that some aspects of work will always remain non-digital. To successfully adopt paperless practices, you need to make electronic communication seamless, but it might be a mistake to completely eliminate paper or other physical representations of data. Make sure that your workplace offers the option of using paper when it is really useful.

Paperless practices only provide maximum benefit when coupled with smart data management systems.

Data in the cloud

Cloud-based services offer the greatest flexibility to workers, enabling them to access information from pretty much anywhere, anytime. In combination with the support services provided by cloud-based service providers, migrating data into the cloud is becoming an increasingly attractive option for companies.

It's a big decision to restructure a company's data system. Careful planning and risk assessment is necessary to ensure safe and seamless operation. This transition also requires training and behavioural change, as workers need to learn to use new tools (e.g. new cloud-based software) and adapt the way they work.

Naturally, some companies are reluctant to make such a big jump. But JobAdder's example (introduced in the previous chapter) is proof that it's possible to successfully run a company, even a software company, entirely relying on cloud-based file management and software infrastructure.

Your data centre

If cloud-based file management is not the right choice for your business, you may still consider hosting your data in an external facility.

Most Australian companies have their own in-house server room (according to a survey by Colliers). There are, however, a number of issues associated with local server rooms. These rooms, while relatively small in comparison to the whole office area, consume a large amount of power, requiring a high-capacity power supply as well as a cooling system and reliable power protection. They are very expensive to build, operate, maintain and relocate.

Furthermore, when a company relocates, the infrastructure required for the reliable operation of an in-house server room can restrict real estate choices. The company may be forced to say no to otherwise ideal tenancy options, just because that building doesn't have the necessary infrastructure in place, and instead to move into a more expensive or less attractive tenancy.

Most companies can free themselves from these constraints by getting their systems (including files, applications, emails and telecommunication services) hosted outside the office, for example in a shared third-party facility that also looks after security and maintenance. While renting space in a professional data centre is significantly more expensive than renting office space, this can still be a worthwhile investment when the broader benefits are considered.

Design implications

Your data management could make a huge difference to the way your workplace functions and what it looks like. Setting up cloud-based or remote access systems will allow your people to access data from anywhere through the internet. This will give your organisation the opportunity to adopt smart workplace strategies such as non-assigned seating (desk sharing), Activity-Based Working and mobile working, which could completely transform your physical work environment.

Strategy 3:
Create a well-functioning floor layout

Traditionally, the starting point of the workspace design process is developing a 'room schedule' – a list of all the rooms to be included in the space, such as workstation areas, meeting spaces, dining area, utility rooms, reception, etc. The next step is to develop a floor layout by fitting all the required rooms into the available (or smallest possible) floor space without compromising good functional connections. For example, the reception area needs to be near the entry, the dining area needs to be near the kitchen, and the utility room needs to be well connected to the workstations.

The problem with this approach is that decisions about room types are made way too early, before thoroughly exploring how information flows within the office. Instead, the main focus is on static items, such as desks for the computers, a conference table for meetings, a dining table for lunch, leading to the creation of unsophisticated environments.

Today's leaders recognise that effective knowledge exchange and collaboration are essential in order to succeed in the knowledge economy. To encourage interaction, they create more open workplaces (by removing walls and partitions), and provide more spaces for social activities and teamwork than in the past. These are usually good first steps, but will only lead to real results if the space promotes the right sort of activities and stimulates the right sort of communication.

To create functional environments, we need to see work as people and knowledge being in a well-directed flow.

Primary work activities

In a 2008 U.S. workplace survey involving 900 office workers, Gensler, a global architecture firm, identified the four primary activities that make up knowledge work: *focused work, collaboration, learning* and *socialising*.

- **Focused work** – Most knowledge workers spend more time with individual focused work than with any other activities. To be able to concentrate, most people need to work in quiet environments, away from distractions and interruptions.

- **Collaboration** – Teams build collective intelligence and solve problems through collaboration, by sharing knowledge and exchanging ideas. Spaces that support collaboration tend to be open, visible, easy to access, and equipped with technology that supports communication and the capturing of ideas.

- **Learning** – Today's workplaces are also learning spaces, as constant learning is essential for keeping workers' knowledge and skills up-to-date in an ever-changing world. Learning occurs in training and meeting rooms, at people's desks through online training, and through human interactions.

- **Socialising** – Social activities strengthen trust and help form vibrant communities, setting the foundations of well-functioning teamwork and business success. Dedicated social facilities such as lounge rooms and kitchens are ideally easy to get to, but are located away (and feel far away) from focused work areas. Socialising can also happen throughout the workplace, for example, in corridors, stairways, and in-between places.

Gensler's 2008 survey found that the workplaces of top performing companies were better designed to support all four modes. Workers in top-performing companies found non-focus activities more critical to individual performance than workers in lower-performing companies, and spent their time more evenly balanced across the four modes.

Interestingly, Gensler's subsequent survey, conducted in 2013, uncovered that the key qualities of high-performing workplaces had shifted: focused work emerged as the main driver of performance. At the time of the second survey, workers in top-performing companies had come to value focused work more highly than those in other companies. It also became clear that the other three modes can only be effective if focused work is well-supported; most importantly, if workers are unable to concentrate, collaboration doesn't work well either.[9]

Designing for all four modes

As these results show, priorities in work activities change over time, and also vary from business to business.

Gensler's framework, as I understand, covers four quadrants of processing information:

	Individual activity	Group activity
Exchanging and processing existing information	Learning	Socialising
Producing new information	Focused work	Collaboration

You might use this framework to guide the design of your workplace, or choose to create your own, one that better describes work in your organisation.

Before jumping into the design stage, you need to consider the attributes of spaces (e.g. sounds, lights, technology, privacy) that help people excel in each of the different activities. You should also look at how these activities could potentially hinder each other, because they can, and often do, clash.

---

9   The survey revealed that the importance of focused work was not reflected by the design of the vast majority of the workplaces. Gensler's report stated: 'Despite many workplaces designed expressly to support collaboration, time spent collaborating has decreased by 20%, while time spent focusing has increased by 13%.' The report also pointed out that the overall effectiveness of workplaces had declined by 6% over the previous five years, which can be largely attributed to the decrease in employees' ability to engage in focused work in their workplaces.

For example, open workplaces designed to promote dynamic interaction can be acoustically and visually distracting for those trying to concentrate. Balancing focused work, collaboration and other modes, without compromising any of them can be a challenging goal.

To create a workplace that supports all activities – and supercharges human performance[10] – you need to set clear boundaries between areas where activities could impose on each other. A straightforward approach is to establish zones, each designed for different levels of noise, intensity of activities, and access.

For example, focused work is a quiet, low intensity activity which benefits from being away from traffic, so a great location could be around the perimeter of a building. In contrast, socialising is a noisy, high intensity activity that needs easy access, so locating the social zone near main circulation paths can be ideal.

Case study: Skype office

Skype's Palo Alto (California) headquarters, accommodating 250 employees, is a fully renovated warehouse. The building was stripped down to its core to give space to a strategically organised workplace.

Skype is a fast-moving, disruptive company that values elegant functionality, and is driven by the purpose of breaking down barriers to communication. They implement a software development strategy called Scrum, which 'enables teams to self-organize by encouraging physical co-location or close online collaboration of all team members, as well as daily face-to-face communication among all team members and disciplines in the project' (as described by Wikipedia).

The company recognises the environment's influence on the thought process, and has created an innovative, highly functional workplace that facilitates different types of interactions and encourages spontaneity.

---

10   Gensler's 2013 survey report states: 'For employees whose workplaces support both their individual work and collaborative work, we see a significant spike in performance.'

Spaces for **concentration, collaboration,** and **contemplation** are laid out concentrically around a central corridor:

- The **concentration** zones (individual workstations) are organised around the building's perimeter, in areas that are quieter and benefit from daylight.
- The **collaboration** zones (meeting spaces, whiteboard areas) are located along the central spine, encouraging team members to 'meet in the middle'.
- The **contemplation** spaces (casual lounges) are sprinkled around the collaboration zones.

There is also a **chill-out area** (kitchen) which provides space for a variety of social activities.

This layout is very effective in managing noise, which is especially important considering that Skype is involved in high-tech development and uses extensive audio-visual technology. The noisiest functions (technology-equipped meeting rooms and phone booths) are located in freestanding, acoustically isolated pods.

The design also promotes casual interaction in the right places. Informal gathering areas near the centre function as points of arrival, and also facilitate way-finding (which is especially important for Skype's transient staff). Movable furniture in the communal spaces supports spontaneous conversations. Mobile whiteboards called 'Skype-Its' are used throughout the office to help staff capture and share ideas.

The office has an open and light feel, and supports teamwork while offering areas for individual work or relaxation. This is a workplace people want to work in, and which helps them perform at their peak.

Strategy 4: Support flexible ways of working

If you allow people not only to meet, but to actually do work in all areas, rather than just at their workstations, you can make much better use of a strategically zoned workplace.

Today's mainstream technologies, such as wireless data, laptops, mobile phones, location-tracking applications, etc., make this option viable, enabling workers to move from space to space and still access all the digital resources they need with minimal friction. Interestingly, technology also assists people to collaborate better in the non-digital world, as they can now more easily organise face-to-face meetings and working groups as work dictates. As a result, flexible work arrangements are increasingly common.

Flexible working is synonymous with 'non-assigned seating'[11], meaning that workers don't have their own dedicated workstations (or cubicles or offices). Instead, they choose a vacant space every time they come to the office, and either use their own laptops, or log into the company's network from a shared computer. You have the option to set up an online system for workers to reserve their desks in advance (hoteling system), or spaces can simply be allocated on a first-come first-served basis (hot-desking).

Benefits for staff and the organisation

Flexible working allows people to work in those areas within the office (or even outside the office) that best support their work, throughout the day. It provides opportunities for better collaboration by enabling people to form self-organised groups as needed, irrespective of organisational structure. This arrangement also facilitates mentoring relationships and communication between work buddies. Furthermore, flexible working offers personal control to people, and thus a more satisfying work experience.

Flexible working can reduce accommodation costs by a better utilisation of the space. In most workplaces, a large number of people are away from their desks at any given time. With this more efficient workplace model companies can minimise the redundant space they pay for and operate from a smaller floor space.[12]

---

11 The following terms also refer to various forms of non-assigned seating: non-territorial working, free address work, unassigned seating, flexi-desking, hot-desking, desk sharing and hoteling. Agile working and Activity-Based Working refer to more advanced forms of flexible working. I'm sure there are many more similar terms; they keep being invented to keep us entertained. Be aware that these terms are often used interchangeably, but incorrectly.

12 Luc Kamperman, who first introduced Activity-Based Working (a form of flexible working), states: 'The cost/benefit in general is that companies are able to allocate up to 10, 20 per cent more people in the same building.' 'On any given day, only 40-50% of a typical office is filled, due to sickness or travel or vacation.'

Potential problems

However, there are common issues with flexible working. In a flexible environment it can be difficult to find other people, let alone to supervise them. Some managers find it difficult to adopt the practice of assessing people's performance based on their results, not on their presence.

With non-assigned seating, workers need to give up their private workstations – a space that used to be only their own, which they could personalise and set up to meet their needs, and where they could keep their work-related items and personal belongings. Instead, they need to retrieve their items from a locker every time they come in, find an empty desk and set it all up. Flexible work settings also tend to be smaller than assigned workstations.

In short, non-assigned seating requires a huge shift in behaviour. When workers don't adapt well, either because they might be stressed or upset, or because they don't know how to, their performance suffers. When change is not managed well, people who find it too challenging may leave.

It's up to the workers to make the right choice about which space suits which task, and then to properly adjust the ergonomic features of their entire work setting every time they shift location. When they are constantly on the move, some may find this a bit too much effort. Incorrectly set up work settings increase strain on the body (especially on the neck and the back) as well as the chance of injury.

Saving on accommodation costs by implementing flexible working is a very attractive incentive for companies. But it can be hard to predict how these changes will impact on people's experience and performance at work.[13]

Flexible working is not for everyone and every business. Unless flexible working suits the organisation's culture and model of working, the losses can quickly wipe out what has been saved on the floor space.

---

13 There is little credible research on how flexible working influences work and business performance, and the results also vary from business to business. Flexible working is a highly debated topic. Not surprisingly, most case studies – written by designers or business leaders who have already invested into the change – rave about the benefits of adopting flexible work practices, while researchers and workplace strategists warn about the downsides.

Setting the foundations

I'm not suggesting that flexible working is inherently problematic. But we need to acknowledge that it takes something important away from workers while also putting demands on managers, and workplaces need to address the emotional and psychological challenges that may arise.

Flexible working is a holistic strategy, so when adopting it you need to carefully consider its impact on the organisation's culture, people's experience and behaviour, technology requirements, and how managers can take care of their teams. Basing the decision on cost savings alone is a recipe for disaster.

To be successful, the changes need to be carefully implemented, and supported by committed leaders and engaged staff – who should all understand the drivers behind the changes, the benefits for them, and how to work productively in the new environment. A high level of trust between all involved is foundational.

Companies that are the most successful in adopting flexible working tend to foster open communication, and to implement change management and/or educational programs.

Design suggestions

- If you're not comfortable with the idea of people juggling with desk spaces like playing 'musical chairs' and risking that some might miss out at times, the safest option is to provide enough desks for everyone, in addition to the short-term work settings such as collaboration areas and quiet spaces.

- Before adopting flexible working, consider testing it out in parts of your office. (For an example, see the Arup case study at the end of this chapter.)

- Keep in mind that flexible working may better suit some people or work functions than others. A hybrid environment – with a mix of allocated and non-allocated desks – can be a good solution; you don't need to go all the way.

- Provide adequate storage, such as centralised lockers, shelves and cabinets, for work-related items and personal belongings. (Using mobile storage units is also an option, but not very practical.) It's important to get the storage numbers and sizes right, since making changes after the units are installed can be difficult and costly. (This may sound like a trivial issue, but it's surprising how often companies find out that their storage units are too small, or that they don't have enough of them, when it's too late.)

- Make this new way of working attractive for everyone, including those who have fixed desks but need to work with others who are constantly moving around. When you need to take something away from people, provide benefits elsewhere.

- You will need to establish new ground rules, for example no talking, no phone calls, or no mobile devices in certain areas. Putting up some friendly signs can help.

Technological suggestions

- Consider using applications that allow people to book a particular desk, or group of desks for a project team, in advance. You could also use a 'check in' system to find out if those who booked have actually turned up, and if not, cancel the booking.

- To help people find a colleague, a vacant spot or a room, you could use applications that capture and show real-time data about who is sitting where.

- A range of tools are available for measuring space utilisation (meaning, to which capacity your different rooms and workstations are used). This data could help you refine your workplace strategy and plan for future changes.

- You could use a telecommunication system which allows people to log in to the phone system from wherever they work in the office, and which directs unanswered calls to their emails. However, more and more companies are giving up their landlines as they become redundant with extensive mobile phone coverage.

Strategy 5:
Make the most of Activity-Based Working

Activity-Based Working (ABW) is one of the most commonly discussed strategies in workplace design, though it's often confused with non-assigned seating.

ABW is an advanced form of flexible working; an agile workplace strategy with a strong focus on improving communication and teamwork, while still supporting focused work. Essentially, ABW combines the two strategies discussed above: a well-functioning floor layout with flexible working.

As its name suggests, Activity-Based Working is all about providing the right types of spaces for the wide range of activities we do at work. The core principle is really this simple, and can be adopted by almost any organisation in one form or another.

Activity-based workplaces typically offer five to ten different types of work settings for individual as well as team activities, for example, open workstation areas, formal and informal meeting spaces, cafe-style lounges, project rooms, and quiet library-type rooms. These spaces are designed to help people excel in each activity, whether it's generating ideas, solving problems, executing plans or sharing knowledge.

ABW workplaces invite people to choose where and how they work based on what they do, who they work with, and how they feel. People and teams move around a lot, usually every day, and sometimes several times a day.

The benefits

The best activity-based workplaces are dynamic environments geared towards teamwork, with collaborative spaces taking up over 30% of the floor area (while in traditional offices this is typically around 10%). This is achieved within the same, or smaller, floor space since with non-assigned seating the space is used more efficiently.

ABW allows project teams to sit together, learn from each other and support each other while implementing a project. This is a much more modern and efficient way of working than managing the project through scheduled meetings only, and then everyone working by themselves in between meetings (typically surrounded by colleagues working on other projects), ticking off items from a to-do list.

ABW is a potent strategy; if implemented well, the benefits are enormous. It creates a less hierarchical workplace that stimulates interaction and knowledge exchange, supports learning and professional development, promotes trust and personal accountability, and makes work more efficient as well as more enjoyable.

The way I see it, ABW is an answer to the decades-long debate about whether open plan offices or private offices are better environments for productive work, or in other words, whether workplaces should be designed for collaboration or for focused work. We don't need to choose either/or; Activity-Based Working offers both, and lets people make their choices in real time.

Spreading like wildfire

The concept of ABW was developed and made widespread by a Dutch consulting firm, Veldhoen + Company. It was first implemented in 1997 in Tilburg for the head office of Interpolis, a Dutch insurance company.

Veldhoen + Company brought the concept to Australia, when in collaboration with Australian architecture firms Woods Bagot and Clive Wilkinson Architects, they delivered Macquarie Group's new workplace, One Shelley Street in Sydney, in 2009.

The financial sector was among the early adopters, quickly followed by businesses in the property sector. Today, professional services, communication and technology companies, and even law firms[14] are following their lead, developing, testing or already using their versions of ABW.

The way ABW is put into practice is constantly evolving as new technologies and work practices emerge, leaders learn from each other, and companies shape the core concept to their specific needs and culture. (For example, the National Australia Bank has recently adopted a workplace model in which

---

14 Until recently, lawyers were particularly attached to their private offices, partially due to privacy issues and partially due to the status their offices represented. This held them back from a more strategic use of space.

not individuals, but entire teams move around within the office together, and the space is designed to enhance communication between different teams. A case study of this building is included in Principle 4: Diversified.)

Good news, bad news

- 'Macquarie Group workplace has yielded over 90% employee satisfaction and up to 30% more people per square meter' (reported by Smith Madden, commercial interior design and project management company).

- After the Sydney office transformation of GPT, a property company, an employee survey found: 'Perceived productivity in the top 10 percent of Australian offices' and 'Number one for occupant satisfaction' – compared to any other office surveyed in Australia!

This kind of news about successful office transformations is abundant and spreads fast, attracting a large amount of interest in this way of working. And in some cases, perhaps a bit too much interest. Due to its radical and transformative nature, many leaders see ABW as the alpha and omega of workplace design. (If this was true, this book would have only one chapter.)

Remember, ABW – like any forms of flexible working – can be done well or done badly, and is certainly not for everyone. (For example, Deloitte found that ABW worked well in some of their departments but not in others.) If you consider implementing ABW, make sure you look at both sides of the story, and ensure that your workplace works for everyone.

Design suggestions

- Get the fundamentals of flexible working right, as explained under Strategy 4. (Without implementing non-assigned seating successfully, ABW cannot be successful.)

- Take a note of the different types of activities (e.g. phone conversations, collaborative design meetings, individual quiet work, social catch-ups) your people do. Find out, using surveys or digital measuring tools, how often and for how long people engage in the different activities. Observe how frequently they use the different types of rooms that you already have, and how that works for them.

Think through how you would like your people to shift their work habits; which work activities need more focus, and which need less. Use all of this information to create a workplace which offers the perfect mix of different work settings.

- Feel free to experiment with different room set-ups and technologies. Spaces do not always work as planned; when you find that a space is not used often, or is used the wrong way, make some adjustments.

- Encourage your people to move around and explore the benefits of working in different types of environments, instead of just sitting in their favourite spot all the time. At the same time, also give them the opportunity to retreat to a familiar place whenever they need a break from constant movement. This is what our next strategy is about.

Strategy 6:
Create 'neighbourhoods'

We all enjoy 'transition' in our lives, like going on a journey or advancing our career. But we also need a 'home', a familiar place to go back to which offers safety and comfort. Seeking a 'home' is a human survival mechanism. A flexible, innovative environment that offers freedom of choice does meet workers' 'transitional' needs, but their need to have a 'home' – a familiar environment to work in when they need a break from stimulation and newness – is rarely looked after.

When teams are intentionally mixed up with the aim of promoting cross-collaboration, people inevitably end up sitting near colleagues they know little about, personally and professionally, and when neighbours are too busy to even say hello, everyone is left disconnected. In such environments, workers are less trusting and are more resentful of distractions. People also feel compelled to behave more formally amongst less familiar faces, which takes effort and makes it harder to relax.

Workers are more reluctant to ask questions of their neighbours, and more likely to communicate with their peers through electronic means, which lack the nuances of the spoken word and can add to feelings of isolation. Maintaining a buddy or mentoring system – to support junior or struggling team members – can also be a challenge, unless there are some rules around seating arrangements.

Flexible working, with its lack of structure, also takes up precious mental resources. For example, people need to make choices about where to sit and who to sit next to for the day. When they arrive late, they need to walk around in the busy office searching for a vacant spot, which can be disheartening and even embarrassing. To avoid this unpleasant experience and secure their preferred desks, workers often use a variety of techniques, such as leaving late after the cleaners have gone and marking their spot by leaving papers behind, thus outsmarting the system.

A flexible workplace often feels impersonal and sterile, since it doesn't offer many opportunities for personalisation. This is especially apparent out of hours when most people are away and all signs of human activities and personalities are locked away in storage units.[15] But even during the day, a space without character can leave people feeling somewhat alienated. Creating a flexible space that people feel connected to is certainly possible, but it takes extra effort.

Peer groups and nested groups

Creating neighbourhoods in the office can alleviate some of these issues without sacrificing the benefits of agile work practices. The neighbourhood is the home of a team, a zone that members gravitate towards unless they have a particular reason to work elsewhere.

Anthropological studies show that in any environment, the number of people who work or live together in a tight group influences the quality of collaboration and relationships. To form close bonds and build trust, the ideal group size is around 6 to 8 people. A group smaller than that can be easily dominated by one person, and a larger group cannot function well without a leader. But in this sweet spot, there is the right balance between individual influence and peer pressure (i.e. getting people to fit in with the organisation's or community's culture and pursue a shared interest) to optimise team outcomes.

---

15   In contrast, think about the home of a person you know well. The space we inhabit tells so much about who we are, and it also shapes who we are. Occupying spaces that don't resonate with our identity is not natural to us, and can strongly impact performance. This will be further discussed in Principle 5: Caring.

In organisations where people are grouped into teams of 6 to 8 they tend to have stronger social ties (including friendships), and thus to be more trusting, engaged and loyal.[16]

Therefore, to support the formation and cohesion of peer groups, create small hubs within the workplace such as team rooms or distinct groups of workstations partially separated from each other. And to amplify the benefits, consider setting up 'nested groups', which means organising small groups into larger clusters. This can look like a handful of peer groups organised around a shared facility (e.g. a meeting space), with these units then combined into departments of 150 or less[17].

The way office neighbourhoods function is not dissimilar to city neighbourhoods, with their family dwellings, building blocks, streets, side streets and public squares, each space supporting the formation of different types of relationships and communities.

Several of today's most effective offices follow this model, building a structure into the system we are all familiar with, instead of putting a mass of people into one large undifferentiated space.

Interestingly, it's not only offices that can benefit from establishing neighbourhoods. Here is an example:

---

16   You might have observed that workers tend to naturally form family size groups, or that teams larger than 8 often struggle to collaborate effectively.

17   150 – Dunbar's number – is estimated to be the maximum number of social relationships an average person is able to comfortably maintain. Large organisations are often structured into departments of 150 or less, as this strategy appears to improve cohesion and morale within organisations.

A non-traditional workplace: Falkenburg Road Prison

At certain times in history, prisons were built for deterring and punishing criminals. But many of today's prisons are thoughtfully designed to influence their residents' behaviour – to calm prisoners, partially in the interest of staff security.

The Falkenburg Road Prison in Florida is a great example. Prison staff had a significant contribution to the design, and their insights helped make the building safer and more functional.

One of the key decisions was to adopt what's called 'direct supervision', the practice of placing guards within the inmates' containment area, as opposed to separating them with a glass wall, which is a more common practice. Decision makers took into consideration the research which found that this arrangement positively influences both violent and non-violent behaviour. This can be explained by the social bond that naturally forms when humans interact face-to-face and which shapes their behaviour, even in a prison yard.

Using a group nesting strategy was another critical decision made to align prisoners' behaviour by increasing social bonding and peer pressure. The facility accommodates inmates in 4 to 8 bed dormitories[18]. Four of these sleeping units, separated from the neighbouring units by half-height walls, form an alcove. And four of these alcoves are organised around a common living area, which also includes the guard station. (From a bird's eye view, the facility resembles a village, rather than one enormous building block, as prisons are usually depicted.)

As a result, inmates are not members of a homogenous group of hundreds; they are members of a small family-sized group, which belongs to a medium size group, which is connected to a larger community.

This layout has turned out to be really successful; the jail has a low number of violent incidents, and is widely recognised as one of the most progressively-designed prison facilities.

---

18   One of the prison's architects acknowledged, '... in terms of behavior, an eight-man cell actually functions pretty well.' However, the design was also driven by concerns of security and efficiency, hence the smaller dormitories.

Putting things into practice

 ## Case study: Arup

Arup is a global engineering, design and consulting firm offering professional services for all aspects of the built environment. Until recently, their Melbourne group was located in two separate buildings, which made interaction between departments difficult. Before moving everyone into one large office, management decided to try out Activity-Based Work in one of the existing offices to find out how it would work for Arup, and whether it was worth adopting in the new office.

In a conversation, one of the masterminds behind this experiment, senior business administrator Lian Heather, brought me behind the scenes.

Making the decision

Before the transition to ABW, Arup's engineering teams (structural, electrical and mechanical engineers, etc.) used to work within their own departments, which made it difficult to bring multidisciplinary project teams together to design a building.

The idea of adopting flexible work practices came from one of the engineers, Cameron McIntosh, who realised that doing so could improve communication between workers in different departments. At that time Activity-Based Working wasn't yet an established concept, certainly not in engineering companies, but after doing thorough research, the core transformation team realised that ABW was the solution to their problem. Once the support of higher management was secured, things happened really fast. Out of the 84 people in the group, around 30 – those who were the most enthusiastic and open to change – volunteered for the six-month pilot program.

What the transition looked like

Interestingly, the transformation happened mostly through changing the way the space was used; the interior was hardly touched, apart from creating new breakout spaces and installing a set of lockers. As Lian explains: 'We had to work with what we had. We've had to take over spaces and say "this is now the concentration space" or "this is now a collaboration space" but nothing has really changed.'

The 'concentration space' was a cluster of workstations where people were asked to stay quiet and leave their phones behind. The 'collaboration space' was a group of desks without divider partitions or any other barriers for team conversations. Other work areas included the enclosed 'design studios' equipped with a projector and a whiteboard (these spaces turned out to be really popular), and the 'drop-in space', an island of bare desks without computer screens, for people who would only come to the office for a couple of hours.

The ABW desks were dotted around the office, so the participants could easily collaborate with those who had allocated desks, and Arup's already existing CISCO telecommunication system made it possible for people to receive phone calls and voice messages wherever they worked.

Challenges

The transition wasn't without challenges; it required a shift in mindset and behaviours, and pushed people out of their comfort zones. For example, participants needed to store their personal belongings in a locker instead of on the top of their desks, reduce the use of paper, and learn to manage their files differently. (Engineers have a culture of using a lot of paper, especially for big drawings; perhaps this is why ABW reached the engineering sector a bit later than other industries.)

The number one complaint was the difficulty of finding people. However, those who participated adjusted quickly, because they knew they had to. Lian was one of them: 'I became more aware of people. So if I walked around the office, I would remember: this person is sitting over here today.' Also, people tended to sit with their peers – unless they needed to work elsewhere in a multidisciplinary project team – which made it easier to find them.

Learnings

A series of surveys of the participating and non-participating staff revealed some interesting findings:

- Those on ABW were just as satisfied with the amount of storage space they had during the program (i.e. a locker and a small shelf) as they were before the program started, when they had a whole desk, a pedestal, and large shelves. In contrast, the satisfaction of non-participating members substantially dropped, despite the fact that the amount of storage available for them hadn't changed.

- Access to discipline leaders is very important in Arup, and so the surveys also asked all staff about whether this was an issue. Those on ABW found that the level of access they had to leaders was about the same, while the others thought that it had decreased. Interestingly, no discipline leaders were on ABW. People with allocated desks just had the perception that they couldn't find people, and this perception became all-encompassing.

From the responses, it appeared that staff who needed to deal with limitations had willingly changed their behaviour, but those who had not received the benefits associated with ABW had a heightened perception of the negatives.

Only those who participated in ABW were involved in the change management program. However, the feedback revealed that this was a failing, since the impact on the rest of the group also turned out to be significant.

Results

According to the feedback, people in general felt more productive after the changes; they were able to do things quicker because they could more easily talk to those they needed to.

The new recruits who jumped straight into the program did fit in spectacularly quickly, since they were not weighed down by ingrained habits.

One of the several graduates who also joined the program felt at the end that he had gained a massive advantage compared to his peers who had fixed desks. He had more opportunities to get to know people and to learn about other disciplines.

The new system also made it possible to invite external team members (architects, for example) to work in the office, which made collaboration more powerful and opened up new opportunities.

The transition wouldn't have worked without managers trusting staff, and treating them as grown-ups. This gave the most empowering feeling to everyone involved.

At the end of the trial period, all but one of the participating people wanted to continue, and many of the non-participating staff were also ready to join in. The trial was a success; it became clear that ABW was a viable option for Arup to pursue further.

Questions to consider

- What tools and technology do your people use for capturing and developing ideas, and for documenting and exchanging information? And how well do these work for them?

- When is it best to use digital tools, and when is it best to use low-tech tools?

- What tools and technology are you likely to use in future?

- When do your teams need to talk face-to-face, and when is it sufficient or necessary to communicate through digital means?

- How do you store and manage data? And how does it affect your people's work?

- What is the role of paper in your business? And do you intend to change this?

- What kinds of activities do your people do in your organisation? What are the different 'modes'?

- How does information travel between people and between teams?

- How do your teams interact? And how could this be improved?

- Could flexible working suit your organisation's work style and culture?

- Are your people ready to deal with the challenges of flexible working? And do they appreciate the benefits?

- How are teams structured? What are the group sizes?

- How would self-organised work benefit your business?

PRINCIPLE

3

PRODUCTIVE

CREATE SPACE FOR A PRODUCTIVE BUSINESS

Creating an environment where we can focus, think clearly and work efficiently

Productive work, in today's knowledge economy, is not about producing as many widgets as possible during a shift; it's about solving mental problems and making efficient decisions. To do well, we need a clear head space, high physical and mental energy, and full presence. However, myriad forces in the workplace test us and pull us away from what we are supposed to be doing. A productive workplace shelters us from internal and external distractions and provides us with the right conditions to make the best use of our knowledge and skills.

Productivity matters

What productivity is and isn't

It's not easy to define productivity, but it is important to do so. Those who take the time to understand what productivity is tend to have more productive teams, because they know better how to create the right conditions for their people to do their best.

The definition I like to use is: productivity is the amount of work of a predetermined quality produced in a set timeframe. In plain English, this means working fast and well, with minimal errors[1]. I believe all productive activities have one common feature: the efficient use of resources (e.g. time, skills, and knowledge) achieved through thinking, communicating and acting to the best of our abilities.

Hipsters call it 'Getting Shit Done' (or GSD). No messing around, no procrastination, no dealing with irrelevant stuff. It involves tackling challenges with focus and high energy, making quick and effective decisions, and bouncing back after setbacks.

You and your team know best what 'fast and high quality work' means in your business. You might include the number and quality of social media posts created each day, phone calls made, clients acquired, reports written, decisions made, ideas generated – whichever activities contribute to providing value to your clients and the organisation.

Productivity does not mean working longer hours; in fact, the longer the hours, the lower the productivity ratio. Old-school productivity measures such as the speed of typing and number of typing errors are far less important today. The number of hours spent in front of a screen is a useless measure

---

1   Productivity is about efficiency, as opposed to effectiveness. Scott Hanselman, Principal Program Manager at Microsoft, states it beautifully: 'Effectiveness is doing the right things, but efficiency is doing things right. That means effectiveness is picking a direction and efficiency is running really fast in that direction.'

unless we have an outcome. The number of interactions in an office is less important than the quality of them.

The new workplace

New ways of doing business

The advances in information sharing have transformed the way we work. In this new economy we have different work habits, do different tasks, use different skills, use different tools, and communicate with different people than we did even just a few years ago. Work has become more complex and challenging; we have more competition, and more new skills and more knowledge to acquire each day.

However, technology cannot entirely replace humans. Most tasks that are simple or can be automated have already either been taken over by machines or are usually outsourced. Thinking and assimilating knowledge are the new frontier.

We need to be 'switched on'

Knowledge work is becoming ever more elaborate and complex. The value of our work depends on the quality of our thoughts and decisions; coming up with unique ideas and customised solutions is at the heart of what we do. To stay on top of the game, we need to deal with complex situations, think and communicate with intelligence and clarity, and take action in alignment with the goals of the project, team and business.

This is a lot to ask. We may not need to be superhuman (though sometimes you may wonder), but we certainly need optimal mental functioning to be able to work well.

New challenges

Maintaining a productive state in our hectic work lives is a real challenge. Physical discomfort, interruptions, and negative emotions (insecurity, self-doubt, frustration and worry) are among the common distractions in the workplace that can deplete our inner resources.

Interconnectivity and easy access to information, while making our work easier and more efficient in some ways, also impose new demands on us:

- **Distraction:** dealing with competing demands on our attention

- **Complexity:** making sense of a vast amount of information quickly (much of which is irrelevant)

- **Intensity:** evaluating numerous tempting opportunities and making many decisions each day, usually under time pressure

- **Overload:** having more responsibilities and obligations than we can handle

Many of these influences are outside our control. However, it is within our control to create a workplace that supports us to stay in the best possible shape to tackle these challenges. When the negative influences we are bombarded with are not managed well, the impact on our psychology and behaviour can be dramatic:

- **Stress** has become normalised, impacting on our mental functioning, quality of work, attitude, and relationships. Many of us always feel behind, regardless how much we work, as we try to keep up with demands.

- People's **attention spans have been shrinking** rapidly. One hundred years ago, the average human attention span was around 20 minutes. According to research, our attention span today can be as low as 8 seconds (2013 data), which is worse than a goldfish!

- We have become victims of **information overload**, a mental state when we are unable to make sense of information at the speed that it is presented to us. In this state we are anxious and powerless, work more slowly, make more errors, and are less creative.

- **Cognitive overload** (often aptly called 'fried brain syndrome') occurs when we simultaneously need to deal with several mental demands and challenges, such as information overload, time pressure, interruptions and work complexity. We become stressed and find it difficult to pay attention and to focus. We become irrational. We juggle between tasks even when we don't need to, and set the wrong priorities by doing things that are easy rather than what is important. We make poor decisions or no decisions at all.

- **Personal problems** emerge when the pressures of work affect our relationships and support systems, further exacerbating inefficiency at work.

These are huge issues not only at work but in many areas of our lives. Creating a clear head space for our work and lives is one of the most important and potent ways of reclaiming our productivity, sanity, health and happiness.

Some office designs don't help

Very few workplaces address the issues triggered by current trends. Instead, there is too much emphasis on the functional requirements of office design, especially fitting all the necessary functional elements such as desks, storage spaces and meeting rooms into the smallest possible space, like a jigsaw puzzle.

Open-plan offices: collaboration vs focus

With collaboration and innovation being the mantras of business today, leaders of organisations are striving to create workplaces that promote face-to-face interaction. As a result, open-plan workplaces have now become the default in most industries. These environments support teamwork and knowledge exchange, promote a culture of transparency, and are more flexible than private offices. They are also cheaper to build.

However, unless the productivity issues created by these workplaces are addressed, the disadvantages far outweigh the benefits (as already mentioned in Principle 2: Smart). Noise issues and the lack of privacy have now become the most common complaints of office workers. In a large open space, many of us have difficulty concentrating due to various distractions. And working in close proximity with our colleagues all the time, without having the option to retreat, can make individual focused work a huge challenge.

So despite focus being the most significant factor contributing to effective work, this is what our open-plan offices compromise most. (According to an Australian research study, open offices had a negative impact on productivity in 90% of cases.)

Unproductive space, people and business

Dark, stuffy, noisy, drab – this kind of workplace offers no support for us to successfully live up to the demands of modern work. It might be cheaper to occupy this kind of space, but it does not help us get our work done quickly, effectively and efficiently. And that comes at a price. Poor workspaces waste time, money and workers' talent, whether that manifests in higher labour costs or in lower profit. But there can be a greater cost – the damage to our brand when the quality of our service suffers.

And sometimes, even when leaders set the best intentions, make thorough plans and engage expert professionals, things can go wrong.

💡 Polar fleece and ear plugs

Shortly after moving to Australia, I got a position at one of the country's most highly regarded architectural firms. The office space was brand new; the team had just moved in. The space expressed beautifully all that the firm stood for.

It demonstrated high quality design in congruence with the company's promise to their clients. It was a spacious, sun-filled, open office with an outdoor deck and stunning views. At first sight, this was an ideal environment for making people feel great and work well.

Imagine the horror of the firm's principals when they found that our billings were down despite the effort made to create this model environment. The culprit? An over-active air-conditioning system left all of us with chattering teeth and numb fingers, despite polar fleece becoming the office uniform. On top of that, the company moved into the new office before it was complete, so we needed to work with distracting beeping, drilling and knocking noises in the background during the remaining construction works. As you would imagine, it was nearly impossible to focus on our tasks; we were stressed and exhausted.

Good design is a demanding task indeed, and even the professionals can make mistakes, as this experience shows.

Closing the gap

Common approaches to design

Of course, design teams do their best to create thriving work environments. So how come the majority of workplaces still inhibit productivity?

A productive environment needs to support people's physical and psychological needs, and some of the solutions for creating the right conditions can be costly (e.g. functional building services, good quality building fabric, and extra floor space). Unfortunately, at times of financial challenge decision makers often feel that compromising on this is the only option.

The impact of supporting human needs is hard to measure, so cost-cutting often results in spaces where people's well-being – and thus their performance – suffers. It's not unusual that businesses move into sub-standard tenancies aiming to save on rent, just to find that the losses in productivity are way higher than the savings.

Designers need to find a good balance between all business and human objectives, rather than focusing on only a few of them. Humans are sensitive creatures, so even if 99% of the environmental conditions are right, it's enough to be disturbed just by one 'tiny' thing – a single noise, a flickering light, an unpleasant odour, or the uncomfortable feeling that someone is watching – in order to lose our train of thought.

Productive workplaces

It's great to see positive trends; increasing numbers of workplaces are designed to provide high quality air, good quality lighting and acoustics, ergonomic furniture, quiet rooms, breakout spaces and bike facilities. Some workplaces go even further, providing height-adjustable desks, gyms, workshop spaces, and lounge rooms.

The leaders of companies that best capitalise on their people's potential know that a productive workspace is not only a setting, but also a tool for looking after their people's internal environment, i.e. their physical, mental and emotional states. They realise that time is not the only limited resource people need to use wisely, but also their mental capacity, such as paying attention, processing information, and making decisions. The environments they provide are tailored to make it easier for workers to excel, and in these workplaces people actually look forward to their work!

What the workplace can do for us

The physical environment can help us optimise our productivity in three different ways:

1. Supporting people's physical needs (see Strategies 1-3 below)

    We are biological beings, just like plants or animals. In order to function properly and thrive, we need clean air, physical comfort, sufficient light, support for our body posture, and regular rest. Provide a space which offers these, so that people feel well, think well, and perform at their best.

2. Reducing negative influences (see Strategies 4-6 below)

    Reduce the distractions and negative influences that can clutter people's head space and compromise their performance. Consider those generated by the environment (noise, glare), by the proximity of colleagues (conversations, interruptions), and those generated by people's own minds (stress, fear, overwhelm).[2]

3. Promoting productive behaviour (see Strategies 7-8 below)

    Create an environment that assists people to take care of themselves (e.g. taking breaks, being physically active), adopt productive habits (e.g. doing one thing at a time), and give up unproductive ones (e.g. multitasking, procrastination). This is especially important today when some of the greatest obstacles to productivity are self-imposed. A well-designed space can help us better maintain our energy, clarity and focus, and make the best use of our most precious resource: our thoughts.

---

[2] Some of the distractions are not related to the physical space (or even to work), such as personal conflicts or family problems. The environment we work in of course does not have the power to make up for all these, but it can help us feel better in many ways.

Key design strategies

Here are the key design strategies to help promote productivity:

1. Provide clean, fresh air
2. Make people feel comfortable – not too hot, not too cold
3. Provide good quality lighting
4. Minimise distractions and interruptions
5. Reduce sources of negative thoughts and feelings
6. Promote good posture, movement and exercise
7. Encourage productive habits
8. Provide opportunities for quality breaks

Once these strategies are implemented, your people will not only be more effective and produce higher quality work, but will also develop a better relationship with their work and the organisation.

Productivity can be further enhanced by enabling people to choose a work environment that is best suited to their individual work style, personality, and the type of thinking required for the task. This will be discussed in the following chapter, Principle 4: Diversity.

Strategy 1:
Provide clean, fresh air

Clean fresh air ... how do you feel even just thinking about it? We go and get some fresh air when we need to take a break or need to think clearly, but we tend to forget how fundamental it is to our everyday functioning. This is the number one thing every workplace needs to provide; without allowing people to breathe good quality air, all other efforts to support productivity are fruitless.

Used air (with too much CO_2 and other contaminants) is an invisible problem. When you notice that your office is unpleasantly stuffy, or that you struggle to stay awake in the meeting room because your brain is starved of oxygen, the problem is already severe. But even when less apparent, bad air quality is a productivity killer.

So how come bad air quality is such a common problem in workplaces? Providing good quality air is a complex engineering and design challenge.[3]

Fresh air can be brought into buildings in three ways: through openable windows, through a piping system (mechanical ventilation), and through the combination of both (mixed-mode ventilation). With each solution, there are a number of issues to watch out for.

Openable windows

Many people (myself included) prefer working in places with openable windows. Open windows offer connection to the outdoors, and provide a sense of control. Air coming in through the windows feels fresher and more natural.

However, with naturally ventilated buildings (i.e. those with openable windows), you rely on people's diligence in opening the windows regularly. And especially when it's too hot or too cold outside, they will likely be reluctant to do that. Another problem with openable windows is that it's hard to avoid draught and to control air circulation so that the fresh air reaches where it's needed most.

If your workplace has openable windows, make sure that your people are willing to take responsibility for ventilating the space. You may need to set some rules to avoid disagreements. You may also need to organise your floor layout around the natural air-flow; for example, locating meeting

---

[3] These challenges include: taking outside air into the building from a location where it is clean (which can be tricky in a city with heavy traffic), distributing it within the building to where people actually are (whether they are spread out at their workstations or squeezed into a small meeting room), blowing it into the space at the right pace (not too slowly, because that would mean people don't have enough fresh air, and not too fast, because that could be inefficient and create draught), making sure that the fresh air brought into the workplace is at the right temperature and that it actually reaches people before being extracted, and doing all these without wasting too much heating or cooling energy.

places close to the windows, and printers (emitting toxic fumes) near those windows where the air naturally exits the building.

Mechanical ventilation

Mechanical ventilation can give you a much better control of air-flow as long as the system is well-designed and well-maintained and is specifically tailored to the layout of your workplace.

Unfortunately, these factors don't always come together. Most of us know only too well how it feels to work in stuffy rooms. I have worked in offices where different odours surprised me regularly – car fumes, chicken parma, glue solvent; sometimes I didn't even want to think about the spaces the air I was breathing in had travelled through. Random odours like these indicate that something is wrong with the system.

Upgrading an existing ventilation system is a very costly exercise. So before moving into an existing building, it's important to check that the ventilation system functions well and has the capacity to provide enough fresh air to the maximum number of people who will occupy the space at any given time. Before committing to a tenancy, it's worthwhile talking to mechanical and electrical engineers or contractors to get a clear picture about what is involved in servicing your new fitout.

Whether you are relocating or changing the layout of your current workplace, it's very likely that some small modifications to the ventilation system will be necessary, such as relocating air-vents. Meeting rooms tend to be bottlenecks with many people using a small enclosed space. Before making any decisions, make sure that the ventilation system can be adapted to the new layout, and all your rooms can receive enough fresh air even when at capacity.

During operation, make sure that your ventilation system is well-maintained, both the air delivery systems and the controls (you may need to talk to the facility manager about this).

Mixed mode ventilation

This solution offers the best of both worlds, as it allows people to open the windows when the outside conditions are pleasant, and also gives the benefit of mechanical ventilation at other times, in which case the air can be heated or cooled by the air-conditioning system. In mixed-mode buildings you also have the 'privilege' of dealing with the issues that both options bring.

It is a good idea to train your people when to open the windows, and when to switch to mechanical ventilation. Also, make sure that there are systems in place which stop mechanical ventilation running while the windows are open to avoid wasting huge amounts of energy.

Strategy 2: Make people feel comfortable – not too hot, not too cold

When we are uncomfortable (e.g. too warm or cold), it's an indication that our body is out of balance. As a natural response, our body tries to restore its normal function by drawing resources from parts of the body that look after non-essential functions and redirecting these to support vital functions. Alertness and high-level thinking are luxuries as far as our body is concerned, and so extended physical discomfort can make us tired and unable to think clearly. (Other sources of discomfort such as bad lighting, uncomfortable furniture or too much noise can cause similar problems. These are discussed in subsequent sections.)

Whether we feel too hot or too cold, both make it difficult to concentrate, resulting in increased errors. Feeling hot can make us sluggish and lethargic, while on the other hand, feeling cold leads to muscle tension as well as emotional tension, and can narrow our focus.

An American case study of a large company's office found that when the workplace was cold (which in this case meant below 20°C), productivity dropped by half and errors increased by 44% compared to when the office was more comfortable (in this case 25°C). And these results didn't even take into account the time people spent away from their desks warming up.

Finding a middle way leads not only to increased productivity, but in pleasant conditions people themselves tend to be warmer and friendlier.

Occasionally, though, slight discomfort can enhance our performance. For example, feeling a little bit cold can make us more alert. And being tired or distracted can enhance our creativity and our ability to learn. At the end of this chapter I'll provide an example of appropriate use of discomfort to enhance productivity; see 'A non-traditional workplace: Tony Robbins training'.

Achieving thermal comfort

How comfortable we feel in a space depends on many factors (not just what's shown on the thermometer). These include:

- Physical attributes: the temperature and materials of surrounding surfaces, humidity, air movement, and also outdoor temperatures

- Personal attributes: our clothing, gender, age, physiology, upbringing, lifestyle and personal preferences

- Psychological attributes: our sense of control over our environment, and our mental states such as whether we are stressed or relaxed

A truly comfortable workplace takes into consideration all of these, by providing generally pleasant conditions, catering for people with different needs, and also making people 'think' that they are comfortable – as explained below.

Start with the right building

To create a comfortable space, you need to do more than just choose the right air-conditioning units. In order for a building to be truly comfortable, it needs to be designed and constructed to the highest standards, with consideration of the climate (and micro-climate), orientation, function of the space, preferences of people using the space, etc. Further to that, the building's heating, cooling and ventilation systems need to be designed as integrated parts of the building (not as add-ons). If you are involved in the design of a new building, make sure that all consultants work in effective collaboration to achieve this.

Modern buildings with high energy efficiency ratings tend to have much better temperature control than older buildings. If you are moving into an existing space, it's worth getting the best building you can afford to start with, because retrofitting temperature control is expensive and often does not have much of an impact.

If possible, choose a building that is well-constructed and well-insulated, has appropriately shaded, good quality windows, and has been designed to stay warm in winter and cool in the summer. If air-conditioning is required, make sure that the existing system has the capacity to serve your teams, and/or can be adapted to the new layout and to new demands.

Although working in a building designed to the highest standards would be ideal, this is often far from our reality. If dealing with extreme temperatures and an erratic air-conditioning system (or the lack of it) gives you constant grief, you still have options. There are design strategies that can make people feel more comfortable (and therefore more productive) without changing the actual temperature in the space.

Taking advantage of our differences

Engineers usually aim to create conditions that are as even as possible throughout the whole office. However, this is a tough goal, so despite all efforts, the temperatures in different areas of a workplace will never be perfectly uniform; there will always be cooler and warmer spots.

But even if achieving 'correct' temperatures were possible, those 5-10% percent of people whose comfort needs are outside the norm would still suffer. What we find comfortable varies to a great extent; a space that's too warm for one person can be too cold for another.

It would be nice to allocate a personal thermostat to everyone, but this is rarely a realistic option. Instead, you could take advantage of the variations in temperature and the differences in people's needs, and make everyone feel comfortable by using the following strategies:

- Consider temperature differences when designing the room layout. For example, it may make sense to locate the breakout space in the warmer part of the building and the meeting room in the cooler part.
- Ask people whether they prefer cooler or warmer temperatures, and allocate their desks accordingly. Alternatively, make it possible for

people to move around and choose which area they want to work in. (These are much better options than having people who prefer warm temperatures freezing on the cool side, while those who prefer cool temperatures feel hot on the warm side, which is not an uncommon scenario.)

'Thinking' comfortable

We can also help people feel more comfortable by changing their perception of their level of comfort. Here are a few options:

- People's perceptions of comfort tend to improve when they have the opportunity to control their comfort conditions to some extent, for example, by opening windows, changing the air-flow by adjusting the vent near their desk, or moving location.

- Interestingly, people who feel they have some control in general have higher tolerance to discomfort even if their area of control is not directly related to comfort. This means that if they can adjust the lighting, choose to sit or stand, or move furniture around, for example, then they will be less concerned about the space being too warm or too cold. (I trust you'll find ample ideas throughout this book for providing choice and control for your people.)

- Happy people tolerate more deviations in temperature and discomfort in general, while stressed people can easily become irritated even by minor discomfort. Good design can contribute to reducing stress and improving the happiness of your people, as I will explain later.

- The colours used within a space also influence the perceived temperature. Rooms that are painted warm colours (e.g. red or orange) feel significantly warmer than those painted cool colours (e.g. blue or purple).

- In naturally ventilated buildings – with windows that open – people accept wider temperature ranges than in fully air-conditioned buildings with fixed windows.

Strategy 3:
Provide good quality lighting

Good quality lighting defines the ambience and highlights the visual appeal of a space. It enables us to see what we need to see without putting a strain on our eyes, and it also improves the function of our body and mind by keeping us energised and alert, as I'm about to explain.

Whether it's a sunny or a gloomy day can make a huge difference to how we feel and what we do, and whether we are having a good day or a bad day. Lighting can put us in a frame of mind which helps us excel in our tasks. For example, it can make us feel more social, which is ideal for team building, or make us more critically aware, which is better for analytical tasks. (See more about this in Principle 4: Diversified.)

While a well-lit space enhances our performance, bad lighting can make even the most beautiful space look unattractive, cause distraction and eye strain, and hinder our productivity.

Natural light

 'Friendly' sunlight

Once I attended a formal presentation about Facility Management, followed by a round-table lunch. Facility Management, according to Wikipedia, is 'an interdisciplinary field devoted to the co-ordination of business support services ...', and this may give you a feel for the sort of conversations to anticipate at such an event. And my experience matched my expectations – up to halfway through the lunch.

The event was held in a posh top-floor inner-city venue with heavy red plush curtains blocking the sun and the views. Everyone around the table was engaged in nice, smart, formal conversations about buildings and their operations. However, what happened next was rather mundane but telling; someone suddenly opened those curtains. As soon as daylight filled the space, the conversations changed; people shifted their voices,

> used more animated gestures and started to smile. They talked to each other like friends, and that was the moment when relationships started to form.

Access to daylight is essential for our health and well-being. There's a reason why residents of northern countries with long dark winters often get depressed, or why people working in windowless rooms for long periods of time often become miserable. (I'm grateful that I never had to work in a place like that. In fact, I refused to do that for this reason.)

Among the many benefits, daylight can reduce stress and fatigue, prevent eye strain and improve morale at work. It doesn't only make us happier, but also supports our optimal mental functioning. An abundance of research shows that workers in naturally lit spaces learn and recall faster, concentrate and think better, and are more creative.

Many workplaces these days are designed to let in as much natural light as possible. However, while daylight is our friend, it can also be our enemy. A number of factors need to be considered to ensure that the Sun is 'on our side'.

Common challenges – and how to overcome them

- Large unshaded windows can result in the **overheating or overcooling** of the space, making people feel uncomfortable and increasing costs associated with air-conditioning (due to the excessive energy use and the need to install larger systems). On the other hand, heavily shaded windows can cut out views and daylight.

    It requires careful analysis to find a balanced solution, develop a smart window shading system that only lets the sun in when and where it's beneficial, and create a space that is attractive, efficient and comfortable. (Computer modelling, typically undertaken by specialist engineers, is a great way of identifying the optimal design solution while also taking your budget into account.)

- When there is a large contrast between different surfaces within our field of vision (for example a bright window next to a dark wall), we **experience glare**, which makes seeing difficult. Glare causes eye strain, impairs our focus and productivity, and should therefore be minimised.

To address this, create relatively uniform lighting levels within work areas[4] through the appropriate use of shading devices and by good lighting design. Also, make it possible for people to turn away from glare. Position furniture and screens thoughtfully, and better still, set up a flexible environment that allows people to change their position or location.

- Many workplaces with great potential to access daylight **use this opportunity poorly**. It's a common mistake to sit people who prefer working in low light near windows, as they tend to keep the blinds permanently closed, depriving everyone of daylight and views.

  When designing the floor layout, think through what would be the best (and most democratic) use of daylight. Keep in mind that different tasks require different levels of lighting, and that individuals have different preferences. (I've heard a story about two people working next to each other in an office; one of them complained about the space being too dark, while the other one wore sunglasses!) So utilise the brightest areas in your workplace well, for example as a lounge room or thinking space. Only those people who appreciate daylight should work permanently near windows.

- Most of us prefer working near a window; however, not all workplaces provide this opportunity. If access to windows is **treated as a reward or the privilege** of a selected few, this may be off-putting for some people.

  If it's not possible to bring daylight to everyone, it is worthwhile to turn some of the naturally lit areas into shared spaces for everyone to enjoy.

- A common mistake is to **position desks** close to the windows parallel to them (i.e. people either facing towards the windows or turning their backs to them). This configuration often leads to glare or unwanted reflection on the screen, unless the blinds are closed, which is not ideal.

  Usually these issues can be avoided by turning the desks perpendicular to the windows.

---

4   ... but not throughout the whole office! (I'll talk about this in Principle 4: Diversified.)

Indoor lighting – lamps and light fittings

Indoor lighting design is an elaborate but rewarding process, providing plenty of opportunities for artistic expression and playing with the ambience of the space.

Following the sun

Beyond supporting our visual comfort and making the space appealing and functional, indoor lighting needs to compliment the ever-changing daylight. Furthermore, it should also meet our fundamental need to connect with nature. Indoor lighting that resembles the qualities of light we see in nature helps us feel comfortable and function better.

Our bodies have evolved to harmonise their function with the changing cycles of nature, including the movement of the sun. (This in-built biological process is called the body-clock or circadian rhythm.) When we are in sync with nature, we wake up at sunrise and get sleepy when the sun sets. We are more alert and dynamic in the morning, and slower in the evening.

A built space with artificial lighting can quickly trick our system and distort our perception of time. For example, in a bright space our body receives the signal that it's daytime, time to be awake and active. On the other hand, in a dim room our body can get confused and make the conclusion that it's evening, time to go to sleep.

It's staggering how often this issue is overlooked, and how many workplaces are so badly lit that they make people slow down and drift off during work, even in otherwise well-designed, high-profile workplaces.

A lighting specialist friend of mine, Landon Bannister, once said: 'It has always seemed strange to me how we prioritise lighting in office buildings. We spend large dollars engaging lighting designers for breakout spaces, lobbies and reception areas, and happily increase the lighting budgets in these areas. Yet for the office floor, where our staff will spend the most of their time, the least amount of thought and dollar investment is made.'

The 'Total Eclipse' of Office Lighting

Using downlights – spotlights and fluorescent tubes (often mounted on black ceilings) – is such a common way of lighting offices that we may not even question it. Here are some of the problems that can arise:

- This type of lighting creates a lot of glare.

- Downlights make it difficult to see the things we really need to see well in a workplace. They are great for lighting up horizontal surfaces like table tops. But when was the last time you spent most of your working day looking down? What we really need to see well are, for example, other people's subtle facial expressions, so that we can communicate and relate to each other better. (This requires more diffuse lighting.)

- Downlights – especially when combined with dark ceilings – create a completely unnatural lighting effect, confusing our body and mind.

The only time in nature when we see bright light coming straight from above is in the middle of the day. This is siesta time. This type of lighting lacks 'spirit' – perhaps this is why it's avoided in photography. Just think about the time when the light is most appealing in nature: morning and evening, when the sun is at a low angle.

At the same time, a dark ceiling with bright spots resembles the night sky with stars. (And even if the ceiling is white, downlights do make the ceiling look dark.) These spaces mess with our body clocks; they make us slower and sometimes even drowsy, since the body's biological response is to go to sleep once the sun is down.

And how do we subconsciously interpret a dark ceiling (night sky) combined with the lighting shining vertically from above the top (midday sun)? This effect is really odd, like experiencing a permanent total eclipse.

This sort of lighting is relatively easy to design and cheap to build, and can be very energy-efficient, since no other surfaces are lit up than what is required by minimum building standards. Some people also find that bright lights on a dark surface look kind of 'cool'.

But do any of these benefits warrant a design that is unnatural and confusing, causes eye strain, makes us drowsy, and makes it difficult for us to see well?

As we've seen, it's not enough to create lighting that is decorative, efficient, and just bright enough to see. It also needs to support our productivity by keeping us alert and energised.

Due to the rapid evolution of lighting technology, we have many tools available for creating good quality lighting. Here are a few suggestions for creating a well-lit space that is not only visually attractive, but is also more supportive of wellbeing and performance:

Design suggestions

- Make sure that not only the floor and desk tops, but also the **walls and the ceiling** are sufficiently lit. Make all the surfaces look a bit like the outdoors, with a bright sky and horizon. This will create a much warmer, more natural and engaging atmosphere, compared to lighting that is only directed towards the floor. Use some indirect lighting such as uplights, wall-wash lamps, or pendants with an uplight component to create the effect of an 'indoor sky'. You may still create darker spaces that resemble, for example, the shady areas under trees, but these should be features, not the norm. (You don't want your teams to work in a cave.)

- As mentioned earlier, different **lighting levels** suit different tasks and people, so it's best to enable people to control the lighting levels in their immediate work area. This can be achieved by installing individually switched dimmable lamps, and/or using task lights in addition to ambient (background) lighting, for example.

- The colour of natural and artificial lights varies, ranging between cool and warm colours; this attribute is referred to as **colour temperature**. Different coloured lights have different effects on people. Lamps with cool (bluish white) colours – resembling the morning sun – are energising and help with concentration, but may bring a sterile feel to the space. On the other hand, lamps with warm (yellowish) colours – resembling the afternoon sun – are relaxing, but may create a tired feel in the space. Unless you can change the colour of the lighting, it's recommended you choose lamps with colours in the mid-range, or that are suited to the function of the space.

- A more advanced option is to install a lighting system (including lamps, switches and controls) which enables you to control the colour and intensity of the lighting as needed. A system like this, programmed to gradually change lighting colour and intensity throughout the day in sync with changes in natural light is called **biodynamic lighting**. This solution is especially effective for improving workers' well-being and performance.[5]

- In rooms that don't have real **windows or skylights** you can make quite an impact by installing digital ones. These lighting panels not only imitate natural light, but also look a bit like real windows or skylights, so you feel more connected to the outdoors. Some of them go as far as depicting nature scenes such as beaches, moving clouds, and trees with their leaves dancing the wind!

- It's important to keep an eye on the **power consumption** of your lighting so as to meet legal requirements, reduce energy costs and minimise environmental impact. With today's highly advanced lighting solutions, it is possible to create good lighting levels throughout the office without using much power, by using energy efficient lamps (e.g. LED / T5 / compact fluorescent lamps) in combination with intelligent lighting control solutions.

To get the best outcome, you need to engage specialists who are open to discussing your specific needs and are willing to design a bespoke lighting system for your teams.

---

5   These systems can also be programmed to draw an extra surge of energy out of people in the afternoon and evening by imitating the bluish morning light which speeds up metabolism. This application, in my opinion, is unethical, since it confuses people's biorhythms and exhausts their energy reserves. I can't help but think of battery hens whose natural cycles are tricked by artificial lighting so that they produce more eggs, and as a result their health is damaged.

Strategy 4:
Minimise distractions and interruptions

Distractions waste time. In a distracting environment we may end up spending more time getting our head around a task than actually progressing with it. Also, constant distraction impairs our mental acuity, focus, attention span and creativity, along with our ability to engage in complex tasks. It reduces the speed and the quality of our work, while draining our energy and sanity.

Nevertheless, most workplaces today are seemingly designed to bombard us with as many distracting influences as possible: ringing phones, noisy air-conditioners and printers, overheard conversations, movement around us, colleagues interrupting our work, and so on. A lot of people say they get more work done at home or outside office hours than working in the office 9 to 5. This shows that something is fundamentally wrong with the way workplaces function these days, since their very purpose should be to help us make progress with our work.

Good workplace design – coupled with effective management strategies – can dramatically reduce the number of distractions that people are exposed to at work.

Too much noise

Noise is seen as the biggest distraction in most workplaces. Especially in a large open office, our attention might be interrupted by some sort of sound every few seconds. Certain types of noises – like beeps, bangs and clanks coming from the office or the traffic from the street – carry no meaning but can simply be annoying. Other sounds – like the conversations we overhear, or music with lyrics – may not sound unpleasant to us but the words might hijack our attention.

Using headphones is a popular strategy to mask external sounds, and many people I talk to swear that it does the job – it helps protect their head space. At the same time, research shows that listening to music to block out distracting sounds also impairs mental functioning. Either way, you should never settle for a noisy office. While those using headphones might be able to escape from noise and hide in their bubble, it will still distract those who are trying to have a conversation or relax.

You can reduce distracting noise in an office thorough strategic design, such as **providing separate areas** for quiet activities (e.g. focused work) and noisy activities (e.g. collaborative work), as discussed in the previous chapter.

Some of the solutions to manage noise are rather counter-intuitive. For example, companies often install high partitions between workstations to reduce noise, but this can produce the opposite effect: when workers can't see their colleagues at the other side of the partition, they feel less empathy towards them, and are more likely to speak louder. So you might be better off **keeping the workstation partitions low**, or removing them altogether.

You may also consider **implementing a music & mobile phone policy**. (There might be better opportunities for your people to show off their wacky ringtones than the exact moment when someone around them is just on the verge of coming up with a breakthrough idea.)

Despite our best efforts, eliminating all distracting noise is an unrealistic goal. The best way to get around this is to provide **enclosed, soundproof rooms** accessible to anyone for tasks that require intense focus. (When we really need to concentrate, our hearing can become so sharp that we can hear the cat meowing in the next street. For a period of time we may need perfect silence, which a shared office cannot usually offer.)

Too little noise, and echo

On the other hand, the workplace should not be too quiet either. In a very quiet space it's easier to overhear every word in a conversation even from a distance, so people tend to talk more quietly and talk less, as they are more self-conscious about being overheard or causing distraction. This could kill the dynamics of the workplace and restrain communication. In contrast, moderate background noise feels more natural and relaxing. If you find that your workplace is too quiet at times, and you can't improve it through space design or management, consider implementing a white noise or pink noise system – an audio system that emits a soft random noise (with a specific range of frequency) via loudspeakers.

All work areas need to have good acoustic treatment. Rooms with lots of smooth, hard surfaces can create echo, making even a normal conversation disturbing and hard to understand. Talking to someone in an echoey space feels like being on stage and hearing your own voice from the speakers, which feels really unnerving if you aren't a natural public speaker. In order to minimise echo, use finishing materials that absorb sound (e.g. acoustic ceiling lining, soft wall coverings, carpet), and/or fill the space with furniture and other items. There are also decorative sound-absorbing ceiling and wall panels available that can be ideal for retrofits.

> ### 💡 Egg trays on the ceiling
>
> Some companies spend a lot of money on creating deluxe conference rooms, with glass and steel and tiled surfaces, just to find that they're terrible places for meetings, with way too much echo. I've heard stories about how some managers have fixed this with cheap solutions, like sticking cardboard egg trays onto the ceiling in desperation to make the space usable. Imagine how terrible this looks! There are so many ways to prevent or fix this problem in a civilised fashion without resorting to cobbled-together solutions.

Movement and interruptions

Most workplaces are designed to promote as much interaction as possible. In a collaborative environment our colleagues may feel free to approach us with a question or request anytime, and we may feel that we need to be available all the time. This comes at a cost; we hardly have any opportunity to focus on our work without interruption, and even when we do, all the movements around us can be really distracting.

To enable your people to concentrate on their task, make sure that they can find a spot in the workplace where nothing 'interesting' is going on around them that could divert their attention. These areas should be away from traffic and activities involving a lot of movement.

Visual distractions

Even when everything is perfectly still around us, we may still get distracted by our busy-looking environment. When a space is too 'interesting', stimulating or cluttered, it can divert our attention from our task. (I am still haunted by the memory of working in an office with hot pink and orange features throughout the space!)

While too much clutter can be a distraction, a sterile environment can also inhibit productivity. (This will be explained in more detail in Principle 5: Caring.) So if you are tempted to implement a clean desk policy, think twice. You need to find balance between making the space too busy or too boring. The level of clutter that is acceptable or attractive is different for each individual, so make sure you find common ground among your team. You yourself may need a perfectly organised workspace to think clearly, but this doesn't mean that all other people will struggle with a slightly messy space.

Strategy 5: Reduce sources of negative thoughts and feelings

Whenever something in our environment – or in our own mind – triggers negative feelings such as discomfort, pressure or anxiety, we experience some form of stress. While a certain level of excitement can boost our productivity, too much stress inhibits the optimal functioning of our body and mind. For example, it narrows our arteries and our field of vision, and limits our creativity, our attention span, and our ability to solve problems, make decisions and think outside the box.

Dealing with negative emotions can be extremely distracting and draining; often we can't help but concentrate more on the source of the stress and less on our task. We also tend to be more unpleasant to the people around us, acting without patience and empathy. Even when we experience minor stresses, the effects can pile up over time, and it may take only a minor irritant for us to lose control – to snap at a colleague, or feel suddenly overwhelmed, unmotivated or exhausted. Beyond lowering individual performance, it can affect the whole team or organisation.

While in today's fast-paced, ever-changing environment you can't eliminate all negative triggers, by creating a well-designed work environment you can reduce negative thoughts and emotions and promote a more positive atmosphere.

The strategies presented below are aimed to protect workers from stress. (You can also support people in building up their resilience to stress by providing opportunities for exercise and relaxation. These strategies are discussed later in this chapter.)

Lack of personal space, and crowded space

We all have a personal space that we aim to protect, and when it's invaded we can become tense and irritable. Furthermore, we can also get very uncomfortable if we feel we are in a crowded space, even when our personal space is not intruded upon. These issues are becoming ever more prominent as workplaces are increasingly crowded, or in other words, the average floor space per person gets smaller and smaller.[6]

Our preferred amount of personal space depends on many factors, including our culture, personality, and relationships with other people. Workplace designers need to take these factors into consideration, especially in high density spaces, and allow workers to maintain a comfortable distance between each other.

How crowded a space feels depends firstly on the number of people in the space and how close they are to us, and also on the physical attributes of the space. The following features can make a room feel less crowded, with the same floor area and the same number of people in the space:

- High ceilings, large windows, wide open views

- Rectangle-shaped rooms (instead of square rooms)

- Straight walls (as opposed to curved walls)

- Light surfaces – achieved either through daylight, artificial lighting or light colours

- Lit-up walls, with even lighting levels throughout the room

- People facing towards each other (rather than turning away)

- Neat and ordered spaces (as opposed to messy ones)

---

6   The average amount of office space per worker globally shrank from 225 square feet in 2010 to 150 square feet in 2013, according to a survey conducted by CoreNet Global (a leading association for corporate real estate professionals).

- Attractive features such as plants, artwork or special furniture
- Clear escape routes through doors
- Having the opportunity to leave the room and work elsewhere

Lack of privacy and insecurity

One of the greatest sources of stress in today's open offices is the invasion of our privacy. It's a core human need to be able to find a place of solitude, as even the most extroverted people need some privacy on occasion, but in many workplaces there's simply nowhere to go. (It can be really discouraging when our only option to have some alone time is to go to the loo.)

When we are forced to conduct all of our business in a public area where everyone can see and hear what we are doing and saying, we can become very stressed, insecure and even at times aggressive.

Having to work in a position where we can't see what's happening behind our backs further adds to our tension. When we feel that we might be monitored – especially when we are faced with a new task in which we have little experience, and the person overlooking our work has more expertise and authority – it can make us feel insecure, and we are more likely to doubt our abilities and worry about making mistakes. These issues usually lead to reduced focus and productivity.

Here are some ideas to improve your workers' personal space without building barriers:

- Have you ever wondered why the seats in restaurants and bars that back onto a wall or partition are the first ones taken? This is because we generally feel more secure with this kind of set-up – we feel protected when we're able to see what's happening around us. Creating a floor layout and seating arrangement in your office where no-one has their back to an open area or door will allow people to feel more secure in their office space.

- Provide enclosed rooms or partially enclosed quiet areas or meeting booths where people can work or rest in solitude or in small teams. Make sure that everyone has the option of finding visual and/or acoustic privacy.

Feeling lost or disoriented

It can be quite an unsettling experience to visit an unfamiliar space where you can't figure out where you can or should go, so areas accessed by visitors or transient workers should be designed to make it easy for them to find their way around. To do this successfully, you need to understand the perspectives and emotional states of visitors and organise the space and signage around that.

We may also feel disoriented or struggle to understand the space around us even when we are fully familiar with the workspace. A space can be disorienting for several reasons, for example, if it has an undefined shape, strange angles, or too many openings to different directions. Having too many different patterns, reflections, or transparent surfaces around us can also be confusing and disorienting. Features that are almost but not quite regular (e.g. forms and layouts that are almost symmetrical, rooms that are almost rectangular, angles that are almost right-angled) can also be confusing, and should therefore be avoided.

Bad news

Bad news comes in many forms and causes us great stress. It can come from an email about losing a highly anticipated job, an upset client's phone call, a wrong delivery from a supplier, or a confrontation with a colleague who thrives on conflict. Sometimes even the anticipation of bad news can stress us out just by sitting next to the phone, in front of our inbox or near a certain workmate.

We can't escape bad news forever, but we can create an environment that allows us to have more control over when we receive bad news and when we don't. Being in a 'safe zone' can help us to be more present with tasks that require our attention.

Here are some ways to create a relaxed working environment:

- Ask your people where they receive most of their bad news from (e.g. email, mobile phone, coworker, etc.), and create areas where they can work without being reached by bad news. This may mean restricting certain forms of technology in some areas.

- Sometimes similar results can be achieved without changing the physical environment, just by creating new strategies or policies. (For example, one of my university professors told me about a policy he learned from Alvar Aalto, one of the 20th century's greatest architects. At Aalto's practice, designers were not allowed to keep their rolls of tracing paper in an unstable position where these could easily be knocked over, causing a sudden 'BANG' and scaring his employees. Aalto wanted to create a calm environment and ensure that people did not stress in anticipation of this frightful noise.)

Mental clutter and overwhelm

In today's business we are expected to be able to achieve so much each day! Even relatively little tasks like emails, phone calls and social media posts can quickly add up and clutter our mind, causing us to feel overwhelmed and sometimes even bringing us to a state of mental paralysis. A single look at our endless to-do list, inbox or a mountain of files on our desk – or any sort of reminders of the tasks ahead of us – can make us feel disempowered and destroy our sense of control.

Although the physical space cannot do the work for us, it can help us accomplish more and work with more presence and joy by allowing us to focus on one task at a time instead of constantly reminding us of our other duties.

Design suggestions for reducing mental clutter and overwhelm:

- Provide storage space where people can keep their project files out of sight, preferably far away from the work areas.

- If you use a project tracking board, make sure it's only showing what's relevant to the day's work (along with what's already been achieved), not a full list of overwhelming tasks to be completed in the next year. However, in saying this, it doesn't mean we should ignore our company's long-term vision. We need a healthy balance of projections and pertinent items that need to be completed to reach our goal.

- Encourage your people to keep only their daily to-do list at their desk, not the long-term ones.

- Establish the habit of keeping work areas dedicated to focused work relatively tidy.

Case study: Excite Print

Excite Print is a print shop owned by a couple who recently upgraded their space with my assistance. Before the changes, the space looked and felt like an industrial facility, primarily designed to accommodate machines. Work areas were located in in-between spaces, and there were no dedicated staff areas. The prime spot in the space, next to the window, was occupied by a printing press.

The workstations and their surroundings were packed with work-related items, notes, charts, and to-do lists. There were no free surfaces or decorations; there was no space for the eye and mind to rest. No wonder that the owners were anxious about the team's wellbeing, and were worried about burnout.

The upgrade had major spacial and financial limitations, but there was still significant scope to address many of these issues. The space was essentially transformed from a factory into an office, and the upgrade also involved behavioural change and education of staff.

As a result, the wellbeing of staff has also been transformed. They all find the new environment calmer, and feel more connected to what they do. Due to the reduction in stress levels, people feel more comfortable and are able to focus more easily; they therefore handle challenges better and work more accurately, which in turn lower stress again.

A manager explains:

> 'The nature of the printing business is inherently demanding, with constant multitasking and juggling of deadlines. At the busiest times, looking after the workplace might seem like a low priority. During the upgrade, we realised that a poor workplace can be depressing, although people are often unaware of stress while it is happening. So we decided to eliminate any unnecessary stress. We didn't have to make the environment perfect; we just needed to deal with all the things we could easily control. We didn't make huge changes, but those several small things made a big difference.'

Strategy 6: Promote good posture, movement and exercise

Sitting still all day, often in bad posture and without doing any exercise, has well-known negative effects on our health and well-being. Most people in sedentary jobs also experience some sort of discomfort in their body, ranging from slight numbness or tingling in their extremities to excruciating pain. While mild physical discomfort can be distracting, more severe pain can also be draining and debilitating. Both are ample reasons for promoting healthy posture and physical movement at work.

The benefits of a physically engaging environment are much wider than just improved comfort and health. Our body can be used as a tool to enhance our mental acuity by quantum leaps. There's a strong link between the state of our body and our mental performance, so engaging our body at work can significantly boost our brain-power and productivity.

Some of the most successful organisations are now taking advantage of this opportunity, after recognising that the traditional, one-dimensional workplace model – promoting sitting still most of the day – limits potential. They provide environments where people's minds and bodies are put to work, and find that the results are exceptional.

Empowering and healthy posture

The way we hold ourselves directly influences the way we feel and think. When we feel energised and confident, we typically hold ourselves up straight, with our heads lifted up and our chests open. In contrast, when we experience negative emotions, we typically hunch our backs, with our heads low and our chests closed.

Our posture and our psychology mutually influence each other. While our mental state can dictate how we hold ourselves, by changing our posture we can change our mental state instantly. While an empowering posture can make us feel more energised and positive; a bad posture can make us feel stressed, drained and even lethargic.

Design suggestions:

- Invest in good quality ergonomic chairs, tables, and other accessories as needed. Make sure they have sufficient adjustable features that are easy to use. (I've seen offices where all height-adjustable desks were set to the factory default, because it required a technician to change the desk height.)

- Make sure that the workstations are properly set up and used. It is beneficial to organise training for your staff about office ergonomics.[7] Although there is an abundance of information freely available about ergonomic furniture set-up, it can be worthwhile to engage an ergonomist.

- Your furniture choices should consider the devices your people use. For example, there are chair types specifically developed to support the use of mobile devices.

Working in different postures

As mentioned earlier, our mind functions differently in different postures. In fact, the neurological connections between our body and brain are so intertwined that when we keep working on a problem in the same position for a long time our unconscious mind learns to associate that posture with that problem. Therefore, shifting our posture triggers changes in our thinking, and this can be used to our advantage whenever we are stuck on a problem and need a fresh perspective. Snapping out of our posture can help us overcome mental blocks and see new solutions.

Whilst I was writing this book, I shifted my position several times a day – I sat at a desk, on a sofa, on a floor cushion, or knelt at a coffee table. Whenever I changed my posture, new thoughts came to me, and this habit helped me to maintain my focus and keep my thoughts flowing. At times, as soon as I stood up, I was hit by an idea that had been nowhere in sight while I was sitting.

---

7 A U.S. research study measuring the impact of ergonomic setup on employee productivity found that people who used an ergonomic chair and also received training about office ergonomics increased their productivity by 17.7% over the sixteen month test period.

Design suggestions:

- Provide different types of seating throughout the workplace, (e.g. chairs, sofas, benches, floor cushions, fitness balls, sitting blocks, tall stools).

- Consider providing standing desks (this could also be a 'hot desk') and encourage your people to try out working while standing. (Working in a standing position is a popular trend today, and can be a great way to keep our moods and energy up.)

Thinking with the body

Our body is a wonderful but often underutilised tool for learning, solving problems and expressing ourselves. Many of us learn or engage with a subject better when we have the opportunity to feel it through touch and/or physical movement, rather than performing purely mental activities (such as immersing ourselves in the digital world). Using our body with awareness – and in congruence with our message – also influences the quality of our communication and our ability to express ourselves with clarity and charisma.

While traditional work environments provide little opportunity for workers to develop and utilise these skills, some of the most innovative organisations (e.g. IDEO, LEGO) have made it a point to make great use of people's body intelligence in solving problems and generating creative ideas. Their work environments promote a physically active way of working, providing space for activities such as:

- Writing and drawing freehand
- Using flip-charts during presentations
- Role playing or simulation
- Building models and prototypes
- Creating storyboards, mind-maps, montages, and posters from physical materials
- Playing with tactile items during meetings or brainstorming sessions

Movement, physical activity and exercise

Beyond its well-known health benefits, physical movement increases blood flow to the brain and enhances brain function, both in the short and the long term. It decreases stress, lifts mood, enhances our intellectual skills, prepares our brain for optimal learning, and also supports brain development. Exercise also improves our memory and reasoning skills, helping us to respond faster.

While there is some awareness around the importance of being active, few workplaces are designed to promote movement and exercise. While encouraging people to go to the gym after work is a good idea, if people exercise in the morning or during the day, it has an immediate beneficial effect on their performance. And of course they are much more likely to do that if the workplace has the right facilities.

I've attended educational events in the past where participants spent time bouncing on rebounders at the beginning of each session, and were encouraged to stand up and move around whenever they felt stiff, or when their mood or attention dropped. I found that taking in new information was easier than I've ever experienced.

Design suggestions:

- Encouraging people to walk a bit of a distance within the office is a common design strategy. You may locate essential facilities such as printers or storage in far corners, or make it easier to use stairs than lifts. This might be a good start, but you shouldn't stop there.

- Provide shower and changing facilities for those who ride to work or exercise during the day.

- If possible, provide a gym or room for exercise within your office.

- Consider providing opportunities for people to work while engaging in physical activities. The 'treadmill desk' is a fascinating recent innovation enabling workers to use their computer while walking at a slow pace. While its health and productivity benefits are not yet established, it is quickly gaining popularity. (Dr James L Chestnut, author of *The Wellness & Prevention Paradigm*, wrote his entire book on a treadmill-mounted laptop!)

- Consider organising walking meetings, or, if you are among the adventurous, you could acquire something similar to Google's 'meeting bikes' which allow several people to meet, work, exercise and have fun at the same time.

💡 The evolution of the office desk

The variety of office desks you see in the most forward-thinking workplaces is a great reflection of how the focus is shifting from sedentary work towards more healthy, dynamic and adventurous ways of working.

- First we saw height-adjustable desks, which enabled an ergonomic setup for people of different heights.

- Then standing desks became increasingly popular. In some countries, there are now discussions around making it mandatory for employers to provide desks that allow staff to sit or stand. And in Denmark, this legislation is already passed!

- Then came the treadmill desk, which enables workers to combine computer-based work with physical movement. There are fierce debates in professional circles about whether treadmill desks are practical, beneficial and safe enough. But based on what I see, this innovation has a bright future.

- And finally, the latest invention is the Hamster Wheel Standing Desk, the brainchild of two creatives at a software company called Autodesk. This is the tongue-in-cheek version of the treadmill desk, allowing you to walk inside an 80 inch wheel while working. Although its practicality is questionable, it is an awesome idea.

Strategy 7:
Encourage productive habits

Not all distractions that hinder our productivity come from the outside world – the space and people around us. Some of the most detrimental ones are those we create ourselves. Multitasking, jumping from task to task, or checking emails and websites too often are just a few of the common habits that can make it impossible for us to maintain deep focus, keep calm, and be in our flow. Habitual multitaskers are less effective at screening out distractions and need more time to refocus once interrupted.

Falling into such habits is easy and can quickly send our brain into mental overload, a state in which we are likely to create more problems than solutions, or spend a lot of time achieving nothing, while still ending up exhausted. While we may perceive that our main problem is having too much to do in too little time, our real challenge is taking charge of our own behaviour.

I often ask my clients if they give in to any 'bad habits' that weaken their productivity and that they would like to change, and the answer is unanimously 'Yes'. We're all guilty of this, so the question is: why don't we change?

The path of least resistance

Although we like to think of ourselves as acting in a fully rational manner at work and in life in general, the truth is that some aspects of our behaviour are beyond logic.

In his brilliant book, *The Happiness Advantage*, which explores human behaviour and presents strategies to drive high performance at work, psychologist Shawn Achor explains that we naturally gravitate towards activities that are easy to start, whether or not they are productive. Our actions submit to what he calls the 'twenty second rule': we are much more likely to choose a task that takes less than twenty seconds to start than those that take longer. And this ingrained pattern often works against us, hindering our productivity.

(I personally used to fall into this trap on a regular basis, for example, using a computer to sketch out an idea just because it was quicker to start than finding the tools I really needed. Sketching paper and pencils were hidden away somewhere in a messy utility room.)

Challenges to changing bad habits

If all we rely upon is our willpower to change our habits, we have little chance of success. Our willpower is a limited resource, and can be quickly depleted by sitting through long meetings, focusing on dry data for hours, or pushing through other demanding work scenarios.

And after having exhausted all our willpower, it should be no surprise that we can't resist the temptation to follow the easy path. As soon as we hit the smallest obstacle – like becoming stuck on a creative idea, or lost in a sea of numbers, or reading something that is technically difficult – we'll switch tasks.[8] Today, when we can find instant entertainment through the click of a mouse, it's inevitable that seeking a temporary escape from our problems is a wide spread addiction.

Design strategies

To break old habits and form new ones, we need help. We need an environment that makes it hard to continue unproductive habits and easy to adopt productive ones. Shawn Achor suggests that we should sway the 'twenty-second rule' toward our advantage: create barriers to old habits that take over twenty seconds to get past, and create such conditions that we can start new, more constructive activities in less than twenty seconds. This could mean creating new rules and boundaries, and taking away some of our choices.

Here are some suggestions for creating a workplace that promotes productive habits:

- Store project-related files far from the work area, making it difficult for people to switch between projects.
- Designate a room for working without computers, and provide easily accessible tools for capturing ideas, e.g. whiteboard, paper, pen, Post-it notes, modelling materials.

---

8 Gregory Ciotti, expert in productivity and work habits, calls these moments 'ah-screw-its', which aptly describes what goes through people's minds when they are about to abandon a task.

- Designate a room or space with no phone and internet access. (This can also be a rule; it's not necessary to disconnect the data source.)
- Create informal meeting areas scattered throughout the workplace where people can easily engage in face-to-face conversations, instead of half-heartedly taking part in never-ending online discussions.

Remember, not all habits can be influenced by the physical space. Some may require adapting your systems or technologies, like creating a half-minute barrier to accessing the internet.

The list of design options above is far from complete. You and your team are best qualified to identify your productive and unproductive habits and to decide what changes in your workplace could best work for you.

Setting new boundaries and limiting choices could trigger some initial resistance. But once your people start experiencing the difference – working in a space that helps them take better care of their head space – it won't be long before the benefits become obvious: improved well-being and performance on many levels.

Strategy 8:
Provide opportunities for quality breaks

Mental capacity and attention span

Being knowledge workers, we spend most of our working hours processing information, solving problems and making decisions. These activities inevitably deplete our mental energy – including our ability to innovate and make effective decisions – and stress, distractions, discomfort and multitasking only add to this. Our mental energy is finite, and can run out faster than the number of hours in a day. Research shows that as the day progresses, people make worse and worse decisions. So it is wise to treat mental capacity as a scarce resource and make careful choices about how to use it and restore it.

Apart from our mental energy, our attention span is also finite. How long we can focus on a task and maintain a peak state of mind depends on many factors, of course. But even if we have ideal conditions to be in the zone – we love what we do, and are working without distractions in a supportive environment – we still need to take regular breaks to maintain our attention and mental energy. It's estimated that the longest time we can effectively focus on a task without a break is around 40 minutes.

Pushing through

Do you know the feeling when you are facing a mental block that you can't seem to get around, and trying to push through doesn't help? You go round and round in circles, with the words and numbers in front of you becoming meaningless, and your mind wanders off to all sorts of places. By this stage you are certainly overdue for a break.

Although we often put pressure on ourselves and our team to maintain productivity throughout the day, pushing through mental exhaustion, instead of taking time to recharge our batteries, is counterproductive. We inevitably slow down and make worse decisions, and we become irritable and impulsive. Ironically, the more we work, the more our productivity declines.

Even when we are aware that it's time for a break, if we don't have any attractive options, it might be easier to just keep working.

Taking quality breaks

Not all activities that we enjoy doing during our break times help us recharge. It can be tempting to surf the internet, chat with friends online or clean out our personal mailbox, but these activities can in fact be quite draining, as they usually involve dealing with distractions, taking in new information, making decisions, and juggling between tasks – exactly as our work does.

An activity can only be restorative if it doesn't put the same sort of demands on our physical and mental energy as our work does. For example, exercise, meditation, socialising, reading a book, watching a movie, or playing games can be good restorative activities after doing intellectual work. And sometimes the best thing we can do is allow our mind to wander. (Research shows that mind-wandering can greatly increase our success in solving creative problems.)

Since many of us are addicted to mental stimulation, taking a break from technology and choosing less stimulating activities requires self-control and planning.

Making it a habit

Just because we know how important it is to take quality breaks doesn't mean it will become a habit. We need to create the right conditions in order to change old work patterns.

We need to feel that we have permission to take a break when we need to, without seeing it as unproductive time. When productivity is defined too narrowly (e.g. as sitting at a desk or making visible progress), it's more likely that we will either skip breaks or feel guilty about taking them, and so won't end up relaxing at all.

We need to listen to the signals from our mind and body, understand which activities deplete or refuel our inner resources, and learn how to nurture our physical and mental energy. Developing and following a restoration routine that works for us – without compromising our responsibilities – takes time, effort and discipline.

And of course, we also need a space that is inviting and suitable for helping us recharge. Taking breaks in the same space where we work is not a good idea for many reasons.

The break space

A break space, in order to support restoration, should ideally:

- Make it easy for us to engage in restorative activities and difficult to engage in those that are similar to our work

- Be a space that feels a long way away from the place that exhausted us. It doesn't need to be physically far, but it needs to have a very different style and ambience, and divert our attention from work. Quality external views, unique decor and objects, artworks, images and music can all serve as positive distractions.

- Be a comfortable, attractive and pleasant environment, a space which encourages us to take breaks, and where we enjoy spending time
- Be a safe space where we are not observed, challenged or judged, and where we can predict what will happen, with no surprises

(See Principle 5: Caring for specific design strategies for making a space attractive, pleasant and relaxing.)

Honouring the needs and limitations of our mind and body, and giving ourselves the opportunity to take breaks in a suitable space, will pay huge dividends. Coming back to work with a fresh mind gives a great boost to our productivity, and substantially improves our long-term results.

Putting things into practice

 ### A non-traditional workplace: Anthony Robbins training

The most unusual learning environment

Anthony (Tony) Robbins is 'the world's #1 success coach', and has been reaching out to millions worldwide for over 30 years. He teaches people how to live up to their potential, and to live a purposeful, active, healthy, fulfilling life driven by values like personal growth, contribution and love.

At his training programs there are often thousands of participants who don't just sit on a chair all day; they shout and sing, jump and dance, (and sometimes even walk on fire!) while engaging all of their senses and experiencing a broad range of emotions. All of this happens in a massive windowless space where artificial lights and sounds are not just distracting but invasive, and the temperature is freezing cold.[9]

Building on the science of performance

For many people who haven't experienced an event like this, it may sound weird, and I was also somewhat sceptical until I had the opportunity to participate. Being there helped me understand that every detail of the space and activities had been carefully designed to support the best learning outcomes for the participants.

---

9 Some of Tony's strategies may appear contradictory to those that have previously been discussed. How can being in an uncomfortable room while being distracted and stirred up be an effective learning strategy? The reason is because we need one set of conditions for performing well in what we are already good at, and another for stretching our boundaries. For the former we need to be able to be focused and present. For the latter we may need to put our conscious mind on hold (by wearing it out), so that our unconscious can open up for new learning. Typically, these transformative activities happen outside of traditional workplaces.

In fact, these programs have been developed based on a deep understanding of human behaviour and psychology. Tony's research organisation, Robbins Research International, has been studying this subject for decades, with a special focus on what drives people's thoughts, decisions and actions. It's been shown that our mental and emotional states determine our life quality, experience and results, and that it's within our control to achieve productive mind states (for example, feeling energised, confident and focused) by using our own resources skillfully. One of these resources is our own body.

The tools of personal transformation

During these trainings, participants practise using their body as a tool to enhance learning, to make better decisions, to make those decisions stick so that they follow up on them, and to access their multiple intelligences as opposed to using only their analytical mind to solve problems. These events truly make an impact, and are known to be among the most effective personal transformational trainings available worldwide.

In your workplace you probably can't jump up and down, scream for joy and party for days. (Or even if you can, some people probably wouldn't appreciate that – good luck trying to explain the productivity benefits of 'being silly'!) But you are probably able to create a space where it is OK to move, laugh out loud, or maybe even dance a little without disturbing others.

Imagine what your team could achieve if it was possible for them to engage their whole body, a range of emotions and a variety of senses in their work. What if they could access thoughts and ideas that remain locked inside when they just sit all day trying to push their minds to work harder?

❓ Questions to consider

- How would you define productivity in your business?

- What sorts of mental and emotional demands do your team members need to deal with on a daily basis?

- What makes the difference between good and bad days? (Think about a day when your teams are in the zone, and their productivity is at its peak. Then think about a day when hardly anything gets done. What caused the difference?)

- How could you make the workspace more comfortable? And how could you influence your people's perception of comfort?

- How can you bring sufficient daylight into the space – where and when it's needed?

- How can you ensure that everyone has the chance to enjoy natural light and outside views?

- What can you do to minimise noise, interruptions and visual distractions?

- What are the most common emotional issues your people need to deal with? And how could these be reduced?

- What opportunities do you have to provide sufficient personal space and a sense of privacy to your people?

- How could you promote a physically active way of working?

- What unproductive habits do your people tend to fall into? And how could the space nudge them towards shifting these habits?

- How do your team members feel about taking a break from work to relax?

- What sort of environment would invite your people to take a break and help them refresh their minds?

PRINCIPLE 4

DIVERSIFIED

CREATE SPACE FOR A DIVERSIFIED BUSINESS

Establishing an environment where everyone can work effectively using different skills and engaging in different activities, regardless of their age, personality or preferred work styles

'A diverse workforce is a company's lifeblood and diverse approaches are the only means of solving complex and challenging business issues. Deriving the value of diversity means uncovering all talent and that means creating a workplace characterized by inclusion.' – *Global Human Capital Trends 2014*, Deloitte

Why do we need diversity

Diversity is everywhere

The way we work and do business is becoming more and more dynamic and diverse. With fast changes, increasing competition in most industries, and customers looking for a complete package of services, companies need to bring a variety of resources together. Leaders recognise that diversity is an asset – that building a team with different skills and backgrounds is essential for their business to remain competitive. Many companies take pride in the diversity of expertise and personalities in their teams, along with the wide range of services they offer.

Multidisciplinary collaboration is seen as the hotbed of innovation. Often three or four generations work together, adding to the diversity of teams, and with younger generations bringing a whole new set of expectations and practices into the workplace.

Knowledge workers rarely do the same task continually for a whole day, let alone for a week or more. Even workers with specialty skills, or those who work in businesses with a narrow niche, need to apply a broad range of skills, draw on a vast knowledge and do many different activities.

Competing for talent, most organisations go to great lengths to attract high-performing workers and to keep them engaged. An important part of this strategy is to provide them with an environment that is interesting, exciting, and offers many choices.

Diversity brings new challenges

Employing 'like-minded' people (meaning people with similar thinking and approach to work) used to be a convenient way of finding consensus and avoiding personal conflicts at work. However, in today's business this strategy is rarely viable.

People who excel in different tasks tend to have different personalities; the person looking after company policies has a very different nature from the one raising the community spirit within the organisation. (Among my past colleagues, one constantly encouraged tidy desks, while another was more enthusiastic about regularly informing everyone about the engineers' division soccer results. We needed them both, but the way they worked was of course very different.) In a socially diverse environment personal clashes are more likely to arise; the design of the workplace needs to address that, helping to minimise conflicts, and making it easier for people to deal with the disagreements that do happen.

Creating an environment which works for people with different skills, personalities and backgrounds is not easy, not only because they may have opposing needs and conflicting opinions about what they find attractive, but because it's generally hard work to figure out how to influence people in a certain way, and thus to shape their thoughts and behaviours. Designing for a diverse team only adds to this challenge.

'People are complicated. They are a hodgepodge of rational and irrational thoughts and emotions, so their responses to places are complicated also.' states Sally Augustin in her insightful book *Place Advantage: Applied Psychology for Interior Architecture*. We are designing for humans, so we can never be certain what the exact outcomes will be.

The good news is that we have a huge toolbox to help us stay on the right track, so why not use it?

The typical workplace

In most workplaces, the majority of work areas still look and feel the same. When you enter, you might be greeted by an impressive reception area and a sophisticated board room, but as soon as you pass this 'facade', you see rows of identical desks and similar looking meeting spaces and private offices. Only 'special' spaces receive special attention – a nice lounge area, a quirky informal meeting space or a colourful feature wall somewhere. It seems that unique design is used as a tool for making statements, instead of bringing the most out of every bit of the space.

Uniformity is a problem

Uniform environments feel inauthentic and alienating, but beyond that, these kinds of offices also make work difficult, for the simple reason that it's impossible to design a single perfect workstation type or room type that serves different individuals well and suits the wide variety of activities required by today's business. (How could we expect to build productive relationships, develop new strategies, execute plans and make critical decisions in the same type of setting – typically sitting on an office chair at a desk, staring at a screen?)

A uniform workplace is therefore **a bad fit for most people, for most of their work**, making it hard to think, learn and communicate well. Being forced to adopt ways of working that are not natural for us[1] is not only unproductive, but can also be uncomfortable and exhausting. And when visitors come to the office, for example for client meetings or collaborative workshops, their experience also suffers.

This sort of office offers no real choices or incentive for people to proactively use their workspace. Instead, it encourages workers to sit still all day like mushrooms, to use the same old tools and strategies, to run the same sorts of meetings, and to **produce the same old results**. Furthermore, unstimulating spaces limit creative thinking and people's ability to solve problems.

A homogenous environment discourages initiative and innovation and promotes **a culture of uniformity**. Feeling that our individuality has no place can be detrimental to our relationship with our work and other people. People tend to be less tolerant and trusting, and personal conflicts are more likely to arise in an environment where personal and cultural differences are (seemingly) not respected and valued.

Furthermore, being surrounded only by 'working spaces' can create a sense of urgency, the feeling that **we should always be actively doing things**, and that it's unacceptable to take time to think or rest.

---

1 The same problem is now receiving a lot of attention in the context of the traditional education system. It's becoming widely recognised that students have different learning and communication styles, and so forcing them to sit still all day and listen to the teachers talk only engages a fraction of them. The rest of the students learn and achieve less than what they would be capable of if they were allowed to learn in a way that is natural for them.

The ideal workplace

Instead of putting our diverse teams into a homogenous workspace, we need to respect people's unique needs and provide an interesting and appealing environment with a variety of spaces for individuals and teams to choose from. The space should encourage people to be conscious of the way they use the space and produce results, and proactively choose or set up the area that is best suited to their task. Also, the environment should celebrate individual differences, enhance fruitful collaboration between people with different work cultures and habits, and assist with the easy resolution of conflicts.

To achieve these goals, the workplace needs to:

- Be designed around how our mind and body function
- Support different types of individual and team activities, and provide access to a range of work tools and media
- Promote different emotional states and ways of thinking through their ambience, for example, incorporate stimulating areas for dynamic group work, along with subtle relaxing spaces for deep contemplation
- Be equally welcoming and comfortable for people with different personalities
- Be furnished in such a way that helps people connect and interact with each other in different work scenarios
- Accommodate different work, learning and communication styles

Diversity vs random chaos: mistakes to avoid

Certain aspects of workspaces (and the teams that work there) should not be diverse. The vision, purpose and core values of your organisation need to be shared by everyone, and be consistently reflected by the space, reminding people that they are standing on common ground and working towards a common goal, and making it easier for them to embrace differences.

Diversity should not be created in a random manner, whether it's about building teams[2] or setting up the workplace. To assemble effective teams, you need to bring together the right mix of skills and personalities. Similarly, you need to create a workplace that has the right mix of space types, and offer choices that align with users' needs. Figuratively speaking, having a restaurant menu in front of you will only excite you if you are in the right sort of restaurant in the first place. (If it's Japanese or Thai, I'm in.)

It's important that your company educates people about the opportunities the space offers, and empowers them to engage with the space. Leaders should also assist workers to explore and better understand how they can work most effectively and with the least friction, to try out new ways of working and to fine-tune their personal work strategies.

 'The misunderstood genius'

> Several horror stories circulate in the building design industry about building projects where no money or intellectual power have been spared in creating an 'intelligent' environment which was able to interact with people in multiple ways. And as it turned out, workers were simply not interested in using the building's features as the designers anticipated. No-one wanted to use the 'collaboration room' or the breakout space.
>
> Had the design team put more effort into finding out what worked for people, and earned their engagement by 'selling' the opportunities to them, the outcomes would have most likely been very different.

Diversity – psychology – performance

Experiencing variability in our environment through our senses, and having choices around the type of space we inhabit are among our basic human needs. Meeting these needs is essential for us to feel well and think clearly.

---

2 Building powerful teams with the right mix of skills and personalities is a whole different science. There are various tools and strategies that can help you assemble the optimal team, maximising individual and team performance, satisfaction and trust. 'Talent Dynamics' is one of them.

When we are able to freely navigate between being challenged and feeling comfortable, we also function better. In a well-designed, diversified environment everyone can find an area that feels a bit like home, as well as other spaces that challenge them to think or work in a radically different way than they are used to.

Nurturing our uniqueness

The way we interact with our physical environment is shaped by the personal attributes we are born with, along with our personal history and culture. As a result, we all have different preferences in the way we choose to work, learn and communicate.

How do we design for such diverse needs? Science can provide guidance; for example, we know from research studies which sort of environments people with certain personality traits are the most productive in.

There are also some overarching patterns in how we all feel, think and behave in certain types of spaces. Place scientists have explored how we tend to respond to colours, textures, ceiling heights, lights, furniture arrangements, sounds, shapes – in fact, just about anything you can see, feel or hear in a space. The information they have gathered can provide great assistance in designing spaces where 'the right thing will happen'[3], whether that is to focus, generate ideas, learn or relax.

Task association

Having access to a range of work areas gives us an excellent opportunity to develop good work habits. When we only do one type of task in one location, we will eventually start to associate that space with that specific task. As an example, when I go to my 'email writing space' (which is a specific desk at one of the flexible workplaces I regularly use), all I am inclined to do there is write emails.

This habit may appear restrictive, but it's an extremely powerful method for staying focused, especially in a workplace where our attention can be

---

3 Using the words of Sally Augustin from the above-mentioned book. (See Related Readings at the end of this book.)

easily hijacked. It can save us from procrastination and multitasking, and also assists us in establishing clearer boundaries between work and leisure.

However, at times you may need to turn this strategy upside down ...

Breaking the loop

When working on a problem in the same place for a long time (for hours or days) it's easy to get into a mental loop. We keep looking at the problem from the same perspective and seeing the same avenues and obstacles. After a while our unconscious mind learns to associate the problem with that place, making it even more difficult to think outside the box. (Scientists estimate that around 90% of our thoughts are repetitive – we all master the skill of going in circles!)

It's nearly impossible to find solutions to a problem while fixated on it, so we need to 'step away' from it – both literally and figuratively – to create space for new thoughts.

Can you remember a time when you couldn't recall the name of a person, no matter how hard you tried, but as soon as you stopped thinking about it the name popped into your head? Or when you couldn't find the answer to a question, but once you stopped trying a whole new world opened up and answers came to you from places you hadn't previously considered?

Shifting our place of work – for example moving to another corner of the room, into another room, or outdoors – prompts us to move away from the problem and to look at things from a different angle. It helps us open up and become receptive to solutions.

Key design strategies

Key design strategies for creating a work environment that embraces diversity:

1. Press people's 'genius' button
2. Allow people get into the right 'work mode'
3. Promote the right sort of thinking
4. Support different types of interaction
5. Accommodate different personalities
6. Accommodate different work styles

Putting these strategies into practice will make it possible for everyone – yourself, staff, clients and other team members – to work effectively, using different skills and engaging in different activities, regardless of their age, personality or preferred work style. Moreover, it will assist team members to better work together and to capitalise on their differences.

All aspects of individual and team performance will further improve when people feel they are in a positive, caring, healthy environment. This will be explored in the following chapter, Principle 5: Caring.

Strategy 1:
Press people's 'genius' button

Have you ever observed in what sort of environments you have the best thoughts?

Most people rarely experience moments of clarity while staring at a computer screen, trying hard to solve a problem, and generally struggle to access their inner genius in a formal office environment. Instead, great ideas often pop up in the most unexpected places.

- Many people have breakthrough moments **in buzzing coffee shops or bars,** while catching up with team mates or friends. This is because being in stimulating places and interacting with others are just the right fuel for some of us to get our creative juices flowing. Perhaps this is why so many important innovations in history originated in coffee houses.

- Some people are in their element **in nature**, and it's not only because the sunlight and fresh air help the body and brain function better. Being in nature also makes us happier and more in tune with ourselves, so our ideas flow more freely. Even just the sight of nature can give a great boost to our creativity.

- **During exercise** we are also more likely to come up with great ideas. Exercise enhances brain function, as we know, and it also gives us the opportunity to be alone with our thoughts (barring team sports). Furthermore, running, cycling or working out are somewhat monotonous activities, providing ideal conditions for our conscious mind to switch onto autopilot, giving our unconscious the opportunity to quietly play and bring up insightful thoughts.[4]

  I've made many of my best personal and business decisions while cycling. While moving with speed I feel more compelled to move forward with those issues I tend to procrastinate on in the office, and I'm more ready to accept risks.

- Many people have great ideas **in the bathroom**. Taking a shower is relaxing[5], and we are alone with our thoughts, in a safe, comfortable place. We might also feel a bit tired[6] (as we tend to wash just after waking up or at the end of the day). For many of us, these are ideal

---

4 This is a similar state to being half awake half asleep, when our brain produces alpha waves, and we are highly receptive to new ideas and unusual associations. In contrast, focusing hard on a problem deactivates the function of the brain that enables creative problem solving.

5 When we are very relaxed, our brain may release dopamine, which not only makes us feel happier, but also boosts our creative juices.

6 Feeling tired can also increase creativity, since tiredness weakens our ability to intensely focus on an issue and to filter out everything we deem 'irrelevant'. Sometimes those stray thoughts are the missing pieces which, when we find them, enable us to put one plus one together and produce a great idea.

conditions for getting lost in our thoughts and experiencing epiphanies. In addition, the negative ions in the steam further improve our mood and wellbeing, and enhance our ability to think creatively.

I'm one of these people; I can credit many of my ideas to hot showers – that's where I've developed most of my design concepts, as well as many of the ideas for this book. This is a habit I share with the late Douglas Adams, author of the iconic Hitchhiker's Guide to the Galaxy, who is known for producing many of his highly creative ideas in his bathroom. In fact, one of the trilogy's characters, the Captain of the Golgafrinchan ark ship – who spent most of his time the bath, and had a very relaxed attitude – was based on Douglas Adams' own habit of taking extraordinarily long baths.

I'm not suggesting that your office needs to provide the facilities for your teams to spend their working hours under the shower, on a treadmill, or having coffee with their mates (though I secretly hope that in the future workplaces will have a lot more emphasis on these.) However, there is a lot you can learn from observing these everyday experiences about the conditions that allow you and your team to access your best thinking.

As you may now realise, some of the ways people come up with their most precious ideas are rather counterintuitive and not what the traditional office as we know it offers.

Environments that support people's best thoughts may:

- Distract people from focusing on their problems
- Encourage people to let their minds wander
- Be very comfortable and allow deep relaxation
- Be social and highly stimulating
- Promote physical movement and exercise
- Allow people to be alone
- Be outside the office

So when it comes to enabling people's diverse skills and qualities to come to fruition, I encourage you to think broadly. Everyone is different; some might choose a quiet library, a noisy lounge room, or a game room with a pool table as a thinking space. Or they might decide to take a walk in a nearby park. Let your people make their choice – so they can unleash their genius.

Strategy 2:
Allow people get into the right 'work mode'

Open and closed work modes

John Cleese, English actor and comedian – and a truly creative writer, as you would probably agree – held a public lecture on creativity, sharing his knowledge from his professional experience as well as research into psychology. Cleese explained in simple terms that the way we operate at work can be described as either being in an 'open mode' or in a 'closed mode'.

In 'closed mode' we are very purposeful, focused on getting on with things, and tend to be a bit impatient. In this mode we may feel under pressure and develop tunnel vision. This is the mode we spend most of our time in at work, and are often stuck in it. 'Creativity is not possible in the closed mode,' Cleese says.

In contrast, in 'open mode' we are less purpose-driven, and are more relaxed, receptive and contemplative. We have a wider perspective, are more playful, and are more inclined to humour. We allow ourselves to be curious since we don't feel the pressure to achieve things quickly. This state is ideal for creative ideas to surface.

We need both modes to get things done at work. We need to be in 'open mode' to come up with a solution to a problem, and then to switch to 'closed mode' to implement it. Then we need to switch back to 'open mode' again to review the results and decide if we are on the right track, and then again to 'closed mode' to proceed with the next stage. We need to keep switching between these two modes to be at our most efficient.

Enabling both work modes

In the last century offices were primarily built for the 'closed mode' – with private rooms and cubicles, and with a minimalist aesthetic. With collaborative work and innovation coming into focus over the last couple of decades, organisations have been more interested in creating workplaces that promote the 'open mode', and so today's offices are geared towards encouraging serendipitous interaction, the cross-pollination of ideas and dynamic teamwork.

But be aware, when the same area in the office promotes both work modes simultaneously you can only expect mixed results. I often see workstations and brainstorming spaces located side by side in the same open space, perhaps designed with the intention to allow workers to overhear interesting conversations and to make it easy for them to join in.

Transitioning from the closed to the open mode can take some time. (Stripping off our sense of urgency and letting our mind quiet down can easily take half an hour.) So dragging workers abruptly out of their closed mode can leave them in no man's land – unproductive (and perhaps even disruptive) in both modes of work.

And it doesn't do a favour to the creatives either. When everything around the so-called 'creative space' suggests a sense of urgency – such as practical furnishing, work charts, ringing phones, and the sight of rushing colleagues – it can make it really difficult for people to get into the right mind-state.

We need to build for both modes, and be strategic about how we support people to get into and maintain the state they need to be in at any given time.

Designing for 'getting on with things'

We need to appreciate that in some tasks we are most efficient when not coming up with new ideas and not considering new options, but just getting on with what we've started.

Supporting people to be focused, present and switched on while being in the implementation mode should not be very complicated. In 'closed mode' people are less receptive to the subtle qualities of their environment, so the most important thing is to eliminate negative influences (e.g. distractions and sources of stress) that may interfere with their work. By putting in place the strategies from previous chapters you will have done much of the work. (Design features and aesthetic qualities that support focused work will be discussed under Strategy 3 below.)

Designing for 'free thoughts'

How do we plan for 'open mode' – for creating new things? And what is creativity anyway?

Creativity is not about coming up with something from scratch; it's about combining two existing thoughts in a new way.[7] Connecting random ideas (like skyscrapers and Swiss cheese) is not difficult; the challenge is to find ideas which, when connected, are meaningful for us and solve our problems.

Creativity is not a talent we are either born with or not, but is 'a way of operating'. While people with certain personal attributes and skills might be able to think more creatively, we are all capable of generating inventive ideas. It really comes down to getting into a mental state in which our natural creativity can surface, and in the right environment this is more likely to happen.

Design strategies

To be able to open up, we need to liberate ourselves from the usual pressures of work; we can't just be creative while focusing on getting things done in a hurry. Hence, we tend to produce more original ideas in spaces that feel like an oasis, away from the everyday work environment with its usual demands.

Rooms dedicated to creative activities should have clear boundaries, both in physicality and in the way they are used. As a general rule, they should look and feel different to other areas where disciplined work takes place, and people in these rooms shouldn't be able to see or overhear any closed mode activities.

---

7   As John Cleese illustrates, creativity is like humour. 'In a joke, the laugh comes at a moment when you connect two different frameworks of reference in a new way. Example: there's the old story about a woman doing a survey into sexual attitudes who stops an airline pilot and asks him, amongst other things, when he last had sexual intercourse. He replies "Nineteen fifty eight." Now, knowing airline pilots, the researcher is surprised, and queries this. "Well," says the pilot, "it's only twenty-one ten now."'

Ideally, innovation sessions should not be held in the same space as, for example, OH&S trainings or formal performance reviews. Put simply, no activities should happen in a 'creative space' that workers would associate with rules and responsibilities. You don't want the space to bring up those associations when someone needs to think outside the box.

Spaces that are pleasant and promote positive emotions are, in general, more conducive to creative thinking. These include spaces that are harmonious, offer connection to nature[8], natural light and outside views, and promote self-confidence[9] and happiness[10]. (In the next chapter we will discuss these strategies in more detail.)

To think freely and share our thoughts openly, we need to have the confidence that we are not being watched or overheard by judgemental people. So ideation spaces should offer privacy, unless you have already established an open culture where trust, respect and the appreciation of eyebrow-raising ideas is the norm.

In interiors that are complex and rich in detail – e.g. which contain many different textures and objects – we are more likely to come up with new ideas than in minimalist spaces. Furthermore, seeing unexpected, surprising elements in a space expands our thinking and helps us generate a larger number of, and more diverse ideas. These stimulating items could be: a pile of toys, pictures on the wall that are non-work-related, or decorations you wouldn't expect to see in an office. You may encourage your people to keep bringing in out-of-place objects on an ongoing basis.

---

8 One study looked at the effects the natural environment had on our ability to think creatively, and found that people who were sent to a park, along with people who remained indoors but were given a picture of a rainforest to look at, performed significantly better than a control group who were in the typical meeting room.

9 Fear of making a mistake is the enemy of creative thought. John Cleese says: 'Well, you're either free to play, or you're not. As Alan Watts puts it, you can't be spontaneous within reason.'

10 According to a study at Pennsylvania State University, participants who were put into a happy mood produced almost 50% more ideas than those put into a sad mood. Another study confirmed that people are more likely to generate breakthrough ideas when feeling happy, or if they have had a recent happy experience.

> 💡 **Creative artworks**
>
> A picture I've seen in York Butter Factory, one of Melbourne's business incubators, is a modern-age replica of Monet's famous painting Bridge over a Pond of Water Lilies, but with a difference: the picture includes a couple of shopping carts and a traffic cone partially submerged in the pond.
>
> Another example: Superhero's Amsterdam office has a large wall mural, featuring a llama with an ice cream cone stuck on its snout, and with floating rubber gloves in the background. Wouldn't you love that ... or being in a space that inspires such insane ideas?

As Cleese puts it, humour 'gets us from the closed mode to the open mode quicker than anything else ... humour is an essential part of spontaneity, an essential part of playfulness, an essential part of the creativity that we need to solve problems, no matter how "serious" they may be.' How to infuse humour into an interior fitout? I don't think I need to tell you that!

Strategy 3:
Promote the right sort of thinking

It's a common mistake to think of creativity as one thing, and to pursue one-dimensional workplace strategies to support innovative outcomes at work. Some leaders have an excessive focus on getting strangers to accidentally bump into each other, or promoting brainstorming, or putting people into highly stimulating, richly decorated rooms.

In fact, the process of creation involves many different activities and ways of thinking. There are many opinions out there about what the best approach is to generating creative ideas and getting them off the ground. The common view among innovation experts is that creativity and innovation are all about capitalising on diversity – combining different ways of thinking, activities, skills and personalities. In other words, innovation grows out of diversity.

The creative process may include any of these mental activities:

- **Research and learning:** investigating and defining the problem, and reviewing available resources
- **Inspiration:** connecting with desired outcomes; immersing ourselves in another world to gain mental energy and an expanded view of what's possible
- **Individual idea generation:** coming up with new, often radical ideas based on our own knowledge and experience
- **Group brainstorming:** throwing ideas back and forth, building on other people's ideas to advance ours further
- **Creative collaboration:** bringing our ideas and knowledge to the table and combining it with other people's contributions to find new ways of achieving an agreed goal
- **Playing:** connecting with the problem and exploring possibilities in an uninhibited way
- **Reflection:** quiet contemplation time, allowing our minds to ponder and explore different scenarios before making a decision without any urgency or pressure
- **Critical thinking:** evaluating whether an idea is feasible, how likely it is to fail, what the costs and challenges are, and deciding if it is worth exploring further or acting upon

Then we need to turn ideas into business results through implementing and testing ideas, preparing deliverables, engaging and servicing clients, liaising with external providers, doing administrative tasks, dealing with technical issues, and so on.

You need a variety of spaces

You need a range of spaces with different qualities to support different ways of thinking.

It's not necessary to set up a separate room for each type of activity. When a room is fitted with changeable features (e.g. lighting, furniture, props and decoration) your teams can use it in many different ways and change the ambience with little effort to suit their work.

However, some activities don't mesh with each other. The greatest inefficiencies in innovation come from trying to do things that are mutually exclusive, such as seeking game-changing ideas while thinking with our critical hat on, or trying to reflect on things while being bombarded with new ideas. Activities involving incompatible mental states should be held in very different environments.

💡 The 'chill out' training room

Once I attended a training session in a new iconic university building in Melbourne. The building was listed among the world's 10 most spectacular university buildings (by CNN); I believe this title is well-deserved, but my experience was mixed.

The training room was windowless and had dim lighting. It had dark surfaces (carpet, walls and ceiling), and very casual furnishing featuring black bean bags and coffee tables. It was an unusual but pleasant space with a relaxing, grounding atmosphere. I felt as if I was in a cellar, and I think it would have been a perfect chill out room in a club.

However, this room was used for teaching rational, business-related subjects such as how to comply with government regulations. The room was set up like a traditional training room, with all seating facing a screen (for the PowerPoint presentation). Sitting on bean bags for an extended time and making notes on my lap was very uncomfortable. The whole situation felt quite confusing, and made it difficult for me to tune in to the subject.

It was an atmospheric space used for the wrong purpose, making my life (and I assume other trainees' too) more difficult rather than supporting our learning.

Before you design or allocate a space for a work activity, consider whether your people should:

- Focus on the big picture, or focus on details
- Focus on possibilities, or focus on practicalities
- Be ready to take risks, or make safe decisions
- Feel energised and excited, or feel calm and relaxed
- Be courageous and ready to be challenged, or feel safe and nurtured
- Feel social and friendly, or compelled to get things done
- Feel cheerful, or feel serene
- Be rebellious, or conform

Working through the senses

The physical space can have a profound influence on our mood and thinking. This is why we find it easier to have relaxed conversations in small rooms with warm colours and dim lighting, to do administrative work in quiet, brightly lit spaces, or to come up with innovative ideas in a somewhat noisy and messy café-type environment.

The best workplaces engage multiple senses; they use everything from colours and lights to sounds and textures to enhance our experience and performance at work.[11] Below are some examples of how different features of a space shape the way we feel, think and act.

---

11   Music and fragrances are also powerful when it comes to altering people's mood and thinking. While it's not a common practice in offices, you could use these tools strategically to elevate performance.

COLOURS

Colours affect us in many ways: physically, emotionally and intellectually. They can be energising or soothing, put us in a serious or a playful mood, make us feel courageous or cautious, and help us learn, communicate or innovate better. Colours also communicate meaning such as friendliness or danger.

While our responses to certain properties of colours (such as saturation and brightness) are instinctive and universal, colour is largely a subjective matter. The meaning we attach to different colours, along with what we find pleasant or irritating, is shaped by our upbringing and culture, our personalities, and also our gender.

The ways colours influence people's thoughts and behaviour is a hotly debated subject. While science can provide some useful guidance for colour choices, it is just as important to choose colours that people actually like.

Warm colours (reds, yellows, and oranges) are invigorating, create a cheerful ambience, and promote divergent thinking. These are also great colours to create an intimate and cosy feel and to support social activities and collaboration.	**Cool colours** (purples, greens and blues) make the space feel calm and peaceful, and can help with concentration or relaxation. These are good colours to use where people work in stressful situations or need intense focus.
Customers cannot fully concentrate and make their best decisions when surrounded by warm colours.	Customers are more able to concentrate and make a decision about a purchase in spaces with cool colours.
Saturated colours (i.e. pure vivid colours without a grey component) are energising and improve mood. However, certain shades can be distracting and irritating when used on large surfaces.	**Unsaturated colours** (i.e. those with a significant grey component, like pastel colours or browns) are more neutral or soothing. However, too much unsaturated colour can make a space feel dull, especially when these colours are not complimented with accents of bold colours or other exciting design features.

Red is a lively, warm, friendly colour. It is physically energising; it raises the heart rate and stimulates faster breathing. Red is great for tasks that require attention to detail or recalling information from memory. However, it may interfere with intellectual performance and promote procrastination. Red can also be perceived as aggressive.

Blue is serene, calming and soothing. It boosts confidence and stimulates the mind. Blue helps with concentration and clear thinking, and supports productivity. However, it can be seen as cold and unfriendly.

Create Space for a DIVERSIFIED Business

Yellow is the colour of intellect and learning. The right shade makes people more optimistic, raises self-esteem, and is a great colour for boosting creativity. However, yellow in excess or in strong shades can be irritating, and may give rise to anxiety, or make people lose their temper more easily.

Green is the colour of nature and it represents balance and harmony. Green is calming and restful for the eyes, and is reassuring, as we associate green with safety. On the flip side, it can suggest stagnation and come across as bland, if incorrectly used.

Violet is the colour of spirituality; it encourages contemplation and supports meditation. It communicates fine quality (as it's associated with royalty), but the wrong tone may achieve the opposite and look cheap and tacky.

Orange is a fun colour associated with enthusiasm and joy. It is warm and playful, and it makes people happier. Orange is energising and stimulates brain activity. However, too much orange may come across as frivolous and immature.

White is clean and pure, and makes rooms seem more spacious. White can also feel sterile and cause eye strain. Environments dominated by white (as well as beige) can be understimulating. People working in offices with white surfaces all around them are more likely to experience headaches and nausea.

Black, as a colour, communicates absolute clarity. It is serious, elegant and sophisticated, and represents excellence. However, spaces dominated by black can feel cold, heavy and oppressive.

SURFACES

Surfaces with a shiny finish are more invigorating.	Matt surfaces are more relaxing.

FORMS, LINES AND SHAPES

Asymmetrical forms and patterns create a sense of movement and dynamism.	**Symmetrical forms** and patterns create a sense of completion, balance, peace and calm.
Vertical lines suggest stability and strength. We tend to find vertical features naturally energising. (The most dynamic natural environments are characterised by vertical lines: e.g. cliffs, canyons, trees, and waterfalls)	We find **horizontal lines** and features naturally calming. (The most peaceful natural environments are characterised by horizontal lines: e.g. river, beach, horizon, clouds).
Diagonal lines bring a sense of movement and dynamism. The steeper the angle, the more energising the space.	

FORMS, LINES AND SHAPES (cont'd)

Rectangular forms suggest action and efficiency.	**Gently curved** forms and lines are more relaxing.
V shapes indicate threat or anger, and attract attention quickly.	We tend to associate more **strongly curved lines** (like the one in a smiley face) with happiness.

COMPLEXITY

Complex spaces (that combine many different stimulating elements, colours, textures and features) tend to be exciting and energising. Spaces that are somewhat disordered or those with an unusual style have similar effects.	**Moderately complex** spaces (that combine only a few variations of colours, textures, features and 'interesting' design elements) are more pleasant and soothing, along with spaces that are neatly ordered and have a familiar style.

It's important to find the right balance in design. The consequences of being in an overstimulating or an understimulating (i.e. boring) environment are equally severe; both types of spaces make us restless, emotional, and less able to concentrate.

CEILING HEIGHT

Rooms with **high ceilings** promote free and abstract thinking, and help people focus on the big picture. Such spaces can be ideal for brainstorming, goal setting and visioning exercises.	Rooms with **low ceilings** support concentration and attention to detail. Such spaces are great for implementation tasks such as calculations or report writing.
High ceilings may also make a situation feel more formal and thus prime people to conform to social norms.	Rooms with low ceiling heights tend to feel more safe, relaxing and intimate, and can be great for informal social gatherings or for quiet 'thinking time'.

The optimal height of a room – and how ceiling height is perceived – also depends on the room size. In general, larger rooms need to have higher ceilings than smaller rooms in order to feel well-proportioned.

In a tall room, you can create the visual effect of a low ceiling by hanging items from the real ceiling (e.g. suspended lining, decorative elements or lighting pendants), or by setting up a structure within the room, like an indoor tent or gazebo.

LIGHTING

In general, **brightly lit spaces** are more energising, both physically and mentally. In bright places we tend to be more restrained and compliant. In general, high lighting levels are optimal for tasks requiring analytical thinking and logical reasoning, as well as administrative tasks.	**Dimly lit spaces** are usually more relaxing and seem more private. In darker rooms we speak more quietly and engage in more intimate conversations. Interestingly, we also have a more positive perception of others, compared to being in a bright room. In dim light we tend to think more broadly and creatively, and may also take more risks.
Of course, when choosing lighting levels, we should never compromise our eyesight, and so the lighting should be suited to the tools and media we use.	
Cool light has a bluish tint, and a bright, clean, clinical feel. Cool light heightens alertness and helps with concentration. On the flip side, in cool light we tend to experience more stress.	**Warm light** gives a yellowish tint. It is calming and helps create a friendly atmosphere. In warm light we are better at solving problems, tend to take more risks, and are more inclined to resolve disagreements with others instead of avoiding a possible confrontation.

SOUNDS

A moderate level of **background noise** enhances creative thinking and problem solving. (Slightly distracting noise stops people from thinking analytically and from having a narrow focus, which are both detrimental to out-of-the-box thinking.) Interestingly, background noise can also increase the likelihood of people purchasing innovative products. The ideal sound level (for this purpose) is around 70 decibels, equivalent to having a TV or radio playing in the room, or being in a café.	**Silence** helps sharpen focus, so quiet spaces are ideal for tasks that require analytical thinking and attention to detail. However, noise levels that are too low may hinder idea generation. Furthermore, in a quiet space even a soft sound can stand out and a distant conversation can be overheard, so it's easier to get distracted.
Too much noise is a problem, as it makes it very difficult to process information and think creatively.	

TEMPERATURE	
A slightly **cool room temperature** is invigorating.	A slightly **warm room temperature** is relaxing.
It is important that the ambient room temperature is still comfortable, even if you're trying to create an optimal space for the task at hand.	

Personally I find these insights fascinating, as understanding space and psychology is my passion. But I appreciate that this avalanche of information can be overwhelming if you are less nerdy about the subject, so please relax – it's really the designers' job to get all of these right.

But remember, you need to do the preparations; understand how your people need to feel, think and behave in different areas of your office, and communicate this to the design team, preferably through a detailed design brief. Only work with designers who understand the implications of the different spatial features on human psychology, and who are prepared to create a customised solution addressing your brief.

Strategy 4:
Support different types of interaction

You can't overestimate the power of rapport and personal connection when working with others; without these we can't build productive relationships, work well in teams or win over clients.

How we are positioned in relation to each other in a meeting – whether we sit or stand, how far we are from each other, whether we face each other or sit side by side – influences how we behave. This can make a difference to the success or failure of the meeting. Therefore, the furniture types chosen for different rooms, and the way people use that furniture are important components of a company's workplace strategy.

Choose the right meeting table

Size does matter

The conference table is often seen as a symbolic item of a business, a piece of furniture which should reflect professionalism and quality, so usually a lot of effort and dollars are invested into obtaining a truly impressive piece. It's great to see that the choice of some office fitout items receives such attention, but when a table is not right for the purpose, it can do more damage than good.

> ### 💡 The curse of the oversized meeting table
>
> Once I was invited to a meeting with the heads of an interior design company to get to know each other better and explore potential opportunities for working together. I went well prepared for the group's agenda, bringing drawings and photos to use in the discussions – after all, designers are visual people.
>
> When I arrived I was directed to a meeting room with one enormous meeting table, complete with beautiful flowers, artworks and a water jug. It was certainly a very impressive table, but it was hard to appreciate it just then ... The three people I met sat themselves down at three corners of the table, so it only seemed appropriate for me to take the fourth one.
>
> Unfortunately, in this setting, showing visuals to the others was nearly impossible, and it was hard work even to have a connected conversation. We held a somewhat awkward discussion; I felt as if I was addressing a large audience, trying to engage people sitting left, right and centre.
>
> By the end of the meeting we had a good understanding and appreciation of what the others did, but there was little energy or buzz – you know, the sort of thing that actually makes you want to put things into motion.

Holding meetings around a huge conference table is a typical scenario, so when a meeting goes flat, we don't tend to blame the table for it. (Imagine if one of your colleagues reported: 'I've lost the sale, but it was the furniture's fault!')

Of course it's not impossible to have great meetings in a setting that's not quite right. (I have had amazing meetings around enormous tables, even in kitchens!) But research studies show that table size does matter; it influences communication and collaboration. Tables are physical barriers that contribute to psychological separation between team members.

Very wide tables disrupt conversation. When we sit too far from each other, we tend to interact in a formal way and to compete rather than collaborate. So large tables (wider than around 1.6m) are more suitable for presentations and for meetings where it's beneficial for people to interact in a competitive spirit.

Small tables are better for teamwork; they help us build social connection and open up. When we are closer to others, we are more likely to collaborate and work toward a common goal. For small group discussions, tables that are just large enough for the number of people meeting are ideal. However, it's important not to crowd people.

To create space for successful meetings, make sure that your teams can choose the tables that best suit their activities. You may provide a variety of table sizes, or use small mobile tables that can be pushed together as needed. And if you need to hold creative group meetings around a conference table, make sure that it is not too wide.

Shape matters too

The shape of the table also influences the way we interact. Round or square tables suggest equality, and so are great for leaderless conversations such as ideation and negotiation. Long rectangular tables suggest hierarchy (with people sitting at the end or at the middle of the table being the focal point) and are better suited for meetings where leaders need to stand out.

Where we sit

The way we organise ourselves around a table is also important. We talk to others more readily when we can make eye contact, so in group discussions everyone should be able to see each other easily. Sitting side by side is not ideal.

When we sit across the table from each other, it's harder to ignore the other person's presence; in this situation we are more likely to feel exposed or confronted, and to challenge the other person rather than cooperate.

In one-on-one meetings, sitting across the corner from each other is great for working towards a common goal, for friendly casual conversations, and also for stressful discussions.

Do you always need a meeting table?

Sitting at a 'meeting' table on an 'office' chair is a very different experience from using, for example, bar style furniture, like tall tables and stools. We are used to having relaxed, casual conversations in a bar. So when we are in a similar setting in the office, sitting on a tall chair, in the same posture as we do when catching up with friends, the way we feel, think and talk is naturally different from when we are in a more formal setting. And when we are meeting in a home style lounge room with a coffee table and sofas, or in a café style environment with long benches or tiny stools, our conversations are different again.

You might also want to ask yourself whether you need a table at all for certain types of meetings. Randomly laid out bean bags, floor cushions or multi-functional boxes might provide just the right setting for conversations where teams need to explore problems from unusual angles.

Standing up

What about not sitting at all? Standing meetings are gaining popularity, and when held for the right purpose can improve team productivity.

A US study explored how the setup of the meeting space – getting people to sit or stand – might alter the way team members interact and collaborate. The study found that participants in standing meetings are significantly more engaged, share more information and ideas, and are less territorial.

Typically, people have a more individually-oriented focus when seated; they feel they own their space in the room, and use their own pen and paper or device. On the other hand, when standing, team members tend to use shared tools (e.g. whiteboard), see the space as a shared workspace, and thus be more involved in the collaboration.[12]

Standing up also engages the whole body, energises people, and helps them connect with the task (as discussed in Principle 3: Productive).

Another sort of 'Periodic Table'

Stanford d.school is an educational institute teaching 'design thinking', and its teaching space is famous for being designed to the greatest detail to best support its students in learning, practising and experiencing their subject, largely through collaborative work. (The school's interior design inventions are published in a remarkable book *Make Space: How to Set the Stage for Creative Collaboration* by Doorley and Witthoft.)

The 'Periodic Table' is one of the school's iconic inventions; it has been designed to shape students' behaviour in the most unusual ways. The table is deliberately annoying; it's a bit too high for sitting, slightly too low for a standing desk, and too small for four students to use. The table has a non-precious aesthetic, and is fitted with heavy-duty castors for easy manipulation; it's meant to be used and moved around. Tables can also be pushed together to create larger surfaces.

These features encourage students to stand up and keep moving. Also, by putting students into a slightly uncomfortable position, it pushes them to get used to slight discomfort, in particular, to get out of their comfort zone. The designers of this table were aware that there are better ways to study design than just sitting, and created a fitout item which nudges students to get into action. As stated in *Make Space:* 'the Periodic Table is more launchpad than anchor'.

(See a full case study of Stanford d.school in Principle 7: Changing.)

---

12 There is a downside to standing: it makes the difference in people's height more apparent. It forces people to look up or down to make eye contact, which affects social interaction.

Strategy 5:
Accommodate different personalities

'There are two types of people: those who can extrapolate from incomplete information.' (I couldn't help sharing this joke here. My apologies.)

We all prefer different spaces for specific types of interaction, for example: meeting rooms for formal conversations, enclosed offices for resolving conflicts, cafés and lounge areas for social activities, and informal meeting spaces for spontaneous meetings and exploring new ideas. However, our preferred work settings also depend on our personality. Having access to spaces that suit our personality type will be likely to enhance our experience and performance.

A 2013 UK survey conducted by Herman Miller investigated the 'psychology of collaboration'; it classified respondents according to the Big Five personality traits[13], and then looked at how workers with different traits prefer to communicate, and in what sort of work settings.

The assessed personality traits, and the key findings were:

- People who are **'open to experience'** are fascinated by novelty, drawn to new experiences, and prefer variety over routine. They are curious and adventurous, have a wide range of interests, and tend to be more imaginative and inventive than 'closed' people.

    'Open' people prefer to meet their team in casual environments, including outside the office, (such as 'huddle rooms', 'brainstorm rooms', cafés, bars) for generating new ideas, rather than in formal meeting rooms. They appear to spend more time on thinking and developing ideas and less time on computer-based work than others.

- **'Conscientious'** people prefer to follow plans rather than to act spontaneously. They are typically well-organised, self-disciplined, focused on achievement, and aim to work efficiently.

---

13 'In psychology, the Big Five personality traits are five broad domains or dimensions of personality that are used to describe human personality.' (Wikipedia). This system is also referred to as the OCEAN scale. There are many other systems to classify personality, but the OCEAN scale appears to be very useful for correlating personality traits with preferred work settings.

These workers prefer to separate social and non-work-related activities from work. They may take the time to relax in a breakout space or hang out with their peers in a café, but they don't consider these spaces to be workspace.

- **Extroverts** get energised by being around others and having stimulating conversations, and often feel the need to draw attention to themselves. They like to think aloud and jump quickly into action. They tend to be enthusiastic and full of energy, they love excitement – and it all shows. They wear their hearts on their sleeves.

    Extroverts prefer to meet face-to-face to brainstorm and discuss ideas, using a variety of informal, social settings rather than formal meeting rooms. They are more in their element in stimulating and dynamic, open environments. The study found that they especially value views out of meeting spaces.

    On the other hand, **introverts** prefer to communicate through email and to work with detailed, logically presented reports. They are more productive in subtle, quiet spaces where they can work autonomously with no interruptions. For meetings, they prefer enclosed rooms or private spaces.

💡 What introverts can offer

Introversion is perhaps one of the most misunderstood personality traits. Introverts think, learn and communicate very differently from extroverts, and thus need different environments to thrive than extroverts do. Susan Cain's book *Quiet: The Power of Introverts in a World That Can't Stop Talking* has brought this issue into public awareness and is prompting designers and managers to reconsider how workplaces could better support introverts to realise their unique potential.

As Cain's book states, a third to half of the population are introverts, and contrary to the common perception, they make great leaders and excel at creativity. They listen well and usually have deep knowledge to share.

Introversion is not the same as being shy; rather, it is a way of processing information and responding to stimulation. Introverted people prefer to process things internally first, to think and reflect before sharing their ideas. They work well independently, without being in the centre of attention, and are most energised and switched-on in environments that are relatively low-key and quiet enough to concentrate.

Today's workplaces are mostly designed for extroverts – with large open, noisy spaces that offer plenty of opportunities for collaboration – driven by the belief that innovation and productivity come from unbounded interaction and dynamic group work (Cain calls this the new 'groupthink'). Sadly, being quiet (and calm under pressure) are often mistaken as signs of under-performance: being too serious, slow, lazy, unimaginative or antisocial.

In fact, introversion and solitude are crucial parts of the creative process. Psychologists find that the most creative people are not only great at exchanging ideas, but are also drawn to going off alone with their thoughts from time to time, which is when they are most likely to have profound revelations.

None of us are purely introverted or extroverted; we all possess aspects of both, and these should be nurtured. Combining introversion and extroversion is also a great strategy for building effective teams; research found that heterogenous teams deliver more well-considered and successful outputs.

- **'Agreeable'** workers are generally more friendly, compassionate and cooperative than their 'analytical' counterparts, and have a more trusting and helpful nature.

    These people prefer group work for generating ideas but one-on-one meetings for socialising. 'They prefer conference suites for sharing information, the breakout space or local café for generating ideas, and clubs for socialising.' notes the researchers' report.

- **'Neurotic'** people more easily experience negative emotions (such as anger, stress or depression) than their more 'secure' and 'confident' counterparts, are more emotionally reactive, and are more likely to see minor frustrations as major difficulties.

  People at the higher end of the 'neuroticism' scale spend more time in solo activity. They prefer working with documented information, sharing information through email, and when meeting others, using quiet and private meeting rooms.

To maximise workers' talents, you need to let them work in places that meet their individual needs and give them the freedom to be themselves.

Strategy 6:
Accommodate different work styles

What is your work style?

Your work style is the combination of your unique work habits and strategies which help you produce the best results. This includes: what sort of place you work most effectively on a specific task, which tools and communication channels you use, which part of the day you are most productive, how long you can pay attention without taking a break, and whether you work best alone or in a team. Different industries and cultures have their own overarching patterns, but work styles are also specific to the individual.

Your work style is shaped by your personality, interests, experience and routine. It builds on your natural communication style (e.g. whether you prefer communicating through written words, spoken words or images), as well as your learning style (e.g. whether you need to see a piece of information, listen to it, analyse it, or apply it in practice in order to take it in). Your work style also encompasses such personal characteristics as being a morning or evening person, and how you handle multitasking and interruptions (which strongly correlates with your gender).

Knowing your work style helps you make better choices about how to work, and for setting up and using your work environment. People who honour their own work style are not only more effective, but tend to enjoy work more.

For example, people who communicate best through images could really work well in spaces surrounded by whiteboards. Those who think better by doing things could work well in workshops that enable them to build and experiment with things. And those who best express themselves in writing may need a quiet space when they can put their thoughts into a document.

For people working regularly outside of the 'office' it can be especially beneficial to be aware of their individual work style. This knowledge can always help them to choose the right time, the right environment and the right conditions to do their best work.

Exploring your work style

Understanding how we can work most effectively takes effort. The most productive work habits are not always the easiest and most comfortable, especially when trying them for the first time. So encourage your people to explore what really works for them, instead of using their 'work style' as an excuse to stay in their comfort zone.

Suggest that they try out different ways of working and observe the results. Perhaps they can work from a room they normally wouldn't consider, use tools and media they normally wouldn't choose, interact with people in an unusual way, stand up when they would normally sit, change their habits around taking breaks, etc. (Spaces outside of the office, such as coworking places or third places – discussed in Principle 7: Evolving – can provide great opportunities for this sort of experimentation.)

Create opportunities for your team members to experiment without pressure. During stressful times we are the least open to explore new ways of working, and so we tend to fall back into old routines, whether they are productive or not.

> 💡 **The starting point: an idyllic coastal town**
>
> One summer, due to unusual circumstances, I ended up in a small isolated beach town in South Australia for two weeks, and decided to use this time to re-energise, read a few books and plan my year ahead. I was essentially free to follow my intuition around how I spent my time, which was a great opportunity to get in tune with my natural rhythm.

Soon my daily activities started to follow a pattern ... I started each day by writing a journal, still in bed. After breakfast I worked on my laptop, sitting on the balcony. In the afternoon I read books on the beach, and then went for walk, contemplating how I could apply the ideas I'd just learnt. Then I socialised with other residents of the hostel. And so on ...

Days passed, and I got more and more in flow. I unconsciously chose the right activities, in the right place, at the right time, and I felt energised, connected and productive. By the end of this period I had read more books, made more friends, made more plans and learnt more (about myself too) than throughout the whole past year. Also, I had heaps of fun, lots of rest, and I felt like a new person!

Exploring my work style didn't stop there; I'm still regularly trying out new ways of working. Of course, in our day-to-day lives we have to deal with many constraints, but there is still plenty of scope for experimenting.

Here are a few things I've learnt about myself from these experiences:

- I work best if I switch tasks and also locations every couple of hours.

- I am naturally creative and switched on in the morning and late at night. My most creative hours are very fragile; I do my best work in a quiet space away from distraction and information overload, in a relaxed, casual setting (e.g. sitting on a floor cushion or on a couch).

- I'm great at doing research and analytical tasks in the afternoon. For this sort of work, I prefer sitting at a desk, in a more formal environment.

- A walk outside, a bike ride or a shower can work miracles when I'm feeling stuck.

Working with others

Considering other people's work style is essential for fruitful collaboration. While working in a team with a mix of work styles is not always easy, it can be really rewarding. The benefits are broader than just finding a channel for communication.

Adapting to other people's work style forces us to approach a task differently from how we normally would, to think about a problem a different way, and therefore, to produce different solutions. It can also help us understand others better, think the way they do, speak their language, and ultimately, come up with a solution that resonates with them.

💡 Diving into the world of Post-it notes

As one of my earliest projects, I worked with a strategic design consultancy, Huddle, helping them design their new space. The brief was unusual and rather challenging: creating an innovation facility where they could design, test and improve services for their customers, and where they could also invite other service organisations to share the space and collaborate. This was a novel concept, so nobody knew what this space should look like or how it should function.

The briefing meeting was held in my clients' current office, which gave me the opportunity to observe their environment and how they worked. It immediately struck me that they had a very dynamic approach to problem solving; they stood up a lot during the meeting, drew on large sheets of paper, put their ideas on the walls, and used A LOT of Post-it notes while exploring ideas.

This was nothing like I'd seen in the corporate world where people tend to automatically reach for their computers when given a problem to solve, and at that time I was also conditioned to do the same. However, after this meeting it simply did not feel right for me to use a computer for developing a design strategy for this team.

So I took a deep breath, dug out some old piles of Post-it notes from my cabinet, and dived into this new way of working, organising my ideas on small pieces of paper – a bit like playing with puzzle pieces. It was a whole new experience, physically engaging and visually stimulating, so I quickly started to enjoy it.

Eventually, when I presented the design proposal which I had created using my clients' work style, they absolutely loved it. (It's not that they were biased; they did not see me working, and I typed up my advice before presenting it to them.) My solution somehow embodied the essence of who they were and how they worked, and set the direction for the design that the whole team was keen to follow.

Creating a space that works for everyone

Knowing your team members' and your own work style will help you to identify the types of spaces that can best support your work, and to set up your workspace accordingly.

Creating a workspace that also accommodates your clients' and other contributors' work style will make your collaboration way more effective, add to an outstanding work experience, and also increase client satisfaction.

Make sure that the space works for your people, and that your people 'work the space'. In some cases, you can greatly improve your results just by changing the way you and your teams use the space, without changing the space itself.

Create Space for a DIVERSIFIED Business

Putting things into practice

 ## Case study: National Australia Bank, 700 Bourke St

Bank buildings are leaders in providing interesting, diversified work environments for their employees.

An extension of our city

NAB's (National Australia Bank) new headquarters at 700 Bourke Street, Melbourne, is a prime example. This 63,000 m², 14-floor building pushes the boundaries of workplace design on many fronts, including the diversity of environment they provide for their people. This is NAB's third key building within the same precinct. With each project they have been fine-tuning their workplace strategy, becoming key players in the evolution of workplace design in Australia.

The building doesn't follow any formula. It sits on a triangular site, in a pedestrian precinct. You enter over a footbridge, and walk through a kind of piazza before reaching the atrium, the heart of the building. This is essentially still 'public space' enlivened by social activities, with a café and a coworking space for customers. From here you can see the whole organisation and access a variety of facilities, including a theatre, a seminar room, the customer and community lounge, and a range of meeting spaces (formal and informal, open and enclosed) – even if you're not one of their employees. You could also take the lift (after making the necessary arrangements, of course) and go up to the landscaped rooftop garden that features majestic views.

Diversity on all levels

The building is designed to accommodate 500 people on each floor, but you won't see endless rows of workstations. The work areas, organised around the light-filled atrium, are divided into 'hubs' for teams of around 50. Each hub has a variety of spaces such as meeting rooms, informal meeting spaces, quiet rooms, work booths and collaboration areas. External consultants and drop-in staff also have spaces in which to work on each floor.

In this large building there are several micro-climates. It was a deliberate decision to allow the climatic conditions to be uneven in different parts of the building, and at different times of the day. (The designers saw the building as a living, breathing entity where everything is in motion, and worked towards creating an environment that feels organic and authentic.) But the term 'micro-climates' is also a metaphor for the variety of workspaces and furniture types provided. The environment encourages people to move around, like they naturally would when spending a day in a city, and choose their spot based on their task and mood.

The solution to future-proofing

This level of diversity was a response to the challenge faced by the designers: creating a workplace that is going to be responsive to the changing needs of the organisation and individuals for many decades to come. NAB is a rapidly evolving organisation with a diverse organisational structure, with most of its workforce already working flexibly. The building provides a platform for the latest generation of Activity-Based Work, a way of working which focuses on the productivity of and interaction between teams, and in which entire teams choose the space they own for a period of time.

With its radical new approach to workplace design, NAB has not only achieved greater organisational efficiency, but has also created a building that is environmentally efficient[14], and is efficiently occupied (i.e. it has a smaller floor area than they would need with a traditional design approach).

---

14 The building has been awarded a six-star Green Star rating for its design. This is the highest level of recognition awarded by the Green Building Council of Australia, representing 'world leadership' in environmentally sustainable design.

Where people and ideas meet

The building has been designed to draw people in, enriching NAB's colourful community. You can use some of its floors as your own, and mix with and work with NAB's staff. This is not a luxurious looking building, but a place that's more authentic, and therefore more attractive to the public.

The building performs around people, not the other way around. By supporting mobility, offering choices and removing barriers to teamwork, 700 Bourke Street provides a unique setting for the free flow of ideas and innovation.

A non-traditional workplace: Vision Villas

In harmony with the elements

Vision Villas is an entrepreneurial training centre and resort-style accommodation in Bali, which also offers a unique setting for visitors to re-evaluate and develop their personal or business vision while taking a break from their routines.

The ultimate purpose of the facility – along with the educational programs held there – is to assist people to follow their path to 'true wealth'. ('True wealth' in this case refers to making the most out of our talents and creating great value, as opposed to being absorbed in the accumulation of material goods.) To achieve this, the setting has been designed to provide the best support for people to be in the right mental state throughout their experience of planning their path for the future.

Vision Villas was established by Roger Hamilton, social entrepreneur, who created the Talent Dynamics profiling system, which aims to help people understand what roles and strategies in business are most aligned with their personality.

Hamilton teaches that any value-creating process has five distinct phases: clarifying our purpose, creating ideas and plans, forming teams, implementing plans, and re-evaluating our strategies for further improvement. These stages require different ways of thinking to achieve optimum results, and can be symbolised by the five elements as described by the 5,000 year-old Chinese divination book, the I-Ching: water, wood, fire, earth and metal.

The five pavilions

Vision Villas is a physical representation of this system; it houses five outdoor pavilions representing the five elements, each designed to enhance people's performance at different phases of a planning project, helping them to be in their flow. Here is how this works:

1. You start every project by spending some time at the Water Pavilion clarifying your purpose. This is a very peaceful and uplifting place, next to the pool. Your **'why'** is at the centre of the wealth creation process, and so the pavilion is at the centre of the facility.

2. You then proceed to the Wood Pavilion to come up with creative ideas and big picture plans for **what** you want to achieve. Here you can work without interruption and think expansively. While the pavilion itself has a minimalist design, the surroundings are visually stimulating.

3. Then you move to the Fire Pavilion to work out **who** to involve in your team and how to work together. This place is designed to support social interaction. It's like a cosy lounge room, with comfortable arm chairs and lots of bright warm colours (reds and oranges).

4. The next step is the Earth Pavilion, which is surrounded by greenery, and as you would guess, feels earthy. This is where you get grounded (you may request a Balinese massage to help with this), and start to work out how to transform your ideas into reality, such as **when** it is the right time to take specific actions in your business.

5. The last stage in the cycle is the Metal Pavilion. It is in an elevated location, is quiet and well-organised, and has lots of cool colours (purples and blues). This is the place where you look at your project from an outsider's perspective and review **how** to improve your systems and refine the details.

At any stage of this cycle, you can go back to the Water Pavilion to connect with your **'why'** whenever you get stuck or disoriented.

Bring it home

Some might be skeptical about applying such an esoteric approach to workplace design. At Vision Villas, there have been experiments to test out how using the different pavilions influences the way people think and solve problems, and the results were consistent: people working in the space best suited to the task always achieved better results.

You don't need to establish a Balinese resort to adopt a comparable workplace strategy. All you need to do is to create a diverse environment that caters to different ways of thinking and working, and to encourage your team members to answer questions like these before starting any activities:

- What do I/we need to achieve with this task?
- What questions do I/we need to answer?
- And what sort of environment could draw the answers out of me/us?

❓ Questions to consider

- In what types of places do your people have their best ideas?

- When do workers need to be in 'open mode', and when in 'closed mode'?

- How could you infuse humour into the work environment?

- What kinds of features could you use that your team members and visitors would not expect to see in your workplace?

- What types of activities are included in your creative process? And is there anything new you would like to try out?

- What are different types of meetings like in your organisation? (Think number of participants, communication style, tools and technology used, preferred setting, etc.)

- In what kinds of meeting spaces would your team members be comfortable?

- When might it be useful to make your team members feel slightly uncomfortable?

- What are the preferred personality traits in your organisation? And what do people with those different traits bring to the team?

- How do people in your company with different personalities communicate best? Where do they prefer to meet? And in what kinds of spaces do they think best?

- How could the workspace also accommodate those who are in the minority?

- What are your team members' work styles? How do they express themselves best? How do they take in information?

PRINCIPLE 5
CARING

CREATE SPACE FOR A CARING BUSINESS

Establishing an environment where we feel valued and cared about, happy and healthy

We are naturally drawn to pleasant and stimulating spaces that resonate with who we are and which send us positive messages. Such spaces provide us with energy, comfort, and the certainty that we are in the right place to be at our best. In our homes or in our favourite places we experience this every day; however, our workplaces also have the potential to become similarly inviting environments. In an attractive, healthy and safe workplace we are more likely to feel valued and cared about. As a result, not only does our work performance improve, but we also become more caring, engage more with our work, and produce more profitable financial outcomes.

Why should we care?

Living in an era when caring matters

Boundaries between work and life, and between professional relationships and friendships, are becoming increasingly blurred. The world of knowledge workers is an entirely different universe from the old-fashioned factory-like office spaces where people were treated as units. There has never been a time in history when we had as much choice and control over our work conditions as today, enabling us to find fulfilment at work in a space we enjoy.

At work we want to be valued, caring and cared about. Leaders and high-profile entrepreneurs are advocating the importance of caring about people in business, and the media is full of stories about companies that 'walk the talk' and really do have an emphasis on caring in their business. An abundance of studies show that a caring work environment not only supports workers' satisfaction, but also makes great business sense. Being treated well at work is thus not only a fair expectation, but it can become reality if we make the right choices.

While technology and interconnectedness have significantly changed our lifestyle, pushing us to focus much of our attention towards the digital world and away from nature, many of us now have a greater desire than ever before to surround ourselves with 'real' things. We also want to connect with nature and engage in authentic relationships where we feel safe to be our real selves.

Along with these trends, the products, services and experiences that customers are seeking are also changing. They are looking for personal connections, face-to-face meetings, complete services and an enjoyable customer experience. These trends are inspiring new business models and new types of workplaces.

Caring in the workplace

These trends impose a new set of challenges that workplaces need to address. To attract and retain talent, organisations now need to invest extra effort into creating attractive work conditions, so that people look forward to going to work. And to draw in business, they need to show they care about visiting clients and partners and provide a positive experience for them too.

In order to successfully address these new expectations and challenges, managers need to genuinely care about their workers, partners and clients, and make their wellbeing a high priority. If this is not the case, even the most amazing workplace design will not be enough to make people feel valued. But when everything is aligned, the physical workplace has great potential to support this goal and to become an environment where people feel valued, appreciated and cared about.

A workplace survey conducted by Gensler asked employees to rate, on a scale from 0 to 10, how much they agreed with the statement: 'My company values people'. Interestingly, the responses were closely proportional to the quality of the work environment (as measured by the Workplace Performance Index).[1]

Most of the principles discussed in this book, including those primarily aimed at improving business outcomes such as profit, inherently contribute to people's satisfaction levels at work. However, in this chapter we discuss initiatives that are specifically designed to make people feel cared about, happy and healthy, and show how these are inseparable from optimal work performance. In fact, many aspects of performance – such as productivity, commitment and teamwork – naturally improve in a caring environment, as I will soon explain.

In order to achieve this, the space needs to be enjoyable to be in and supportive of people's wellbeing; it needs to promote positive experiences and caring relationships. In other words, it needs to be a 'caring' space. Once this is accomplished, the rewards are likely to be substantial.

---

1 There was a big range in results. In the lowest quality offices workers felt 2.8 out of 10 valued, while in the highest quality offices they felt 9.7 out of 10 valued.

The status quo

Different companies respond differently to new demands. As a result, there are a wide variety of workplaces ranging from inhumane and depressing to amazing places that people can't wait to go to and never want to leave. Unfortunately, the vast majority of workplaces are closer to the former.

Many workplaces are unhealthy or promote unhealthy habits, or are unattractive, crowded, or simply unpleasant places to be in. Many of them are uniform, purely functional (or not even that), and provide no opportunities for people to actually enjoy being in the space.

We often hear about organisations that used to provide small benefits like indoor plants, fresh fruit or coffee machines, but then decided to withdraw such 'benefits' in times of financial pressure. Others remove all unnecessary items from the workspace with the intention of enhancing people's focus and productivity. Either way, what remains is often a barren, soulless office space where workers feel they are being treated like machines rather than humans.

Then there are those workplaces that superficially tick all the boxes. They allocate areas for fun, play and relaxation, yet at the same time management discourages people from spending time in activities that are not, strictly speaking, immediately productive.

Finally, some workplaces only provide a wonderful environment for a privileged group, not for everyone. For example, they may have spectacular reception and meeting facilities to delight their visitors, but dull staff facilities, which sends a signal that the workers' experience doesn't matter that much.

'Uncaring' environments

A work environment that people don't appreciate and where they don't feel appreciated can undermine their relationship with their work and the organisation through self-doubt, lack of trust and disengagement. These issues manifest not only in their work, but also in their attitude towards each other and their clients.

An 'uncaring' environment can therefore compromise the culture of the organisation, the quality of the service provided, and customers' experience, testing everyone's loyalty. Even if leaders genuinely care about their people and it's only the physical environment that gives them grief, the consequences are still significant.

An unhealthy workplace contributes to an increased rate of absenteeism, and is undeniably detrimental to workers' productivity and morale. It's simply impossible to feel valued at work when you need to risk your health to get things done. Also, although it's easy to assume that working in an unhealthy place for only a short period of time won't do much damage, a sick work environment can have immediate effects on health and performance, manifesting as fatigue, drowsiness, dizziness, difficulty in concentrating, and so on.

Having unhappy people at work also leads to further problems. They need more supervision and management, and they also demand higher payment for their services if they are to stay. They are harder to communicate and collaborate with, and are less tolerant of small annoyances and discomforts. Also, their negativity is contagious, leading to a toxic atmosphere.

Why caring falls off the radar

Mentioning the word 'happiness' in the context of work is still often seen as unorthodox, a fluffy, airy-fairy concept which doesn't have much to do with delivering results – despite an abundance of evidence showing otherwise. Wellbeing is seen as 'nice to have', but a low priority in the context of 'commercial reality'. Even worse, some managers actually see a conflict between valuing people and getting them to deliver results.

Even those who genuinely support the wellbeing and happiness of the people they work with and believe that they're essential for success in business can get hijacked during the design process when it comes to making specific decisions about investing in the space. It's too easy to overlook the benefits of people's wellbeing when decisions are based on cost calculations and hard data (e.g. m²/person). **The financial benefits of a 'caring' workplace are probably the hardest to quantify, so they are often simply ignored.**

💡 What if you were investing in a new home?

Imagine you are looking to purchase a new home for yourself or your family. Before making a decision, would you seek hard evidence that a house you really like will support your happiness and a harmonious family life? Can you imagine saying to the real estate agent, 'I love this house, but I'm hesitant. Could you please show me the data you have about how much my quality of life will improve if I decide to live in this place?'

Would you choose a cheaper, less attractive option in the absence of such proof?

Or would you just know that it's a place where you could live happily because it reflects who you are and what's important to you?

When it comes to the people we care about, we are confident in our personal judgements about what sort of environment will work for them. So why would anyone choose or create a workplace based on entirely different criteria?

There are three likely reasons:

1. Not caring enough for the people who will work there
2. Overlooking the fact that places effect emotions and emotions effect performance
3. Not recognising that a fulfilling life and high-performance work are in fact supported by similar conditions

Caring and work performance

'A person who feels appreciated will always do more than what is expected.'
- Brian Tracy

Astoundingly, many business owners still see no connection between caring and work performance. Not only do they miss out on the pleasure of having happy, contented workers on their team, they also operate less efficiently and profitably. In contrast, the best leaders also consider the less tangible aspects of managing a business, and understand the importance of human needs and emotions.

We are emotional beings

It's hard to overstate the importance of emotions in the way we think and behave; they affect our interpretations of what's happening to us as well as how we respond. Even though we try to think and act logically most of the time, it's actually very difficult to override our emotional reflexes. In simple terms, what we do is often based on how we feel. (If you still question the importance of emotions, just think about how you perform as a parent or partner or friend when you're really happy, and then when you're upset.)

We are irrational beings. The vast majority of our thoughts, decisions and actions are driven by our unconscious mind, which is also responsible for processing emotions. (Research suggests that 93-98% of our thoughts, decisions and communication come from our unconscious.)

We are impressionable

We are easily influenced by what other people think about us. Studies show that even subtle suggestions about our identity and abilities can have a huge impact on our performance. For example, we perform significantly better at tests when it is suggested beforehand that we are smart, capable and able to do well. However, when our abilities are doubted, our test results drop dramatically. **Basically, when we are valued we are more likely to live up to expectations.**

We are the recipients of our own unconscious self-talk (or head-chatter). Scientists estimate that we have somewhere between 50,000 and 60,000 thoughts a day, the vast majority of which (about 70-85%) are negative. For example, when we are not happy, our inner voices keep telling us what's wrong or what could go wrong. We are usually not even aware of most of the chatter in our head (unless we pay close attention to it, for example during meditation). **Since we are easily suggestible, we are the targets of our own irrational, silent suggestions!**

> **Our head chatter**
>
> Imagine being put into an unpleasant environment and being told to produce results to the best of your abilities. What sort of thoughts would occupy your mind? Typically these might include:
>
> - 'They don't care about me; why should I care about them?'
>
> - 'I'm replaceable, and I don't make a real difference here. I'm probably not that good at what I'm doing.'
>
> - 'I've sold my soul to this organisation; I give them my time and they pay me for it. Why would I bother going that extra mile?'
>
> - 'The person I am in this space is not the real me. And I don't like this person. What am I still doing here?'
>
> Just think about the impact of such negative thoughts on people's creativity, communication, decision making, and other areas of work performance!

Fulfilment promotes high performance

We're all driven to fulfil our core human needs. While our priorities and strategies are different, what we are all seeking is fundamentally the same, whether it's in the context of work, family, or other areas of life.

Some of our core needs include:

- Experiencing change and variety, facing challenges
- Engaging with others through connected relationships
- Evolving constantly, improving who we are and what we do
- Making a difference, providing value to others

Living a fulfilling life and doing high-performance work do not need to be in conflict. In fact, these activities support each other.

The Happiness Advantage by Shawn Achor (as mentioned earlier) is a brilliant book about happiness and how it fuels performance and success at work. Achor explains how this can be achieved by putting a set of scientifically tested principles into practice. He states: '**Happiness leads to success in nearly every domain, including work, health, friendship, sociability, creativity, and energy.**'

An abundance of data shows that in a positive state we have higher levels of productivity, produce more sales, work with fewer errors, perform better as leaders, and are less likely to take sick days, to quit, or to become burnt out. According to a Harvard study, a decade of research indicates that in a positive state the brain is 31% more productive than when negative, neutral or stressed. Happy people also make 37% more sales, and work 19% more accurately.

Happiness is a biological process which makes our brain function better, as it expands our information-processing capacity and activates the learning centre. It also opens up our minds to new ideas and opportunities, and helps us see out-of-the-box solutions. In a positive state our intelligence, creativity, optimism, and energy levels rise, and we also become more resilient. Essentially, every single business outcome improves.

Successful companies know how to support the positive psychological state of their people, and how to capitalise on the benefits. Case studies consistently show that investments into happiness and wellbeing pay back many times over.

Key design strategies

Key design strategies for building a caring, welcoming environment:

1. Create a healthy workplace
2. Create a pleasant and harmonious space
3. Boost positive emotions and happiness
4. Help people to connect with the space
5. Promote caring relationships
6. Design a positive overall experience

Applying these strategies will not only increase satisfaction with the environment and happiness in the workplace, but will also substantially improve performance, engagement, and commitment to the organisation.

Enjoyable ways of working, having fun, playing and work-life integration are also great contributors to our wellbeing and happiness; these will be discussed in the following chapter, Principle 6: Culture.

Strategy 1: Create a healthy workplace

Our work environment can influence our health in various ways. The sources of potential health hazards in any building are numerous, and our work-related activities and habits also make a huge difference to our health. We don't need to be factory workers or miners to be at risk of acquiring serious health problems at work. In fact, working in an office could lead to equally grim outcomes.

If we do work in an unhealthy environment, the short-term damage to our health might only be minimal. We may not even notice at first, or might quickly recover if we give ourselves the chance. It's all too easy to ignore and gradually get used to unhealthy places and practices. (Who would complain about a slight tension in the neck or the unpleasant odour of the printer room?) But over weeks, months or years, the cumulative effects of minor health issues can lead to serious problems.

Unfortunately, relying on legislation and OH&S regulations alone is not sufficient to create a workplace where our health is well protected. The fact that many types of health hazards are invisible, odourless, cause no pain, cannot be identified before serious damage is done, and are perfectly legal, makes it especially difficult to manage this issue – unless conscious effort is put into the design process to protect the building users' health.

All health problems are caused by either toxicity, structural damage to the body, emotional issues, or a combination of these. A well-designed environment helps us to prevent each of these problems and to support healthy habits.

Below are some of the most important health considerations in the workplace.

Sick buildings

The combination of health syndromes associated with an unhealthy building is called Sick Building Syndrome (SBS). Some of the most common symptoms include: eye, nose and throat irritation, increased airway infections and wheezing, fatigue, drowsiness, dizziness, nausea, headaches, depression, and difficulty in concentrating.

Most of these are related to **poor indoor air quality**. The air we breathe inside a building can contain dangerous amounts of toxic chemicals (e.g. gases and vapours referred to as Volatile Organic Compounds or VOCs), toxic particles (e.g. heavy metals, asbestos, dust) and biological contaminants (e.g. bacteria, mould, fungi). These pollutants can get into the air from building materials, dampness in the building, objects and products we use, and from the outdoors. A sub-standard air-conditioning system can add to this problem by accumulating and carrying around these pollutants.

(Non-toxic materials are odourless. A healthy building, even if new, has no smell at all. If it smells 'new', what you are really smelling is the chemicals.)

Another invisible health hazard is **Electro-Magnetic Radiation** (EMR), which refers to the electrical and magnetic fields generated by electrical cabling and appliances (e.g. lights, computers, routers, phones, chargers, microwave ovens, aerials, power lines). EMR can disrupt the body's electrical communication system, lead to Electrical Sensitivity symptoms and increase the chance of cancer (to mention only a few of the potential health concerns). The safe limits of EMR are widely argued, but building biologists believe that the legal radiation levels are many times higher than what is actually safe.

Design suggestions:

- Choose non-toxic (low VOC) building materials, finishes, work tools[2] and cleaning products.

- Isolate laser printers and copiers; ventilate the copy room separately.

- Ensure the air-conditioning / ventilation systems are well-designed and well-maintained, so as to provide sufficient clean air to people (as discussed in Principle 3: Productive).

- Ensure the building has adequate weather-proofing (i.e. sufficient and continuous thermal insulation, good quality window frames and glass) to prevent dampness and mould growth.

- Avoid materials and surfaces that are hard to clean properly (e.g. long thread carpet).

- Consider using negative ion generating technology to improve air quality (such devices are shown to reduce air pollutants).

- Keep devices with high EMR as far from people as possible; these devices include cordless phone base stations, routers and servers.

---

2 I realise that the concept of non-toxic work tools might sound a bit odd, so let me illustrate this with an example. At one of the consultancies I worked with, management one day decided to provide everyone with a brand new business manager folder, which was lined with fake leather. While the company was proud of its healthy work environment, the overpowering, toxic smell the folders quickly filled in the otherwise clean fresh air of the office. I had to hide mine in a cupboard to be able to concentrate again.

Food and water

While this is not strictly a design consideration, building users often don't have access to good quality drinking water or healthy food at work.

Unfiltered tap water can be contaminated with chemicals and heavy metals leached into the water from the piping system, and it also typically contains added chloride and fluoride[3]. On the other hand, drinking bottled water all the time is a waste of resources and money. Filtering water is a low-cost and effective solution to this problem.

Access to healthy food options largely comes down to location and catering. But there is more that can be done. Offering people good quality fresh fruit is a popular and effective way of supporting people's health. Providing people an opportunity to heat up their lunch is also a good idea. However, microwaves destroy nutrients in the food and spread harmful radiation into their surroundings. It might be worth discussing with your team if they are interested in using a stove instead.

Computer culture

Health issues associated with a sedentary lifestyle, poor posture and lack of exercise are reported all over the media, and we are all familiar to some extent with the consequences. A VicHealth study of the relationship between prolonged sitting and various health problems reveals some staggering statistics (as published in the article *How Is Working In The Office Killing You?*):

- In Australia, office workers spend an average of 75% of their working hours sitting down, increasing the risk of serious health problems and an early death.

- In 2008 the total direct financial cost of people being overweight was estimated to be $8.3 billion. Of this, $3.6 billion was associated with loss in workplace productivity.

---

3   Adding fluoride to drinking water is a controversial topic. Some research suggests that this practice is useful and safe, while other research suggests the opposite. Water fluoridation is used in countries including Australia, the USA and the UK. Other countries including Germany, Sweden and Japan have stopped this practice.

- About 44% of all workers' compensation claims are for musculoskeletal disorders, costing businesses on average $7,400 each.

(The impact of prolonged sitting, bad posture and lack of exercise on people's mental performance, as well as associated design strategies, have been discussed in Principle 3: Productive.)

Unhealthy emotions

Our emotional wellbeing is also a critical factor in maintaining good health. Many of our workplaces constantly trigger negative emotional responses such as stress and worry due to overcrowding, invasion of privacy, noise and other issues. The pressure of our work only adds to these problems. (Strategies for minimising unhealthy emotions have been discussed in Principle 3: Productive.)

Frequent negative emotions significantly contribute to physical health problems, many of which are severe. On the other hand, positive emotions and happiness boost our immune system and support our recovery from diseases.

Benefits of a healthy workplace

The easiest way to measure the financial benefits of a healthy workplace is through absenteeism rates. A large number of case studies show that a healthy work environment can dramatically reduce sick leave. It also substantially reduces workers' compensation claims.

However, this is only the tip of the iceberg. The overall benefits of a healthy workplace are much broader and encompass improvements in productivity, morale, and people's commitment to the organisation.

Strategy 2:
Create a pleasant and harmonious space

Think for a moment about your favourite places where you connect with friends or recharge at difficult times, or your treasured holiday destinations, or maybe your dream house with a 'million-dollar view'. Attractive and pleasant environments are not just 'nice' places to be; they also help us become the best versions of ourselves. This is such a rewarding experience in our lives that most of us are willing to go to great lengths to make it happen. If our workplace can offer similar experiences, our relationship with work, and thus our performance, will inevitably improve.

Connecting to nature

The types of spaces we prefer are rooted in our history as humans. We can best relax and recharge in spaces that capture the essence of our primordial homes, the environments where our ancestors lived for thousands of years. For example, we like sitting in places that are somewhat similar to sitting under a tree – in rooms with lower ceilings and dimmer lights, adjacent to a brighter area with a higher ceiling. That's why we enjoy sitting in sheltered spots in open spaces, for example under a pergola, in a gazebo ... or indeed under a tree.

We are instinctively attracted to spaces that are connected to (or remind us of) nature, that are sensorily rich, where we feel protected, and where we can see what's happening around us.

It's possible to literally **bring a piece of nature** into the workplace. For example:

- Indoor plants, when well-maintained, can substantially enhance the quality of a space, and improve performance, mood and wellbeing. Bringing plants into spaces with no external views or natural light can be especially beneficial. Some plant species also filter air and thus improve air quality. When selecting plant species, make sure that they are suitable to the specific conditions of the space (i.e. temperature and lighting level). If possible, choose plants with roundish leaves as they have better psychological effects than those with pointy leaves.

- The use of materials such as timber, stone, bamboo, clay and paper for furniture and finishes or decoration can make the space look and feel more natural. Natural materials also age well. (Natural-looking fake materials may also have beneficial psychological effects on people, but they can be off-putting if they are of bad quality or obviously fake.)

We usually find a space more pleasant when natural attributes such as **patterns, forms, proportions and colours** are used in the design. This can be achieved by the following strategies:

- Using organic forms and patterns in the design (i.e. the shapes of natural objects such as trees, leaves, animals and snowflakes) can make the design more satisfying. Patterns that are not too complicated have better psychological effects.
- Well-proportioned spaces and features foster balance and harmony. Use ratios that look aesthetic and natural to the human eye, such as the 'golden ratio' (1:1.62). Viewing this proportion actually triggers pleasurable brain waves.
- Photographs or pictures showing nature scenes can have similar effects to looking at those scenes in real life. (Studies have demonstrated that artworks showing nature scenes reduce stress and anxiety.)
- In general, we find objects and patterns with curved features more pleasant than those with sharp angles. Research has shown that we associate circular and curved shapes with positive emotions like happiness, love and joy. In contrast, we link squares and sharped edged forms with negative emotions like anger, sadness and hatred.

In nature there is a sense of **smooth movement** (e.g. clouds, waves, leaves, birds, lights) which is usually missing in built environments. There are various ways to add movement to interiors, bringing them to life:

- Installing a water feature is a popular solution. The fact that we enjoy being around moving water is not accidental, as it represents life, nature and purity. Seeing and hearing the flow of water is a delightful, relaxing experience.
- Adding a fish tank is another option, though it needs to be done well to be truly effective, and it requires a lot of care and maintenance.

- 'Biodynamic' lighting systems (as mentioned in Principle 3: Productive) imitate the change of natural light inside the space by gradually changing the colour and intensity of the light throughout the day.

Nature **engages our senses** – just think of how it feels when you're in a forest, or on the beach, or in a cave. You could create a similarly rich experience in the built environment by using a range of tactile surfaces, creating spaces with different sound qualities, and harnessing the natural fragrances of different materials.

And perhaps most importantly, natural environments are amazingly **diverse, interesting, and rich in detail.**

'Enriched' environments

Unfortunately, many companies like the idea of creating a uniform, often sterile environment for their employees to work in. They do this with the aim of eliminating distractions and enhancing focus and productivity.

Dr. Craig Knight, a specialist in both social and organisational psychology at the University of Exeter (UK), has conducted extensive research to study the influence of the work environment on employee productivity. The results show that the once widely popular sterile, minimalist, so called 'lean' environments are actually not conducive to employee productivity. In comparison, when people work in an environment that is enriched (particularly with art and plants), productivity can increase by up to 15%; this is because people feel more comfortable and content, and are also better able to concentrate. This result is consistent across different nationalities and cultures. In this regard we are not very different from animals. Dr. Knight states: 'If you put any other animal into a similar impoverished space, it really isn't happy. If you put a butterfly into a lean glass jar, it is unnatural.'

Another study in the US observed the brain development of mice kept in different environments, and the results showed that the brains of mice increased by 15% in volume when they were kept in stimulating environments, compared to the brains of mice kept in sterile, bare cages. This suggests that sterile surroundings could result in smaller brains, while having a stimulating environment could optimise our performance and abilities.

Finding balance

Remember, the design needs to strike a balance between being too low-key and too stimulating (apart from those areas that are specifically designed to energise or relax people). While the space should not be boring, too many objects and eye-catching design elements can be distracting. Also, it's best not to combine too many different styles, colours and patterns.

What one person finds too minimalist, another person may find too busy or cluttered. To ensure that the space serves everyone, you need to allow your team members to 'enrich' their space according to their personal preferences. (This needs to be within limits of course; hoarders will need to be kept in check.) Alternatively, you could let people choose between spaces with different levels of intensity. You may find a minimalist environment productive, but imposing your preference upon the rest of the team would be a mistake.

Strategy 3:
Boost positive emotions and happiness

Increasing happiness is arguably the most potent strategy to enhance performance and make work more enjoyable. The benefits of being in a positive emotional state are numerous: our brain functions better, our attitude and confidence improve, we communicate better, and we become more resilient when dealing with obstacles and setbacks. Our relationships with other people and the organisation improve, and we spread positivity to the people around us, including customers.

Being in a positive emotional and mental state involves much more than just eliminating negativity. Our physical environment has the potential to improve our mood and raise our level of happiness – through the activities it supports, the messages it expresses, and its qualities and ambience. While the space alone cannot make miserable people happy, it can initiate major shifts in our focus and habits.

Activities that raise our mood

It's a common view that happiness and emotional wellbeing are determined by our personality and circumstances. However, extensive scientific research shows that our own actions also have a great influence on our emotional wellbeing.

Some of the proven ways to improve our moods include: meditation, physical exercise, and exercising a signature strength – doing things we are good at doing. Beyond giving us a quick boost of positive emotions, if these activities are practised regularly, they can help permanently improve our emotional wellbeing.

There are several other simple things we can do to boost our positivity at challenging times, for example reading a funny article, listening to music, playing a game, or making a personal phone call. Though these suggestions may seem mundane and irrelevant to work, their power to improve performance is backed up by science, so why not use them?

Creating opportunities for your people to practise some of these 'tricks', for example, setting up a quiet relaxing space suitable for meditation and a social space for games and music, will likely empower them to take charge of their own emotional wellbeing.

But keep in mind that just offering such facilities is no guarantee that workers will actually use them; it's important that your people actually feel comfortable engaging in activities that may have nothing to do with work. So make sure that not only your workspace, but also your organisation's policies and culture give them the permission to take time to enjoy themselves and lift their mood.

(Creating spaces for playing and fun will be discussed in the following chapter.)

Focusing on the positive

Our language is full of phrases describing how the quality of our thinking leads to success. While these words may sound general and simplistic, they contain a lot of truth which is supported by scientific evidence. The following phrases summarise how our mind works, and how a positive outlook helps us create better results:

- *You attract what you focus on.* When we focus on past mistakes or potential failure, we can become preoccupied with these thoughts. As a result, we instinctively move towards the very outcomes we want to avoid, and fail to notice other opportunities that can bring us the results we want. So when the outcome of our work is uncertain, with a lot to gain and a lot to lose, it's a much better strategy to remind ourselves of the positives, rather than getting stressed out by the potential negative consequences.

- *Whether you believe you can or you can't, either way you're right.* Our confidence in our own abilities and success can determine how we perform. If we believe in our ability to succeed, it's more likely that we will. It's possible to enhance our confidence in our abilities – again, by using the power of focus.

- *With every failure comes an opportunity.* Setbacks at work inevitably happen, especially when working towards challenging goals. Bad news can be disheartening and demotivating. However, if we bring our attention to new opportunities instead of what is lost, we recover from bad news faster, and we are more likely to find the desire to move forward with enthusiasm and make the most out of what has happened.

You have many opportunities to express positive messages through the physical environment, and thus to draw people's attention towards the positive – enhancing their confidence, motivation, trust (in others as well as in their own abilities and success), and love for what they do. For example, you could display items that remind your team members of their achievements as well as the anticipated rewards for ongoing successful projects. Also, consider setting up message boards where everyone can share uplifting images and words, including ones that reflect on their personal interests, virtues and strengths.

> 💡 **Superpowers and 'Kryptonite'**
>
> I recall visiting the office of a service design company which pinned up on the wall its team members' signature strengths and key personality traits, along with their 'Kryptonite' (meaning their challenges, as even superheroes have flaws).
>
> This is such a simple idea, but it works on many levels. It reminds us what we are good at, and shows that we are recognised and appreciated for it. It also makes it clear that we cannot excel at everything, so it's safe to acknowledge areas where we need help. Seeing what our team mates are good at also helps us develop deeper respect towards them, and knowing their challenges makes it easier for us to offer them the right support when they need it.

Positive ambience

The use of specific fragrances can be a powerful way to put us in a good mood and change the way we think about and solve problems. Beyond improving mood, certain smells can also help us become energised or relaxed, enhance our memory, and improve our ability to do mental tasks.

Music, as we already know, is also an effective way to improve mood and trigger positive emotions; however, it can also give rise to negative ones. We can have very different preferences in music, and specific songs can trigger personal memories from our past. When music is played, it's important that it doesn't disturb or annoy anyone. Having access to a quiet room or a music room is one way to ensure peace.

Our memories of a place

Memories of a place also make a difference to how we feel in it. Imagine having had a traumatic experience (or several of them) in a particular room; maybe you were intimidated by someone, or received some really bad news. Being in this room (or even other ones with similar colours, smells, sounds, pictures or other features) could remind you of that painful situation and stir you up every time you're there – even several years after that experience. Most of this happens unconsciously, but the emotions you experience are very real. And it works the same way with positive emotions.

To prevent such negative emotional triggers, it can be worthwhile changing a space after very unpleasant events, or doing something really enjoyable there, to create positive memories that are stronger than the negative ones.

Having a laugh

Smiles and laughter can work miracles; making us happier, healthier and more relaxed. They also help us become more confident, approachable, supportive and creative, to mention just a few of the benefits. The physical space offers many opportunities to enhance our mood and encourage smiling and laughter. Here are a few of them:

- Place within sight personal items that remind you of joyful memories
- Use graphics, cartoons, etc. that bring a smile to your face
- Use humour!

> 💡 **Laughter builds instant rapport**
>
> When I visited one of my clients at his office for the first time, I couldn't help noticing a poster on his desk which showed his face montaged on the body of a posing body-builder. It immediately made me smile, told me a lot about the culture of the company, and helped me relax and build instant rapport with him. This sort of 'display' may not be appropriate in all workplaces, but there are so many non-controversial ways you can bring humour into your environment. Feel free to be creative!

Strategy 4:
Help people to connect with the space

In places that resonate with us as individuals we are more present, empowered and happy. On the other hand, arriving every day in a place that we can't relate to, and which makes us feel as if we have just landed on another planet, can be a real turn-off. In such environments we are likely to feel alienated, withdraw and seek some sort of escape. (I believe this is one of the main reasons why so many workers resent the concept of the traditional corporate office.)

So how can you create a workspace that your people can identify with? Here are a couple of ideas:

- Make sure the fitout communicates something about who your team members are (their goals, values, interests, competencies, personalities and culture) – as a result, they will develop a sense of belonging more easily.

- Allow your people to make themselves comfortable and to adapt the space to their needs – being able to influence their environment will strengthen their relationship with it.

- Involve your team members in the design and creation of the space – this will give them a sense of ownership and pride, and make them more invested in the changes to the workplace.

Feeling at home

Many of the most successful, high-performance workplaces look and feel domestic, and this is not a coincidence.

Most people don't see their workspace as a channel for self-expression, even though the concept of expressing our identity through our built environment is not new. Just think about all the thought that goes into choosing or creating a family home which is just right for the people who live there and represents who they are. The world is full of places we can go to to purchase furnishings, fittings and other goods for our home. When we walk into a furniture store, we can choose from a vast selection of products. The range of available kitchen units alone is enormous, even though the only practical purpose of a kitchen is to prepare food.

On the other hand, if we walk into the average office furniture store, the quality and the range of options can be depressing. Why is there such a gap between office and home furniture? At work or at home our aim is to be at our best, whether our goal is to cook dinner, connect with family members, immerse ourselves in our hobbies, relax ... or connect with our clients and team members, learn new skills, and communicate with clarity.

What mainstream office furniture design represents is simply an expression of the values that our society associates with work. Most of us are brought up with the notion that work is something we have to do in order to make a living, so what really matters is only what we do, as opposed to who we are and how we feel in our workplace.

When we design or choose our home, some of the most important questions we ponder before making a decision are: 'Does this home reflect and support who I am and who I want to be?' 'Is it a place where I can be happy, inspired, proud and at peace?' On the other hand, when decisions are made about a workplace the most common questions asked are: 'What do we have to do?' and, 'Can we do that here?'

Such thinking implies that connecting with the environment that we work in is irrelevant, and making it 'feel like home' is an unnecessary expense and effort, or even inappropriate. As a result, many of us are even ashamed to admit that we'd like to feel more 'at home' at work.

But what does feeling 'at home' really mean? Doing what you want, whenever you want? For me it means being in a pleasant environment that reflects who I am, a place where I am at ease, connected to the space and the people around me, in touch with my purpose, and in flow. Feeling 'at home' means being in a place where I can focus all my energy and resources on what is really important, instead of struggling to find my way around obstacles, distractions and insecurities.

Aren't these qualities similar to what we all seek in a workplace? Establishing an environment that in many ways feels like home certainly contributes to high performance. And it all starts with the question: 'Who are we?'

Switching, turning, opening, moving ...

At home it's perfectly natural for us to switch on the lights, close the blinds, open the windows or turn on the heater. When there is too much noise around us we can move to another room; when we are tired of sitting in the same spot we can stand up and go somewhere else.

Being able to maintain and control our personal comfort is a basic human need, so in workplaces that provide these sorts of opportunities we feel more comfortable and reassured that we are in the right place. (Design solutions that allow workers to maintain thermal, visual and acoustic comfort as well as good posture have been discussed in Principle 3: Productive.)

Interestingly, when you give people a reasonable amount of control, their tolerance of conditions they cannot control increases. For example, if they can open the windows, they are less concerned about the office being too cold or too warm than if they were working at the same temperature but had no control at all. In other words, they are easier to please.

Allowing your people to make changes to their workspace and to choose where and how they work – the concepts discussed throughout this book – will further strengthen their sense of connection to the space.

'Empowered' environments

Dr. Knight's study (mentioned in Strategy 2 above) – which found that enriched work environments can contribute to productivity by up to 15% – also revealed that when employees participate in the development of their own work environments, productivity increases even more, by up to 32%! However, people's performance can drop dramatically if, after their involvement in the decision-making process, they are criticised for their choices and their decisions are overridden.[4]

---

4 It's best to only seek people's input where you can likely respond to it. For example, it can be a good idea to ask them about the sort of artwork they would like to see on the wall, or the type of chair they would like to sit on. But don't ask them if they need larger workstations if you know there is no space for that. After these though, it's important that you don't ignore what they have told you, otherwise they will likely become unhappy and resentful of the new space. It's inevitable that a few of the ideas discussed cannot be addressed, but this is not a problem as long as your people feel heard, and their input is acknowledged.

These outcomes also show that identifying with our work environment is essential for optimum performance. Dr. Knight states: **'If you go into a space and can see something of yourself, your identity realised in that space, then that's a good space.'**

For small businesses or teams, a particularly viable and cost-effective strategy is to involve building users (and even customers and other stakeholders) in the decision-making process. It doesn't mean that everyone needs to participate in every discussion and reach a consensus about every single detail of the space; that approach would be neither practical nor beneficial. However, they need to be able to influence those attributes of the design that are really important to them, for example, what they want to express about themselves, and what would make them feel that the space where they work is where they belong.

In order to create a design which considers these views, managers and designers simply need to be ready to share their authority, and not just try to decorate the office in the way they think is best.

Having discussions with the users about the design has many benefits beyond improved satisfaction with the environment and increased productivity. These discussions can uncover potential challenges, opportunities and solutions not yet considered, and prepare people for the change. Ultimately, the design experience and its outcome – the physical space – can contribute to an increased sense of ownership and autonomy, and strengthen people's commitment to the organisation.

My experience is that whenever I talk to building users about their workspace – asking their views about what's working, what's not working, and how things could be done better – or whenever I explore possibilities with them and ask for opinions about design ideas, they always become really excited and start looking forward to the changes. When their insights are considered, they become invested in the changes and start to see the space as their own.

Strategy 5:
Promote caring relationships

The price of resentment, mistrust and conflict in the workplace is huge, as these are detrimental to wellbeing and performance. On the other hand, caring relationships based on mutual respect and trust are the foundation of feeling safe and empowered at work, and a catalyst for engaging in effective teamwork.

We have already discussed several principles that contribute to caring relationships, such as providing opportunities for people to move between interaction and privacy, supporting different work styles, eliminating the sense of being in a crowded space, and creating a space that reflects a shared vision and identity.

This section focuses on the foundations of building these caring relationships: familiarity, safety and social equality. In the following chapter we will discuss strategies that can help work relationships further evolve and support a flourishing community in which people feel they belong, where coworkers are not afraid to call each other 'friends' or 'family'.

A caring team

In Principle 1: Visionary, I mentioned a presentation by Michael Rennie (Managing Partner of McKinsey & Company) entitled *Love, fear and high performance*, in which he talked about the two key elements of high performance. One of these is always a big, meaningful, almost impossible, scary goal – one that creates fear. The second key element is a safe team environment characterised by care, respect and trust. That's what he refers to as love (even though you don't often use the word love in business). He goes on to say we can only tackle a scary goal if we find safety in the team.

If you are facing an almost impossible goal, but don't have the support of a caring team, 'then you have *fear* and *fear*, and that's exhausting'. On the other hand, 'if there is love in the team, together we can take on something even scarier, bigger and more fearful'.

Caring managers

A US study found that consultants who know their managers well are likely to perform better, and are more likely to accomplish a project. In the study, employees with strong ties to their managers also brought in more money; they each generated $588 (USD) additional monthly revenue compared to those with weak ties.

A Gallup research poll asked ten million employees worldwide if they agreed or disagreed with the statement: 'My supervisor, or someone at work, seems to care about me as a person.' The results showed that those who agreed were more productive, contributed more to profit, and were more loyal to their company. The research also confirmed that outstanding managers acknowledge the value of getting to know each of their people – including their backgrounds, interests, personal goals and ambitions – and are ready to invest time to care. The dividends of such investments in enhanced working relationships and trust are substantial. The summary of this study states:

> 'Gallup's research indicates that caring can be translated into the phrase, **"Caring means setting each person up for success."** A productive workplace is one in which people feel safe – safe enough to experiment, to challenge, to share information, to support each other, and in which team members are prepared to give the manager and the organization the "benefit of the doubt". None of this can happen if team members do not feel cared about. Relationships are the glue that holds great workplaces together.'

Design suggestions

A physical environment that promotes familiarity, safety and social equality inherently supports caring professional relationships. For example:

- A workplace where everyone can enjoy the 'best spots' promotes a sense of social equality. Even if the space has limited natural lighting and external views, everyone should be able to access some of the most attractive areas. This can be achieved by locating shared facilities (e.g. breakout spaces, collaborative areas) near windows with quality views, or by rotating workstations regularly (or hot-desking). Other 'benefits' such as comfortable chairs, indoor plants and artworks should also be equally distributed wherever possible.

- The types of furniture used, and the way furniture is organised in a space, can also influence our perception of social equality or hierarchy. For example, as mentioned earlier, sitting around a rectangular table suggests hierarchy, while sitting around a circular table – or in a circle without a table – suggests equality. Make sure that you and your teams always have the option to find or create a setting that is right for the dynamics of the conversation or team activity.

- Make it easy for people to engage in casual conversations. Provide 'hot spots' throughout the workplace where it feels natural to have a social chat. It's not essential to put armchairs and coffee tables everywhere; these conversations may take place at a bench, at a standing table, or even on cushions on the floor (depending on the culture and dress-code of the organisation). I've seen offices where the best conversations happened in the kitchen or on the landing of the stairs between two floors. Initiating personal conversations at someone's workstation or in a boardroom can be rather awkward, making it particularly challenging to relax and build rapport. Despite this, many workplaces don't offer any other options.

Strategy 6:
Create a positive overall experience

So far we have mostly focused on creating a series of different spaces that support people's positive experiences at individual locations. However, it is also possible to design their entire experience as they move through spaces throughout the day (or during their visit), from the moment of arrival until they leave.

Designing a positive overall experience is a process that is more commonly used in the context of public buildings such as museums, shops, banks and hospitals – buildings that serve many visitors, customers, or patients. Nevertheless, this process can also be applied in workplace design, with the aim of creating an outstanding experience both for team members and visitors.

This approach involves combining all the strategies discussed so far, and organising them by looking through the eyes of the different users.

Meeting the needs of different users

The foundation of this process is a thorough research and understanding of all the different types of people you are dealing with, including their backgrounds, personalities, goals, preferences, insecurities and fears. This informs the design of the space, ensuring that all the different needs are met.

This strategy is essentially the integration of two different disciplines: service design and space design. (While it's not yet widely practised, by looking at currently emerging trends it seems that this design approach will soon become more common, and will transform our relationship with our built environments as well as the services associated with them.)

Since the design needs to fulfil a very complex brief incorporating many different perspectives, the development of the design cannot be a linear thought process building on a single consultant's knowledge and experience (like the traditional architectural design process used to be). It needs to involve several tests and experiments (whether using sketches, renders, role playing, computer simulation or a physical space prototype) in order to capitalise on the knowledge and insights of many different people.

The outcome is a unique space that takes both workers and visitors on a journey that is engaging, enjoyable, rewarding and memorable.

Case Study: Luxottica

Luxottica OPSM Eye Hub, designed by e2 Designed Experiences, is a great demonstration of this strategy.

Luxottica's OPSM Eye Hub is an extraordinary eyewear store in Melbourne. It has been designed with a sharp focus (excuse the pun) on creating a positive experience for all customers with different needs and life stages. It is a space that engages with all the five senses. The immersive experiential design initiates a two-way dialogue with the customers, and leads them on a journey that embraces education, service and health, beyond selling products. This store is now seen as the future standard for retail environments worldwide.

Alex Ritchie, creative director at e2 Designed Experiences, explains the research process that his firm followed to inform the design of the space:

> 'We worked with a company called Leading Edge, and they did quantitative and qualitative research. We conducted seven workshops with seven different groups of people, and we understood why they would go to an optical store, what they felt nervous about, what they felt excited about, and what they felt frustrated about.'

> 'Somebody is going to buy a pair of sunglasses to go on a holiday and they want to look good on the beach, so they are excited. Somebody might have virtually no eyesight left, so they are stressed. A small kid might come in need of their first pair of glasses, so they're nervous. You might have someone coming in because something is broken, so they are angry. Each of these seven different types of users has a different journey.'

> 'Once we understood how these people use that space, then we designed the store around that. So you walk in and you find, "Oh, I know how to use this space." It's intuitive. "I'm not going to get lost; it's very easy to navigate my way around". And it makes the journey a positive experience.'

> 'You can do the same for the workplace environment by understanding how different people use a physical space, the types of groups that they work in, the type of quiet spaces, activity spaces that they wanted to use, and you map the different individuals and the different teams within an organisation.'

Imagine how your customers and staff would feel if you provided them with a space and experience with similar qualities, and how that would influence retention rates. Ask yourself the question: how can an ultimate customer and staff experience benefit my business?

Putting things into practice

Case study: CO2 Australia's South Melbourne Office

The way CO2 Australia's South Melbourne office was chosen and redesigned can teach us a lot about creating work environments where people feel genuinely valued and cared about. (Their strategies for aligning their space with the brand have been discussed in Principle 1: Visionary.)

It's a clear, bright, inviting space with an air of honesty, and without any hint of trying too hard. While this office does not have the sort of 'creative' features that call for attention and would be displayed in architectural magazines, it is special in its own way.

Philosophy

Andrew Grant, managing director of the CO2 Group (at the time of our interview) explained the philosophy and thought processes that led to the creation of this workplace:

> 'The workplace should be an environment that optimises the likelihood that people can do their best work. The notion of sitting behind a computer screen is an awful way to work, and we all become slaves to that. A lot more value could be achieved through creating work environments that really harmonise ideas, support collaboration, and stimulate a better quality of work.'

> 'A workplace is part of our self-esteem, our sense of belonging, and we have a connection to it. You give someone a junk environment, you're going to get junk performance. If you're going to spend 30 or 40 years of your life, most of your time spent at work, why would you accept mediocrity? I can't work in a mediocre work environment. I don't want to be there, I'm not very effective.'

'There's a lot of work done that shows that we all have discretionary effort and we like to give that extra effort to an organisation depending on how we feel about the job, how we feel about the organisation. The great organisations are the ones where discretionary effort is given freely and regularly, and it shows in the outcomes. The question is, what do you need to do to secure that discretionary effort? And part of it is the physical environment.'

The new workplace

CO2 Australia is an organisation that embodies sustainability and nurtures a culture of valuing people and collaboration. When searching for a new tenancy, they looked for a green building which would allow people to connect with nature and to access open spaces and good facilities. They aimed to create a work environment which would be inspiring, conducive to creativity and collaboration, and supportive of productivity, happiness and good health.

The space is filled with natural light, and is all open, with separate areas for conversations and for quiet, contemplative work. There are showers and a changing room so that people can cycle to work or exercise.

'One of the little things we do here: we have a series of flowering gardens, and it's a tiny expense. We also have simple things like never-ending amounts of fresh fruit. I've seen other organisations where they view it as a cost and cut it out because it's an efficiency measure, where I think it's round the other way. You spend a little bit, you get payback 50 times. Just subtle things that make you happy about being where you are.'

Decision making

CO2 Australia aimed to create a space that would improve productivity, but being a young organisation, they didn't have the history and baseline data that could have been used for comparison. So when decisions needed to be made about the design, they simply used their judgement:

'You can intuitively determine a good workplace, or you can use metrics and process and practice to arrive at the outcome. An intuitive person might go: "I just know it's going to be good". So we were probably more intuitive.'

Results

Andrew Grant believes the results speak for themselves:

> 'I have staff in different regions. I never wanted this to be viewed as a head office where field staff and regional staff are fearful of coming. I wanted this to be a place where they feel as connected as the people who work here full time, and as comfortable. And I think we succeeded; the fact that they happily spend time here to do their own work is one of the measures of success.'

> 'It has created a culture where people feel excited to go to work, they like where they work, they like the people they work with, and they collaborate naturally and regularly. Our clients like coming in for the same reasons.'

> 'The happiness index – we don't have conflict, I see incredible levels of effort and connection and ownership and high quality work. It shines through. You don't need to measure it; you just know it makes sense.'

A non-traditional workplace: ORA Dental Studio

Ora is not a typical dental facility. It has been designed to provide the most pleasant experience for its patients from the moment of arrival. Do you recall your experiences of walking into a dental clinic? Echoing rooms, the noise of drilling, the smell of chemicals, a sterile-looking waiting room with crammed chairs and dated magazines?

Some of the online reviews for ORA say: 'I love this place.', 'Can't wait to go back. Have you ever said that about your dentist?', 'Who LIKES going to the dentist?! I never thought I would say this, but, I do, now! From the moment I walked in, I felt like I was visiting a high-end spa. The space was beautiful, immaculately clean and so relaxing.'

While they couldn't achieve this without outstanding service and care, ORA's success can largely be attributed to the physical environment. The following are just some of the design initiatives that ORA implemented to achieve the ultimate in patient comfort:

- Providing connection to nature and natural elements (views from the treatment rooms, cultivating a meditation garden connected to office, sky-lighting)

- Creating separate entry/exits for non-sedated patients versus sedated patients to encourage relaxation and improve privacy

- Patient's positioning facing room entrance/exit to eliminate uncomfortable feeling of having 'blind spots' and having one's back to the entry/exit of a room

- Creating welcoming spa-like environments for patients and families

- Providing positive distractions for both patients and families in waiting areas and exam rooms (multi-cultural reading materials, nature HD satellite programming, lounge music, in-wall iPod and iPhone docking stations, Wi-Fi, Flexview 330 degree flexible monitors to accommodate any patient position, Bluetooth wireless headphones)

- Utilizing non-off-gassing materials and adhesives and paints to prevent 'sick-building syndrome'[5]

Beyond all of this, ORA is an exceptional example of a green building and practice.

---

[5] These principles are quoted from the website of The Center for Health Design. (See Related Readings at the end of this book.)

 **Questions to consider**

- What are the potential health hazards in your workplace? And how could these be addressed?

- What sort of decorations or messages could boost your people's confidence and help them focus on the positive?

- What would make the space comfortable, pleasant, attractive and inspiring?

- What are the opportunities for bringing nature into the space?

- What are the opportunities for promoting laughter and humour?

- What activities could increase the energy and happiness of your people?

- What kind of environment would make your people look forward to going to work?

- What are the best spots in the space? How could these be accessible to everyone?

- How could the environment resonate with people's identity, reflect who they are and support who they want to be?

- Which design decisions could you involve your workers in?

- What opportunities could you offer to your people to decorate and personalise their space?

- Who are the different types of people – workers and customers – visiting and using the workplace? What are they passionate about, what are they nervous about, and what are they seeking?

- What would make workers and customers feel that they had an outstanding experience in the space?

PRINCIPLE 6

ENGAGING

CREATE SPACE FOR AN ENGAGING BUSINESS

Creating a home for a thriving community where we feel we belong

'We call this "the organization of your dreams." In a nutshell, it's a company where individual differences are nurtured; information is not suppressed or spun; the company adds value to employees, rather than merely extracting it from them; the organization stands for something meaningful; the work itself is intrinsically rewarding; and there are no stupid rules.' – *Creating the Best Workplace on Earth*, Harvard Business Review

Why should we engage?

What is workplace culture?

We often find ourselves in conversations about 'workplace culture', but many of us would struggle to explain exactly what that means.

Culture sounds like an abstract concept, but it's not very hard to define. Essentially, it is HOW people in an organisation behave.[1]

In Principle 1: Visionary we talked about an organisation's values (the principles that guide the organisation towards its vision), as well as its personality or brand (the image it portrays to the market, and which gives an identity to the team). Culture is how all of these manifest in the day-to-day life of the organisation, the code that helps translate principles into actions.

Culture encompasses:

- The ways team members connect and communicate with each other
- Established ways of making decisions and getting things done
- Workplace habits, rituals and celebrations
- Rules around what is expected and rewarded, and what is not
- Rules around what is not appropriate or tolerated
- What happens during a crisis
- What happens within the team – beyond doing work

---

1 According to Wikipedia: 'Organizational culture is the behavior of humans within an organization and the meaning that people attach to those behaviors. Culture includes the organization's vision, values, norms, systems, symbols, language, assumptions, beliefs, and habits. It is also the pattern of such collective behaviors and assumptions that are taught to new organizational members as a way of perceiving, and even thinking and feeling. Organizational culture affects the way people and groups interact with each other, with clients, and with stakeholders.'

Why is culture important?

Culture is an important factor in successful recruitment; not only in attracting skilled candidates, but also in filtering who is likely to be the best fit. In recent years, the trend is for companies to recruit very carefully to avoid the astronomical costs associated with hiring someone who is the wrong fit. Instead, they often invest in creating an environment and culture that attracts the right people.

Culture goes hand in hand with engaging and empowering workers. Engaged employees are not only more committed to their work, their team and the company, but perform better on many fronts, and thus elevate their company's performance.

Culture is all about people – aligning team members and developing productive relationships. It's a very different experience to be part of a group that comes together to make a living, and to belong to a thriving community. In companies with great cultures people are more loyal, and many of them never want to leave.

Organisations with great cultures offer outstanding customer experience and are better in sales. As a customer, when you are dealing with a business with a great culture, you can immediately sense it. You can feel whether the people you're dealing with care about each other, whether they want to be there, and whether they care about you, the customer. In teams where people feel they belong, they also want to make you feel that way.

Put simply, businesses with a great culture and an engaged work community are much better prepared to compete and to navigate through challenging times. Research by the Hay Group indicates that 'companies with highly engaged people outperform firms with the most disengaged folks – by 54% in employee retention, by 89% in customer satisfaction, and by fourfold in revenue growth'.

Before looking at how to design for a great culture, you need to identify what that really is – what makes a workplace a 'great place to work'.

The Best Places to Work

The Great Place to Work Institute has been researching for over three decades what makes a workplace great, with the mission to 'build a better society by helping companies transform their workplaces'.

Their annual Best Places to Work in Australia award recognises the top 50 organisations that go the extra mile to keep their people engaged at work and build a culture their people desire. The award is based on surveys that assess the levels of engagement, trust, pride and camaraderie among the employees of the competing companies, along with managements' commitment to maintaining a great workplace culture (achieved through 'policies and practices, and procedures in hiring, inspiring, speaking, listening, thanking, caring, developing, celebrating and sharing'[2]).

Learning from the stars

Over recent years, software companies have been leading the way in providing the best working conditions. This is understandable if we consider that there is a great scarcity of highly talented software developers (note that there is an enormous difference between the performance of a good and a terrific developer[3]), and that most of these people are well-educated Gen Ys with high expectations.

These people want to have a say in how they work and to influence the direction of the organisation. They seek to have fun in their jobs and to work in a social, collaborative environment. They want little distinction between work and life and to be able to commit time to passion projects. In short, they expect a high level of involvement and autonomy. (When these expectations are met, it's no surprise that tech employees are happier and more satisfied with their jobs than average employees. What's more interesting is that, according to studies, they also have an above-average focus – despite working mostly in open, supposedly distracting environments.)

---

2   Quoted from the BRW article, The Best Place to Work survey. (See Related Readings at the end of this book.)

3   According to Chris Murphy, President and Chief Strategy Officer at global IT consultancy ThoughtWorks, '... a good one is 10 to 100 times more effective than a mediocre software developer'.

To attract, retain and engage high-performing people, today's most desirable workplaces use very different strategies from those of their predecessors (e.g. large financial services companies that used to spend lavishly on building spectacular state-of-the-art office buildings.) They achieve their results through a more people-centred approach, and provide great examples for other industries to follow.

Looking beyond the perks

There are many different ways of motivating people in the workplace, and companies that take culture seriously often use creative, clever and surprisingly simple methods. However, the surveys show that what works in one organisation may not work in another. Managers of the most highly rated workplaces understand who their employees are – what's unique about them, why they work there, and what their needs and desires are – and shape their workplaces accordingly.

Employees appreciate perks such as pool tables and massage chairs. These things, when thoughtfully chosen, do help build loyalty; however, none of them can ensure that workers will never leave. Over 30 years of research shows that it is not the perks and benefits that make a workplace great and why top talents choose to work in a company.

However, free lunches are something that pretty much everyone seems to be excited about, regardless of industry and culture, and are offered by the vast majority of the top 50 companies. And this makes sense; sharing meals together regularly is a great way to build camaraderie, whether it's at lunch breaks, at Friday wind-downs or at special events. Family-friendly policies are also very common among the top-performing companies.

These examples show that at the best workplaces, employers are looking beyond the perks and are investing in building positive relationships and an inclusive culture. They have a firm commitment to transparency, openness, trust and respect – the key factors for building a genuine, vibrant community. Furthermore, there is also a strong focus on flexibility, ownership, and offering meaningful choices. Leaders of the most attractive workplaces know what makes their people tick and treat them like adults.

Cultures are shaped by their environments

Cultures can't exist in a bubble – the space either supports or interferes with culture and human behaviour.

We read our physical environment the same way we read body language; we draw a meaning from the look and the feel of the space around us: why we are here, who we are when we are here, and what we are supposed to do. Furthermore, the design of the interior determines what we actually can do, including how we can interact with others.

Knowing this, leaders of the most attractive workplaces always make sure that their office spaces are designed to promote the right behaviours and enhance relationships, and that their teams are proud of where they work. When the design is in sync with the organisation's culture, people are more confident about what to do and how to do it, find it easier to do what's expected of them, and feel more connected to the team and the organisation.

Of course, we need to remember that the physical space is only a part of the big picture. In a low-trust culture, with conflicting values, workplace politics or ineffective management, a well-designed space alone can't turn things around. However, the physical environment can act as a catalyst to organisational transformation.

Common mistakes and consequences

Spaces without spirit

On the surface, workplace culture doesn't immediately seem to be dependent on the physical space. In many organisations, culture is routinely perceived as a management and organisational issue independent of design, and thus not really considered and aligned with the physical environment.

Perhaps this is why so many old-style offices are still out there sending messages like 'the purpose of this place is only to do work' and 'bringing your whole personality to work is non-professional'. Management might not think this way, but these messages are still in your face.

Environments that are flat and impersonal are demotivating and drain the passion from workers and the energy from their relationships. These kinds of offices might have done some service to organisations in the past; but today, when workers have different expectations, and the competition for talent is fierce, these workplaces act as a filter, only retaining those that are not driven or fit enough to find a place that helps them fully come alive.

Spaces with mixed messages

Confusing culture with gimmicks and perks, or superficially copying the most fashionable design features are also common mistakes, resulting in spaces that might look exciting (to some), but do nothing good to align workers' behaviour or foster a sense of community.

And then there are those leaders who do invest in an engaging office environment, and do it well, but then neglect the culture during challenging times, and perhaps even discourage their teams from utilising the social features of the space.

Spaces that give people mixed messages can be confusing, contributing to indecision and conflicts. Toxic cultures are more likely to develop in an incongruent environment. And being distracted and drained by personal issues has devastating effects on all aspects of our work and our morale.

These sorts of environments not only make it difficult to attract people with the right skills and personalities, they take a toll on people's creative thinking, innovation and problem solving skills. Employing unhappy, disengaged, burnt-out workers also impacts on the quality of services provided and the customer experience, and ultimately influences the market position of the business.

Taking the next step

None of us want to create or work in environments like these. How come there are still so many scary office spaces around? The underlying cause of these mistakes, in my experience, is that the culture of the organisation is rarely well-understood and valued.

Before you can create a space that supports your culture, you need to identify it and get clear about why it is important. This will not only help you create a better workplace, but will also give you the confidence that your efforts and investment will pay off.

Creating an engaging workplace that supports your culture is not only the privilege of big companies who have a fortune to spend on benefits. It doesn't have to be expensive, though it does require your commitment, creative thinking, and the willingness to dig deep and get to know your people better. However, this investment will certainly pay off.

Key design strategies

Key design strategies for creating an engaging environment that supports a thriving culture:

1. Set the foundations for a strong community
2. Make the workplace open and transparent
3. Provide a sense of ownership and influence
4. Let your team play and have fun
5. Integrate work and life
6. Smooth out cultural differences

Applying these strategies has already delivered exceptional results for many companies in terms of creating engaging workplaces. Once successfully implemented, you will notice greater trust, passion and energy in your teams. Your people will become more proactive and committed team players, eager to bring their whole selves to work.

Flexible ways of working (both within and beyond the office), along with the opportunities to alter the work environment to the changing nature of work, will further deepen engagement. The associated design strategies will be introduced in the following chapter, Principle 7: Evolving.

Strategy 1:
Set the foundations for a strong community

We need relationships to thrive in life. Knowing that we can count on our community – whether it's friends, family or work mates – expands our personal resources. We accomplish more, recover from setbacks faster and develop a stronger sense of purpose.

Therefore, with solid social relationships in our workplace we are not only happier, but also perform better. In a positive environment characterised by trust and respect, we collaborate better, share ideas more freely and participate more fully. We are more willing to listen, delegate and provide support. It is much easier to work at our best when we feel that our team is behind us. We are more creative, more confident, happier at work, and happier with our work.

Connecting with our work mates is always great fuel for our drive and confidence, but when we are under greater pressure getting social support can be a lifesaver. Ironically, when companies are going through a rough period – when we need one another most – is the very time when managers tend to withdraw the social 'perks' that could help us stay at the top of our game.

Others completely overlook the importance of a strong community and refuse to put effort into building one. They might be too busy, be worried that their staff will waste time socialising, or might have the belief that work and friendship don't mix and therefore getting too close to their staff will undermine their authority.

In exchange for staff spending more time on aspects of work deemed 'more important', these companies risk paying the cost of staff burnout and plummeting morale. By ignoring the value of social capital, they not only undermine their team's performance but also their own.

Getting people to talk and connect

The most successful organisations take the exact opposite approach; instead of nudging their staff to turn inwards, they encourage their teams to stick together. Today's most sought-after workplaces have plenty of social facilities such as cafeterias, dining rooms, lounge rooms, casual meeting spaces, game rooms, indoor picnic areas, you name it.

And even those companies that don't have a very sophisticated workplace strategy, but just want to create a nice social environment, get some positive results. The reason why this works is simple: these typically relaxed and cool-looking spaces give us the permission to chat with our team mates, and also provide the opportunity to do so.

However, there is much more you can do to help your team members build, improve and maintain healthy personal relationships. To build firm connections, people need to meet first, then engage in conversations, open up, and develop authentic relationships. To get the best results from your space, you need to plan for each of these steps.

1. Increase the chance of people accidentally running into each other.

   Regular casual encounters have a great role in building and strengthening relationships over time; when we bump into someone we don't know well, we may only engage in small talk or just say hello, but every time we meet, there's a chance that these conversations will become deeper and more real.

   You can achieve this with your floor layout. For example, provide shared facilities – e.g. kitchen, meeting space, staff area, utilities – where members from different parts of the organisation can connect. Alternatively, create circulation paths that force people to walk through other departments. (Unfortunately, this is where workplace strategy often stops.)

2. Make sure that these casual meeting spaces encourage people to talk.

   In an interesting piece of research at Google, they figured out that 4.5 minutes is the optimum time for employees to wait for a coffee. If this time is shorter, they are unlikely to talk to others waiting, and if it's longer, they won't bother getting their coffee. So providing a coffee machine with the right settings is one possible solution.

   You can also prompt conversations by giving people topics to talk about. For example a 'notice board' or 'ideas board' in sight, with regular updates, could present interesting conversation starters.

3. Enable people to organise themselves into small groups.

   People tend to open up more and form tighter bonds in smaller groups. Create a furniture layout for the casual meeting areas that puts people into groups of 6-8 or less. And if your organisational structure allows, follow the same principle in the design of the working areas.

4. Create an authentic ambience.

    The interior design should inspire people to show their true selves. Perhaps go outside, observe what sort of environments allow your people to be most true to themselves, and capture that atmosphere in your workplace.

Workplace design and trust

Each year, the Great Place to Work Institute is in touch with over 5,500 companies and 3 million employees globally, and its research continually indicates that an essential characteristic of a great workplace – regardless of industry, location or company size – is trust.

While trends, expectations and popular incentives change, the importance of trust does not; it is the foundation of productive relationships, loyalty and commitment, and is a major factor in accepting new ideas and changes.

Trust works in all directions:

- Peers need to trust each other in order to interact and work well together.

- Companies need to trust that their people are doing their jobs. As mobile work practices emerge and business cultures change, monitoring workers in traditional ways is no longer an option.

- And perhaps most importantly, employees need to trust their leaders. The ability to earn trust is now widely recognised as a form of competence in business. The Great Place to Work website says: 'Trust is the defining principle of great workplaces – created through management's *credibility*, the *respect* with which employees feel they are treated, and the extent to which employees expect to be treated *fairly*.'

In many organisations trust is at an all-time low, causing major headaches for leaders who are aware of the costs: diminished performance due to toxic culture, inefficient communication, and excessive regulations.

The Trust Research Project

Workplace design can enhance or erode trust between anyone in the workplace. A recent Australian study explored how workplace design can influence organisational trust between staff and management. The 'Trust Research Project' project, which was a collaborative effort between Geyer – an interior design and research company, Swinburne University Faculty of Design, and the Great Place to Work Institute, came up with these insights:

- Putting staff into an older style, 'dictatorship type' office – with luxurious rooms for the bosses but with sub-standard staff facilities – could quickly undermine trust, giving the impression that management is not thinking about the way work changes and what their employees' needs are.

- Employees understand if managers have larger offices or work settings if they truly need them, and maybe more powerful computers. But seeing leaders getting better technology or spaces irrespective of what their work requires does impact on their trust.

- Inequalities around the 'health qualities' of the personal work areas can really jeopardise trust. There's no reason why a manager would need or deserve better lighting or more ergonomic furniture, and therefore better health, than anyone else.

- Clear communication is the greatest contributor to trust, regardless of the type of workplace practices employed (i.e. assigned desks or Activity-Based Work). Design solutions that promote open communication will be discussed in the next section.

The other strategies in this chapter all help contribute to building trust within the entire team, along with empathy, authenticity and respect.

Working with friends

Of course, building a strong community does not require that all colleagues can work without friction all the time, and that all team members become best friends. That would be unrealistic. However, friendships are important; according to studies, having a good friend at work is among the top 10 reasons why people stay in their jobs.

I am impressed how many people I meet from really successful companies see their colleagues and coworkers as friends. These managers, entrepreneurs and staff members simply don't see a reason why creation, learning and socialising should be kept separate, and so they just want to have friends around at work. 'Life's too short' – they say.

You don't need to be one of those business owners who is lucky enough to be able to recruit for friends. Workplaces that provide plenty of opportunities for social encounters (as discussed above) do support forming friendships. And the design solutions explained in the following sections, when implemented, will further strengthen these connections.

Strategy 2:
Make the workplace open and transparent

Transparency and openness are common attributes of workplaces where people love to work. Employees want easy access to management and senior staff to talk about problems and solutions. And managers know that encouraging their teams to share information and ideas will empower them and thus help them deliver better results. 'Knowledge is power.'

Traditional offices designed around a hierarchical organisational structure tend to suggest the message that there are few opportunities for advancing our career, whereas the more open and casual work environments acknowledge that good ideas can come from anyone, and suggest that the keys to our progress lie within us – in the quality of our work. This is a great contributor to attracting and retaining people.

An open environment encourages friction-free communication. When it comes to approaching the boss or a colleague with a concern, it can be tempting to simply opt out and remain silent until the problem escalates. The same applies to sharing those 'crazy' ideas that go against the status quo; so many transformational ideas remain untold for fear of being knocked back. Therefore, making it easy and safe for your workers to talk to managers and each other is really important both for the early resolution of conflicts and for capitalising on your team's knowledge base.

The office environment may also influence employees' opinions of their managers' competence and attitude. In one study, managers in open offices appeared in a more positive light (e.g. being more inspirational as leaders, and having higher integrity) compared to those in enclosed offices. Another study found that in offices where managers were physically present (visible and audible), they were perceived to be more friendly.

💡 Australia's best place to work in 2013

The Sydney office of the international trading company, Optiver, has been named Australia's best place to work in 2013, and this achievement is largely due to bringing the concept of transparency to mastery. Their website states:

> 'We believe our company culture is one of our most valuable assets and key for our long term sustainability. ... Despite the strong growth we have always managed to maintain a highly informal atmosphere and relatively flat organisational structure. And for a reason – as we believe this provides our employees with the flexibility they need to be creative, to research their ideas and to act upon them.'

Optiver's informal office environment is well suited to its inclusive culture. The building is literally very transparent, feels open and light, and the door of the CEO, Paul Hilgers, is always open. He says: 'As a CEO of a company, sometimes you underestimate your title. You want to make sure there are no barriers for people to talk to you.'

Optiver is known for its generous salaries and perks, but the real reason for their win lies elsewhere: people working there love the atmosphere of the workplace and what they do.

Getting a position at Optiver is famously difficult; beyond demonstrating exceptional technical proficiency, candidates also must be a good fit for the team without dropping their personalities. But the transparent environment enables them to meet as many staff as possible during the recruitment process, making it easier for everyone to make the right decision.

> Those who get in enjoy a non-bureaucratic culture that gives way to people's brilliance. Workers get almost immediate feedback and rewards for their efforts, which can make their already interesting and challenging work very addictive.

Design suggestions

- Design a non-hierarchical setting. Make sure that people from all positions are able to share the same space, and that this is an attractive option. (You many need hierarchy on an organisational level, but not on a human level.)

- Minimise barriers such as fixed solid walls and screens in areas where privacy is not needed.

- In areas where privacy is occasionally required, consider using mobile partitions or large sliding doors, so that the space can be opened up as often as possible. Glass partitions are great where only acoustic privacy is required. Curtains and blinds are great for providing visual privacy. You may use these in combination for maximum flexibility.

- Use low height screens (if any) between workstations, so that workers, when standing up, can see each other.

- Create casual 'drop-in' meeting spaces which can be used anytime without booking.

- Find a system that you and your team can use to give each other a visible signal indicating whether it is a good time to be approached or you're in a 'bubble'.

- Give your team a not-so-scary option to ask for help. I saw an office once where workers stuck cartoon graphics on the wall to express if they felt 'sunny', 'cloudy' or 'stormy' about their projects. In my experience, in workplaces where it's safe to be honest about struggles, and where the community is strong, team mates are genuinely there for each other.

Risks to avoid

Make sure that your space does indeed match your culture. Fitting a non-transparent culture into a transparent office space, in my experience, causes more damage than good. I worked in offices where managers regularly discussed staff issues (without any involvement of staff) behind glass walls. With these meetings happening right in front of our faces, focusing on work and keeping our spirits up was, as you would imagine, hard work.

Avoid creating independent departments. In separate self-contained groups occupants commonly develop their own subcultures, with their own rules and behaviours. Colleagues from other departments (i.e. 'the outsiders') are treated with suspicion. This can make communication and collaboration very tricky, along with getting consensus on any shared organisational objectives.

Remember, an open environment is not the same as one large open-plan office with no walls, which more likely makes people feel exposed and protective of their personal space! It is a workplace where people can connect with each other without jumping hurdles, and which invites them to express themselves with authenticity and honesty. So while focusing on transparency, be mindful of your people's need for privacy and occasional solitude.

Strategy 3:
Provide a sense of ownership and influence

Studies show that knowledge workers who are in the position to decide where and how they work perform better[4] and are more motivated and more creative. I have also observed in my practice that workers with a sense of autonomy and control over their work experience have a more proactive approach to problem solving, have a more responsible attitude, and are more adaptable to change.

---

4 Gensler's 2013 survey indicates, for example, that employees who are given a range of choices for when and how to work are more focused and collaborative, and are better learners. Another study of 320 small firms, conducted at Cornell University, found that companies that offered their employees a choice in how they work grew four times faster than those with controlling management policies, and had a third of the turnover rate.

On the other hand, workers with little or no influence over their work experience can become intolerant to even small annoyances, and at the same time, become obstacles to problem solving. They tend to see themselves as recipients of the problem, and so they disengage from addressing it.

For example, when staff don't have the choice to move around and engage with the space as their needs dictate, there is a good chance that they will get rather attached to their personal work area – the only part of their work experience they can actually control – and disengage from what's happening outside their 'zone'.

💡 We don't like our office, but don't touch it

One company I worked with had needed to relocate some years before from a spacious high-end office space to a temporary, much smaller and more basic tenancy with many functional and comfort issues. They had no break space or casual meeting space, so apart from the workstations people had nowhere to go. In addition, the workplace didn't reflect the company's values at all.

Understandably, staff felt that some benefits had been taken away from them, and that they were living with a decision that they had not been able to influence. Further to that, they had little control over their current workplace.

Eventually, management decided to upgrade the office, with the goal of improving the quality of the environment and staff amenities, and of introducing new workplace practices and technologies that would make teamwork easier. Staff were also invited to contribute with their ideas, requests and comments to the design; however, some of the responses were rather counterintuitive!

Staff found that the office was crowded, despite the fact that workstations were rather large (most people had 2 desks). They were also disturbed by thermal discomfort and noise, more than seemed to be warranted by the actual physical conditions. However, what was most surprising was that many staff members showed strong resistance, skepticism or indifference towards change – although the upgrade was aimed to make their space more pleasant. They had learnt to cope with the way things were.

After rearranging the floor layout and creating a break space / informal meeting area, staff responses changed substantially; there were far fewer complaints about crowding and noise (although these issues had not been directly addressed), and staff became more willing to engage in further change. Nobody wanted to go back to the old ways.

It is worth mentioning that apart from the time invested, this upgrade had virtually no cost.

Providing choice, flexibility and control over how work is done

There are many ways to provide people with choice and control over their work experience using design. Some of the solutions have already been discussed: providing a range of different work areas to choose from, enabling workers to control their comfort conditions, involving them in decision making about the design, and giving them the opportunity to put their personal stamp on the space.

It's a growing trend to create fitouts that allow people to adapt the workplace to their needs, for example, to tailor the floor layout to support their projects, or to configure their workstations based on personal preference. This requires the use of interior elements that are easy to move around or reconfigure.

Offering staff the flexibility to manage their personal lives and time is also becoming increasingly important. This is not only a management issue; having people working with flexible hours and/or remotely adds a new dimension to workplace design.

(Adaptable design solutions, along with the implications of flexible work practices will be discussed in Principle 7: Evolving.)

Providing a sense of influence – making a difference to the world

One of the most effective ways of motivating people is to acknowledge them on a regular basis. Saying 'thank you', both in formal and informal ways, will inspire your team members to give their best. A great work environment is already a reward in itself, but recognition that is specific and personal can skyrocket engagement. (According to one survey, employees who receive strong performance recognition are more than twice as likely to be highly engaged as those who only receive weak or no recognition.)

So how can we design in opportunities to provide positive feedback?

- Find creative ways of exhibiting your team members' achievements, large and small, and also encourage your team to join in and acknowledge each other. (Keep in mind that singling out people can be damaging – forget the 'employee-of-the-month' certificates!)
- When displaying awards, remember that they have a bigger purpose than just making an impression on visitors. Put them in a location where your team can also see them and receive the subtle message every day: 'well done for your wonderful work'.
- Recognition from clients and the wider public are especially valuable, showing workers that their contribution makes a real difference. This can be as simple as dedicating a wall to unsolicited endorsements from clients.

Having a sense of progress is another great motivator. But sometimes it can be difficult to see the difference a day's worth of our work makes, especially on large projects. So bring into your people's awareness the progress they have already made.

- Make sure that your project tracking wall not only shows what needs to be done but also highlights what's been completed. You can be really creative here. I've seen many great examples of colourful project tracking walls that really invite people to add their progress each day, large or small.

Other strategies introduced in this book that help empower people include: communicating a shared purpose throughout the space, and displaying messages associated with past achievements and future rewards.

Case study: Wealth Enhancers

Wealth Enhancers is an exclusive community, providing financial advice, coaching and accountability and events for its high-performing Gen Y members. In our interview Sarah Riegelhuth, one of the co-founders, explained how focusing on culture has helped her and her team create an office where they all feel at home while performing exceptionally well.

'We like being close to each other'

In early 2012 they moved into a domestic-style office, a refurbished 3-storey terraced house, and both the choice of the location and the design of the fitout were largely driven by staff requests. They gained the biggest insight almost accidentally, shortly before the move:

> 'We were away on a staff retreat for a couple of days, working in a big house. One night we all sat at a really long table, side by side on kitchen chairs, working with laptops, and in that moment staff said, "Do we have to work in a typical office environment? Why don't we work somewhere like this? This is so nice." And we said, "Yeah, why not?" And so we started to look for something that would fit what they wanted: an open plan environment where they could all work closely together.'

> 'Not all decisions were made by staff; we would pick and choose which decisions we involved them in. They certainly initiated the main idea at the beginning, and we got their feedback all along the way.'

An office of choices

In everything they do, Wealth Enhancers want to ensure there is a return on investment. All of their business activities have targets, and are measured and tracked. However, when it came to the design of their office, they didn't feel the need to use any specific formula or analysis; it was sufficient to ensure that their new space supported their culture.

The team has created an office that offers many choices:

- The fitout makes it possible to regularly change the space: to rearrange the furniture layout, to set up different types of work and staff areas, and to change what's stuck up on the wall.
- Staff can choose where they want to work: in the open area, in the staff room or in one of the two meeting rooms. (In the open area, sometimes three people work around a single desk, which would be unimaginable in most corporate environments. But this certainly works for them!)
- One of the meeting rooms is somewhat formal and the other is more casual. When meeting clients, staff can choose the room that best suits the type of conversation they plan to have.
- They also have better food options than in standard offices, since they have a fully functional kitchen with a stove.
- Directors have their own offices, but they prefer mixing with staff: 'I want to be up there, working with my team side by side, working with my friends.'

Smiling clients

Wealth Enhancer's job is not a casual matter, but they have managed to make their workplace casual and comfortable without losing focus on the difference their work makes. The company values are *Get Rich Slow*, *Community of Tall Poppies*, *Innovate and Embrace Change*, and *Commitment to Coaching*, and the space inspires staff to live up to these values each day. There are photos of their smiling members on the wall, and the words, 'we ♡ our members'.

Creating their own paths

> 'Everyone in our business is a fairly motivated type of person, the kind of people who wouldn't work somewhere if they didn't like it. They create their own paths.'

> 'I've learnt that letting the staff be involved in the direction of how they're going to work is really important and leads to success. Because they're all happy, and they would never complain about their work, because they picked it. And it plays into other areas of their work.'

Managers are very satisfied with staff performance; staff live up to very high expectations, regularly meet their individual targets, and are willing to go beyond their core duties to help each other out.

> 'We love the decision that we've made, and they were right! ... I love my company, I love work, and I really hope that all my staff love what they do as well. That's the kind of environment we're trying to create, where everybody's happy to be there and loves being part of this team, this family.'

(See the second part of Wealth Enhancers' case study in Principle 7: Evolving.)

Strategy 4:
Let your team play and have fun

Fun is not only for the younger generations

The majority of the most sought-after workplaces employ young staff. This is because Millennials have an especially high expectation of enjoying their work, and so companies that want to attract young talent know they need to make work fun.

This does not mean that younger workers have very different desires from previous generations; they just feel they can ask for working conditions that an employee 5, 10 or 20 years ago would not have considered asking for.

Companies like Google – where dogs are welcome in the office – or Yahoo – with an in-house massage parlour – have successfully challenged the long-held notion that work and fun are incompatible, and are now seen as role-models for organisations that want to make work both enjoyable and profitable. (Number four of the 10 reasons to work at Google: 'Work and play are not mutually exclusive. It is possible to code and pass the puck at the same time.')

Providing football or ping-pong tables is now the norm, and office slides are the new cool. These kinds of features, when well chosen, are not just PR gimmicks. As discussed previously (in Principle 5: Caring), every time a worker experiences a burst of happiness their thinking shifts and they may see solutions they would otherwise have missed. Sir Richard Branson, CEO of Virgin has famously said, 'More than any other element, fun is the secret of Virgin's success'. Fun is not just about having a nice time; it also adds to the bottom-line.

'Let's get a cool-looking workplace!'

Fun can exist in any organisation. Businesses – small or large, highly or loosely regulated, established or start-up – are now realising that they could use their physical environment to make work more enjoyable and to attract and retain talent.

But there is a trap: copying anything that appears to work for others, buying into the latest trends blindly to get a 'cool-looking' workplace, will likely take you down the wrong track. You need to look beyond the surface and choose the benefits that resonate with the people you are working with.

The young employees of a call centre who need to keep their spirits up might be more energised by a themed setting than, for example, a team of accountants. A creative agency is probably more inspired by an artistic environment than a group of geeks who are most excited about getting their hands on the latest gadgets.

You may also consider offering your team such perks as massage, or the opportunity for a nap (which also have implications on the design of your workplace). But these sorts of benefits will only make a real difference if they are customised to your culture, and if enjoying work is a genuine, deeply rooted value in your organisation.

Play helps us survive and thrive

Play is an essential part of human development and plays (excuse the pun) an important role in various aspects of daily life. It supports physical and cognitive development as well as social skills, and can help us integrate into new environments.

In the context of work, play is not only a pastime, but a powerful tool for working, learning and team-building. Plato said, **'You can discover more about a person in an hour of play than in a year of conversation.'**

Play helps us to accept ourselves and our colleagues better, and to be open to different perspectives and provocative ideas. Play improves our capacity for improvisation, collaboration and learning. It makes us flexible and resilient, and therefore fitter to thrive in rapidly changing conditions and to survive times of crisis.

Unfortunately, play is still widely perceived as frivolous or even inappropriate at work, something we are supposed to set aside for our free time. Accordingly, 'work ethic' is most commonly associated with a person's willingness to work hard and long hours, not to their commitment to get better at, for example, thinking out of the box or building rapport with a range of people.

To create a non-judgemental environment for productive play, you need to understand how play can help your team get better results, and appreciate its value. It needs to be embraced by the organisation's culture; physical surroundings alone cannot do the work.

Design Thinking and the Power of Play

Brendan Boyle is a professor at Stanford d.school – an educational institute teaching design thinking – who has a passion for innovation and play. In his presentation at the Creative Innovation Conference (Melbourne 2011) he talked about the intersection of these subjects:

> 'Most people think that the opposite of play is work. I think it's boredom. Most companies, at best, think that playing is recess, most of them think it's fruitless. But I believe if you make it the part of the process it increases innovation.'

Boyle identified three phases of play (i.e. principles of design thinking) to support innovation:

1. **Role play:** This is all around exploration, 'getting out into the world' to gain insights. Role play involves having a good time while having different, new experiences – just like when we were kids. It helps us gain empathy, as well as insights and inspiration.

2. **Encourage the ridiculous:** This phase is around creative play, exploring different possibilities, really going wild. We need to acknowledge that sometimes the best ideas are born after all the realistic options have been explored, and people start to come up with seemingly ridiculous ideas.

   Boyle explained the insights from a study in brainstorming: 'Out of 100 ideas, the first 60 ideas produced 5 that were actually new and different, the next 20 produced nothing but laughter. And ideas 80 to 100 produced another 10 that were amazing. ... To get brilliant ideas, you have to be close to the ridiculous ones ... There are tons of good ideas out there in the world but those aren't going to change it.'

3. **Think with your hands:** This phase involves people feeling and experiencing an idea through experiments, constructive play and implementation (such as building quick prototypes). 'How would this experience feel?' When you think with your hands, your hand is your prototype.

If you can incorporate play into your innovation process, your team will not only enjoy it more, but will produce better results. But to make sure that everyone fully participates, you need to establish a physical and social environment that helps your team members to let go of their fear of judgement, along with their habit of judging themselves.

Your play space needs to:

- **Be safe and non-judgemental.** This is not about creating comfort, but about providing a space which gives your team members the permission to open up, and in which they are willing to be exposed. Create a setting (with furniture, decoration and props) that is creative, playful and ridiculous, in other words, possessing the very qualities you want to encourage. And if play is not (yet) integrated into the culture of your organisation, make sure that the play space is sheltered from onlookers.

- **Invite your team to do something new,** to get in touch with their creative side by doing something unfamiliar. Many of us automatically reach for our computers – or other familiar media – when given a problem to solve. To break this habit, create a 'play space' that attracts people like a magnet; that is easy to access and use, and which is energising and fun.

- **Be equipped with the right furniture and tools,** making it possible to play, explore and experiment. Use flexible, multi-functional furnishings so that your team can easily organise themselves in a way that suits their activities. (We will have a closer look into this in Principle 7: Evolving.) Provide access to props for such activities as role playing or model building, and ensure there is sufficient storage space for these.

- **Be aptly named.** Just the way we name an activity already makes a difference to how we relate to it. For example, some people might find 'role playing' unprofessional, but not 'service simulation'. Choose names for your rooms that sound appealing to your team.

Stanford d.school's campus is a prime example – with rooms that allow you to draw on the floor and all walls, colourful Post-it notes everywhere, piles of foam cubes and timber boxes you can use as building blocks for creating your own temporary setting, a lipstick pink ladies toilet with disco balls hanging from the ceiling, and spaces named 'instant studio', 'peanut gallery' and 'campfire'. (See a full case study of Stanford d.school under Principle 7: Evolving.)

Strategy 5:
Integrate work and life

This book is about creating space for work, so it might seem counterintuitive to talk about 'not work'. Not all business owners find it a popular idea that the workplace should make people's life better. (Some already find it hard to digest that flexibility, socialising, play and fun do not take staff away from work, but bring them closer to it.)

However, **discussions today are moving away from 'work-life balance' and towards 'work-life integration',** a concept which implies that work and life do not need to be separate (and therefore balanced); rather, they can and should enhance each other.

Tony Bacigalupo, mayor of 'New York City' (a community-driven coworking space) expresses beautifully what today's workplaces should be about:

'We came up with this really toxic relationship with work, that it's something that I have to do for somebody else, and the fun and joy that I get from life is something that I'll do in between ... We shouldn't have to be so disconnected from the work that we do ... When it's all said and done, if more people see their work as an opportunity to realize their potential as human beings, then I'll have done my part.'

The benefits

So how does a workplace that is designed to become an attractive part of people's lives actually improve performance?

- It makes the workplace and work itself more attractive.

- It invites us to bring our whole selves to work, to give more of ourselves and to be more open to receive support from others.

- In a workplace where we are free to share our passions, personal challenges and achievements, we become better people; by being inspired and encouraged by others, it's more likely that we will achieve our individual goals (whether it's about improving our health, learning a new skill or developing our character).

- Sharing all sorts of experiences with our work mates – meals, games, hobbies, rituals, celebrations – helps build camaraderie and maintain a close-knit team.

- Feeling welcome to express our authentic selves increases our commitment to the organisation, our performance, and our drive to help others.

Bringing 'life' into the workplace

More and more companies are offering a lot of flexibility to their staff to manage their personal lives and time. But a few of them go a step further, and provide the facilities for bringing 'life' into the workplace, knowing that it will elevate their business to another level.

Google is a famous example; they invest heavily into attracting their staff to 'live' in the office. Google's cafeterias not only employ their own chefs preparing superb quality food, but stay open well after working hours, inviting staff to dine together. Google also offers on-site day care, while encouraging employees to spend some time with their kids during the day.

Google's approach would not work for everyone. Also, there is much debate as to whether it is a good idea to get staff to spend most of their living (and some of their sleeping) hours in the office, and to wipe out the boundaries between work and life almost completely.

But there is a great lesson here. Google makes these investments in a very frugal manner (even though the image they project may suggest otherwise). Every detail of these strategies is carefully thought through and designed to yield high returns through improved productivity and performance. It's not about just throwing money at people.

You don't need to have a large budget, or a high-profile brand, or hundreds of employees. You don't need to be like Google in any way – apart from having the commitment to elevate your culture – to be able to create and benefit from a workplace where your team feels they belong. I often find out about small businesses who have achieved this so successfully that they wouldn't consider going back to the old ways.

Design suggestions

- Make the space as authentic as possible, in other words, not only 'practical', but easy to relate to.

    An authentic space lets people be themselves. What does your authentic office look like?[5] Well, it depends on your team members' personalities, world views, habits, etc. But most of us would agree on what it isn't: a uniform space without a soul, characterised by composite wood joinery, plastic laminate desktops, halogen

---

5   I wish I could say that an authentic office should feel like an office – that's what authenticity is about, isn't it? But sadly, we have too many negative associations with the traditional concept of the office. I trust that your new workplace along with the increasing number of brilliant examples out there will change the way we all think about workplaces, and one day we will see them as places that are real in every conceivable way.

down-lights, metal filing cabinets, grid ceiling, in-trays – all those items which you rarely see anywhere else but in offices, and which you really don't miss when working elsewhere.

- Bring the 'outer world' into the workplace.

  Find inspiration for the design from places outside of work that people are naturally drawn to. You may create an office that resembles a bit of a neighbourhood, with areas that feel like home, or a café, or a sporting facility, or a market, or a park.

  Themed design (for example, a corridor looking like a streetscape, or a meeting room looking like a ski resort) likewise has its own charm, but also its limitations. If you opt for this type of design, make sure you consider how it actually enhances performance beyond providing the wow factor. (Spectacular office interiors are great for impressing visitors and making people proud, but their merits shouldn't stop there.)

  A wall mural can provide an excellent opportunity for bringing pretty much any theme into the space with an impact. It's a relatively simple and low-cost tool which provides space for unlimited imagination.

- Make space for activities not related to work, such as hobbies and recreational activities (e.g. yoga, dancing, meditation, knitting, etc.), office rituals and celebrations, food-related events, games, and just chilling out. You don't need to provide lots of room, just a smart fitout that accommodates many uses.

- Invite conversations unrelated to work. Provide opportunities for your team to communicate their interests, personal goals and achievements to their coworkers. You might dedicate a shelving unit for personal items and trophies, or a wall surface for sticking up random articles, photos, and invitations (for example, for joining a new running group).

- Make the workplace welcoming for family, and perhaps also for pets.

Helping people think outside the box

Sometimes the best ideas for solving work-related problems are inspired by experiences that have nothing to do with work. The ability to apply knowledge and insights from outside the work environment to solve work-related problems is a potent skill (also called 'cross-application of experiences'), and can help us come up with truly innovative ideas.

This is the foundation of Google's famous '20% time' initiative: encouraging employees to work on side projects – experimenting with their own ideas – for roughly one fifth of their paid working time. Many of Google's significant advances are attributed to this initiative, including Gmail and AdSense (which now accounts for a significant part of Google's revenue). And seeing Google's success, many other tech companies have implemented similar initiatives.

One way to help your team think outside the box is by giving them the opportunity to deepen and share their knowledge in their fields of interest and to explore how this might be applicable to the problems that require creative solutions. Consider setting up a library with books and resources about different subjects, and providing a space for passion projects and research that is different from the usual working area.

(Activities that happen outside the office also influence office design. This will be discussed in Principle 7: Evolving.)

Strategy 6:
Smooth out cultural differences

With a distinct culture and a workplace that reflects this culture you are more likely to attract like-minded team members and clients whose values and goals are aligned with yours. Of course, it doesn't mean that your people will be like clones. Team members with different personalities, cultural backgrounds or from different generations will still have their own ways of thinking and working. And sometimes they will have disagreements.

Apart from dealing with differences between your team members (discussed in Principle 4: Diversified), you also need to prepare for situations where teams from different cultures – your employees, clients, other stakeholders, and perhaps different 'departments' within your organisation – will need to collaborate. When businesses merge or move in new directions, these situations are especially likely to occur.

We already know that diversity within a team, when managed well, is an asset that fuels performance. (This is a reason why you often see corporates mixing with freelance consultants, social entrepreneurs and hipster coworkers.) But a cultural clash can be a real problem if not handled skillfully.

> ### 💡 A modern age tale of 'the princess and the tramp'
>
> Once upon a recent time, the owners of two professional services firms decided to merge. These two firms had very different cultures: the smaller one had a relaxed, youthful, light-hearted culture and flexible work style, while the larger one was more traditional, disciplined and regulated.
>
> After the merger, the smaller team moved into the premises of the larger one, without the owners giving much thought to making the space ready for this move. From this moment on, things went downhill. Clashes in culture triggered tension amongst staff; the smaller team found their new office boring, uninspiring and claustrophobic, while the larger team found the newcomers' work area messy and unprofessional, and perceived their work ethic as careless. (There might also have been some envy in the mix of emotions.)
>
> The conflict persisted despite major investments in coaching and change management programs. This prompted the owners to seek other solutions, and so they started to talk about creating a breakout space in the office that would be strategically designed to help bring the two teams closer. Unfortunately, this project was delayed until it was two late.
>
> Within a few months, most of the smaller team left. The situation also took a toll on the performance of those who stayed. Due to fear and skepticism around introducing any new change, innovation came to a halt. And since people couldn't agree on training styles, professional development came to a halt, too. Doing nothing had became the only 'safe' option. The merger had essentially failed.

No-one can tell for sure if redesigning this office could have prevented this disaster and led to a happy ending instead. Workplace design can only make a finite contribution to what is largely a management issue, but this is often sufficient to make a vital difference.

Several strategies mentioned earlier in this book naturally support the collaboration of people with different cultures, and help smooth out differences. Here are some examples:

- Enable people with different work habits to work in close collaboration. For example, provide team spaces with a range of mobile furniture elements that can be arranged in different configurations, and are equipped with modern AV technology along with traditional work tools.

- Offer spaces that will likely appeal to everyone. For example, create a pleasant breakout space. Everyone loves nature, views to the outdoors, sunshine, plants and natural materials, so include as much of these as practicable.

- Encourage playing, humour and fun. For example, provide areas for playing, and use fun decoration. There's nothing like laughter to get people to connect, build trust and start enjoying working together.

- Involve your teams in the design process of your office, encourage them to collaborate, and let them share their ideas and make some of the decisions. This will not only bring people closer, but they will have a stronger sense of connection to the new environment.

While a well-designed office can't perform miracles, it can help you to get the right people on board when building teams or taking on clients, and thus to maintain a unified culture that still allows for individuality. Here is an example:

Case study: Huddle

Earlier I introduced Huddle, a Melbourne-based strategic design consultancy specialising in designing innovative, effective services for organisations. Founder Melis Senova explained the way they approach cultural differences, and how Huddle's space is an integral part of this strategy.

Bridging cultural gaps

'Huddlers' have a strong family culture which they protect and nourish. Since they are particularly sensitive to it, it's really important for them to find productive ways of working with clients whose culture is very different from their own.

Sometimes this is really challenging. When there is a values clash – when clients' motives or goals are fundamentally different – 'Huddlers' find that they are not at their best. Often more effort is spent on trying to bridge the cultural gap than delivering a really great outcome.

But as long as the values that drive the culture are aligned, navigating between different cultures and ways of working is not a problem.

> 'We work very closely with our clients, so value alignment is really important. For example, our values are around "can do and will do" – anything is possible. We are courageous and honest, we will tell you what we think, and we are happy for you to say you don't agree. We're not precious; we don't think that we're right.'

Every bit of Huddle's office interior reflects these values: the decorations, the messages on the walls, and the ideas in progress, which are all publicly displayed. As soon as you enter the office, you get a sense of what they stand for, and if this resonates with you, you know you're in the right place.

> 'We've worked with organisations with vastly different cultures, but similar values. There was mutual understanding, and we all knew where everyone was coming from. They loved working with us. Loved it. They bought us chocolate.'

Getting ready to jump into play

With the right clients, it's not only possible to work in a different way and in a different type of environment from what they are used to, but it can be really productive and energising.

> 'At Huddle, we think at an ecosystem level – not just about the project, but how the outcomes will impact other things around it: the people, the systems, and the organisation's strategy. And we're thinking outside of the norms as well. So when we are exploring

what's possible, this exercise takes us all over the place. How could we offer that service if we were in the desert, underwater, or on the Moon?'

'In these sessions you need to give yourself permission to be silly and playful, and in a serious environment it would be very hard to do that. Which is why we have an office that is playful, multi-coloured, with cartoon figures of fighter pilots on our doors. We're trying to inject a sense of fun. It helps us think.'

Using play – including role play or simulation – for designing serious things (like bank processes) is a relatively new concept, and so not everyone is ready to just get up and act, let alone to look ridiculous. But Huddle's seriously playful environment makes it easier for their clients to get involved, drop their guard and cherish the experience.

'Our office is open, warm and friendly, and it invites people to leave the work personas outside and just bring the self. It's much better to work that way.'

Using 'cues'

Huddle's team is deliberate about the way they get visitors to interact with the space so that they don't feel alienated when they come in, thinking, 'I don't know this stuff, this is primary school'. Even though they have colourful wooden chairs in the meeting room, walls covered with Post-it notes, and fun decorations throughout, there are cues all over the space – like rows of desks with computers – that send the message: 'this is a professional organisation'.

'For example, today I'm running a workshop with a board – men in their sixties and seventies coming in their suits – and just walking into this environment can give them some discomfort. It's important for us to acknowledge that, and to give them tools that are familiar to them, like white papers, and black pens instead of pink ones.'

By seeing these cues, visitors feel more confident that this is a serious business, and are more ready to play.

Putting things into practice

 Case study: JobAdder
(Part 2, continued from Principle 1: Visionary)

Earlier we introduced JobAdder, a Sydney-based software company.

JobAdder's office evolution

CEO Brett Iredale started JobAdder 12 years ago, and is now working from his seventh office. Each office got progressively better as he started to learn what he liked and what worked well. 'And the next office will be better again,' he says.

Last time JobAdder moved, Brett looked for an open clean space with windows all the way around, and with a decent outdoor area (which is almost impossible to get in Sydney). It also needed to be spacious enough to accommodate the training room, the gym and the lounge.

> 'It's really important that we have a nice place, where we like to come – that's why I started my company'.

Not a copy of Google

JobAdder's culture balances hard work and play, so Brett wanted to create a place that's neither a sea of cubicles nor a theme park.

> 'I have experimented with both ends of the spectrum. I came from a very traditional corporate environment and I hated going to work. So I decided to make a nice little place where I like to go. My first reaction was to go to the extreme opposite direction where there are no rules and it's anarchy ... But then we brought it back a bit, to a midway point.'

> 'I hate when people come in here and go, 'Oh, it's like Google'. I like a lot of what Google does. But in the IT industry, there are a lot of

companies who just set out to copy them without thinking through why they do it. Without thinking: What are our values? What do we try to achieve? Are we just trying to be a cool funky place?'

'I've been to offices with themed meeting rooms, with crazy bits of dysfunctional furniture and decorations, that were just uncomfortable and weird. What we are going for is relaxed, easy and comfortable. Everything here has function and purpose.'

Work, play, life

Brett has made a real effort over the years to build a balanced, healthy and vibrant culture. It can be hard to attract women to work in software companies and Brett has been conscious about creating a culture and environment that appeals to both men and women. Part of that is around integrating work and life. Family members, along with dogs and cats are regular visitors, and there is space for them to feel welcome as a part of the JobAdder extended family.

'We play at every opportunity we get. We work hard, play hard, and by play hard I don't mean we all go drinking late at night. We have a gym, and we also do yoga and boxing classes in here. At least once a week we either get together in our beer-garden or go out. We do a lot of fun things; we go skydiving together, or go away for a weekend.'

What happens beyond 9 to 5 is a really important part of JobAdder's culture and success.

'I've got a policy here, that at 5.30 everyone is out of the office. Go and pursue life from 5.30 onwards.'

JobAdder recently introduced a program called 'LifeAdder', in which each person puts down some goals for the year, outside of work – 'really unusual crazy things' – and then they support and encourage each other throughout the year to achieve those goals.

'I've just completed mine, a 110km overnight kayak marathon, and I've never paddled before. Someone has created a father-son club, one guy's learning a language, and another is learning to play a musical instrument.'

The results

'We work harder, because we care about what we have here. If people like and value what they have, they work harder to keep it.'

'One of the best business decisions I've made was this office. We invested a little bit more than what we ordinarily do, but it had a huge impact on sales, staff attraction, and – definitely – on productivity. Everyone here loves working here, and they tell me all the time. In 10 years I've never had a staff member resign. It's testament to the environment that we have here.'

A non-traditional workplace: Circus Oz

Do I need to introduce Circus Oz? They have been entertaining audiences worldwide since 1978 with their self-crafted performances. As stated on their website: 'Celebrating breathtaking stunts, irreverent humour, cracking live music and an all human ensemble, Circus Oz promotes the best of the Australian spirit: generosity, diversity, death-defying bravery, and a fair go for all.'

I had a chat with Mike Finch, Artistic Director and co-CEO, about the culture of Circus Oz and their new home:

> 'Our culture is collaborative and inclusive. Everybody shares ideas, and the show is made by the people who are in the show, who are directed by a director. It's not that everyone is equal, but everyone has a voice; all their ideas feed into making the show'.

Making the move

The new headquarters of Circus Oz opened in early 2014, after 10 years of planning and coordinating with the government (the owner of the building). The building is partially new and partially a renovation. Originally, there were 3 buildings on the site; the middle one got knocked down and replaced with a new section.

This was a highly anticipated move, from an old building which was not only too small, cold and noisy, but also separated people. Acrobats and administrative staff would only meet when eating together in the kitchen.

All places are connected

In the new building, the performers' room (used for training and rehearsals) is at the heart of the facility, surrounded at ground level by the rooms of technicians and musicians; above them, also surrounding the rehearsal room, are the administration offices. The arrangement of the building reflects the support structure of the company.

Every feature of the building has been designed to allow interaction and cross-over. Every desk in the building has a close connection to the central space, which is surrounded by windows. Administration staff can easily see from their offices what's happening there.

> 'The whole building is almost completely transparent; everyone can see each other.'

Interestingly, the Artistic Director's office is right on a circulation path.

> 'This is all about being permeable. Yeah, people walk through my office constantly.'

This new place functions a bit like a café. People are always running into each other, so of course they see and talk to each other more. Their relationships are stronger.

Welcoming the public

The building is open to the public, and the entrance hallway is designed to encourage people to come in. And while staff areas are more private, there are no locked doors stopping people coming in from the street and walking around.

> 'We actually call it the street, its nickname is "Handball Alley". It's designed to be like a Melbourne laneway. All the signage is going to be hand-painted. One of the early ideas was to hang out drying costumes on washing lines, because the washing area is upstairs.'

Decision making

Ironically, Circus Oz – a community nurturing open communication – got this building built through a convoluted bureaucratic process. The project took a really long time, but even so, some major decisions were made in a hurry. They know that the outcome could have been even better if a layer of bureaucracy could have been removed.

But they are very happy with the building, and have plans in place to improve it even further.

What's next?

The building offers little privacy; it's difficult to find a place for confidential meetings, so people tend to see or hear each other's conversations. Mike Finch thinks that's not actually bad, though he realises that the building could still be improved, for example, to give introverted members a better opportunity to engage their talent.

And there are other changes planned:

> 'I would have preferred the finishing to be scruffier and more raw, which means the artists could then impose their own aesthetic on it.'

> 'When this floor was brand new, and one of our performers dropped a bit of gear, it made a mark on the floor, and he was like, "I'm sorry I'm sorry I'm sorry" and we were like, "Don't worry don't worry it's fine". There was that fear of damaging things.'

But now, people are encouraged to be creative with the space, for example, to stencil the doors. And some staff member even took the courage to spray paint a message on the floor!

Management wants to encourage all members to be playful, but building a culture of playfulness is a journey.

> 'We often get office staff gathered around the windows watching a new trick happening on the floor. But I'm still trying to work out whether that leads to a sense of "play happens in this room" or whether it gives people a sense of "we can all be playful, because we are connected; we are all here to support the show".'

❓ Questions to consider

- What sort of work culture and what benefits do your ideal recruits seek?

- How could you stimulate more conversations and connections in your workplace?

- What fears and concerns might hold your people back from sharing their ideas? And how could you address these?

- What level of autonomy do your people want and appreciate?

- What contributions are your people most proud of?

- What motivates your people? What's important for them beyond work?

- How could you make work more playful and fun?

- How could you make your people feel more comfortable about looking 'ridiculous'?

- In what sorts of environments are your team members most relaxed and genuine?

- Where outside the office do your team members hang out in their free time?

- To what extent do your people want to separate their work and personal lives?

- Do families visit your workplace? If yes, how could you comfortably accommodate them?

- What are your clients' cultures like?

- What are the different subcultures like (if any) within your organisation?

- What would you like your people to say about your workplace when chatting with their friends?

PRINCIPLE 7

EVOLVING

CREATE SPACE FOR AN EVOLVING BUSINESS

Creating an environment where it's easy to adapt to and thrive on change

'We're in kind of a transitional time. Institutions are shifting, the economy is shifting, technology is shifting. Optimizing space is important, but you need to be able to respond to changes in the marketplace, in people's needs, changes in the environment. There's an underlying need to be flexible, responsive, and innovative, and that's the case whether it's an educational institution, a business, a nonprofit, or an individual.' – Scott Doorley, co-director of the d.school's Environments Collaborative.

Why should we evolve?

Living and working in the age of change

If we needed to define the age we are living in with a single adjective, 'changing' might be the most accurate one. Most areas of our lives are characterised by increasingly fast changes – it's only this tendency itself that doesn't seem to change!

Whether you are looking into the future with fear, excitement or mixed emotions, escaping change (in business and in personal life) is not an option. But your environment can make a difference to whether you are just coping with change, or thriving on it.

The new workplace

We have discussed previously how changes in technology, social trends and ways of working have redefined the meaning of 'high performance', and led to new standards in workplace design. Late adopters still operate in inflexible, formal and uniform workplaces designed to reflect the status of 'decision makers' and to maximise the number of people in the smallest possible space. On the other hand, leading-edge workplaces tend to be more diversified and authentic environments, tailored to assist learning, community building and self-organised work. These spaces are designed to promote problem solving, maximise the attraction and retention of talent, and let people be the best version of themselves.

New work practices are still emerging. For example, an increasing number of people work remotely – part-time or full-time – from home, from collaborative workplaces (coworking spaces), or from third spaces (spaces that are neither a home nor a workplace, such as coffee shops and libraries). Each workplace type is taking on its own role in our newly emerging workspace structure, and along with these changes, the role of the traditional office is also shifting.

Challenges in making the right decisions

There is not a simple recipe for future-proofing the workplace. Nobody really knows what the workplace of the future will look like, and how it will operate. (In fact, this is one of the few views that workplace specialists seem to share.) We need to accept that many of our questions that come up during the design will remain unanswered, so we need to prepare the workplace for unforeseen conditions.

Here are some of the aspects of work that can and often do change, influencing how the space is used:

- Technology and media (e.g. shifting from desktop computers to laptops and mobile devices, from face-to-face meetings to teleconferencing)
- Workplace model (e.g. shifting from fixed workstations to Activity-Based Work)
- Type of activities (e.g. doing less individual focused work and more teamwork)
- Culture (e.g. business acquisitions, new generations reaching the workforce)
- Number of people in the space (e.g. due to business growth or contraction)
- People using the space (e.g. employees, customers, external team members and coworkers)
- Work arrangements (e.g. adopting teleworking)
- Expectations of new generations (e.g. making work more social and fun)
- Outsourcing work (e.g. to other countries)

Designing a workplace in the midst of so much uncertainty, with industries transforming, new opportunities arising, and new challenges being presented by the economy, requires a strategic approach.

Workplaces stuck in time

Surprisingly few organisations respond well to these challenges and operate in environments that help people stay current in the way they work. Physical workplaces, in general, evolve way more slowly than technology, businesses and work styles. You might have noticed that many offices still look very similar to those of the 80's and 90's; the only obvious changes are larger and thinner computer screens, the presence of laptops (perhaps), and the distinct lack of fax machines.

This gap between the evolution of work and workplaces might be due to designers and decision makers being overwhelmed by fast changes, or being risk-averse. Also, in my observation, design teams rarely consider the broad context: how the industry and the market will change over time, how these will shape the strategy for the business, and how people will work differently as a result.

Several misconceptions contribute to the creation of workplaces that are stuck in time and hinder business progress. I often hear objections along these lines:

- 'We are trying to implement changes, but it's too much hard work. We are facing resistance.'
- 'The workplace is made up of solid stuff; it's rigid and static.'
- 'To improve our workspace we would need to move office or have an upgrade.'
- 'It's impossible to predict how we will work in future, so how could we plan for that?'
- 'Mobile working or coworking are not going to be relevant to us.'

> ### 💡 Are you looking for a 'miracle vehicle'?
>
> When an organisation decides to change its workplace, the process they follow is often like this: (1) they list their wants and needs, (2) they get some plans organised, (3) they find the people to get it built, and (4) they celebrate the completion of the project and then turn their attention to other duties. Creating a new workplace is seen as a one-off job where the outcome is a physical space that is static in nature, meaning that what the space looks like at the end of construction is what it will look like for several years.
>
> This approach is not dissimilar to buying a new car and expecting it to serve all of our changing needs for the next twenty years. Nobody sane would buy a sports car with the expectation that it will fit a growing family, or buy a ute with the plan to keep it as a city car after moving from the country to the city. Most of us are used to the idea that we can sell and change our car as our lifestyle and priorities change. We don't expect our cars to be 'miracle vehicles' that will suit us for decades into the future. Why do we expect this of the office?
>
> And here is the good news: unlike with a car, we can change our workplace very easily and as often as we want to, without having to replace it – if we make the right decisions at the beginning.

Trying to create a space that works well for practically any situation is a daunting (or may I say, impossible?) task, putting enormous pressure on designers and decision makers to make the right choices and to minimise risks, and it usually shows in the outcome. Such a 'try hard' design risks turning out to be **too conservative**, a 'bland' space with features that have been proven to work in past circumstances, but that lacks new and innovative solutions. Alternatively, it may become **too alien**, with so many radical changes made at once that the space will disengage people.

Despite best efforts, these workplaces will soon become dated, because they hardly ever evolve.

What can go wrong

Here are some common design mistakes that prevent users from fully embracing change at work, and the consequences:

- Design teams often give little consideration to how well the changes to the workplace are aligned with the culture of the organisation, and how people will be affected. No matter how forward-looking the new workplace strategy is in theory, it won't deliver results unless people feel willing to use the space as intended.

- Workplaces often lack the flexibility and 'intelligence' to suit new ways of working. They may not support the adoption of new work styles, tools and technology. An inflexible environment also affects people's approach towards work, making them less proactive and creative. A workplace as set as concrete will set people's way of working into concrete.

- Design decisions made on paper often produce different results from what was planned. If the fitout is 'finished' by the time its doors are open, users lose their chance to make improvements to the space based on their experience of working in it (which is the best possible opportunity for gaining insights into optimising the workspace). Furthermore, this kind of environment sends the disempowering message: 'you only have one chance to make it right'.

- Workplaces that employ mobile workers function differently from 'standard' offices. Also, when they are in the office, mobile workers need different conditions to perform well from those who work there full-time. Where these issues are not addressed, mobile working may create more problems than benefits.

- Supporting collaborative work between different disciplines, industries and cultures, or between 'insiders' and 'outsiders' requires strategic design. Businesses that are not able to adopt collaborative work (or coworking) due to the limitations of their space risk being left behind.

The evolving workplace

Of course, we can also find plenty of great examples of workplaces that are agile enough to facilitate rapid change, both on an individual and an organisational level, but solid enough to offer a sense of stability to people along with a distinct character that is unique to the organisation.

These workspaces not only assist people in their journey of constantly improving the way they work, they also condition people to better deal with uncertainty and ambiguity. In today's economy this is an invaluable skill.

Change also brings a special energy into the way people see their work and life. Having something new in the space or doing something new creates momentum, anticipation, and a sense of freedom – all qualities that can skyrocket performance.

 What is the right amount of change?

We all have the natural desire to experience change in our life – to try out new things, learn new skills, visit different places and see the change of the seasons. Without change we would quickly get bored, and life would begin to seem purposeless.

We also need some stability. We want to be able to retreat to a place that is steady and safe, a familiar place that we can go to when we are exhausted from dealing with uncertainty and stretching ourselves. This can be a physical space, like our home or the spot under our favourite tree, or a non-physical space, like our own mind, or our relationships and friendships. (How important is familiarity in our lives? Just think about how disappointing it is when you go to a music concert and your favourite band only plays its brand new songs.)

In business this translates to innovation and execution: there are times for challenging how things are done, and times for building on existing resources and performing like a pro.

Good design helps create the right balance.

The three driving factors

To maximise your results when planning and implementing changes to the workplace, you need to consider the following three factors:

- Your people's relationship with change (see Strategy 1 below)

  Changes can't happen without the participation of people. Any improvements to the workplace will trigger some questions, and possibly some resistance. To ensure that the changes deliver results, you need to bring people on board, help them see the benefits of new ways of working, and make it easy for them to make the transition.

- Changes happening in the workplace (see Strategies 2-3 below)

  Good workplace design enables people to constantly evolve the way they work. The space needs to be able to evolve, as people and the organisation evolve. The design should never be seen as complete – just as your skills and business strategies are never complete – but should be as fluid as your approach is to dealing with any issues that come up at work.

- Changes happening beyond your workplace (see Strategies 4-5 below)

  The workplace should be able to respond to changes happening beyond the 'main office' and beyond the business (such as changes in your industry as well as other disciplines). It should become a functional part of the new ecosystem of workspaces, consisting of traditional offices, home offices, coworking places and third places.

Key design strategies

Key design strategies for creating a setting where people, the direction of the business and global trends are all fully aligned:

1. Bring your people on board
2. Create spaces that are easy to change
3. Test, evaluate and refine the design as you go
4. Consider people working remotely
5. Get ready for coworking

Adopting these strategies can be transformational. The environment will maximise people's ability to effectively respond to new opportunities, demands and challenges, and solve problems that previously seemed insoluble. They will be able to make the most out of any conditions, whether unprecedented opportunities or crises, and assist the business to progress in quantum leaps.

Strategy 1:
Bring your people on board

By now, you should have quite a few ideas for improving your workplace. But before jumping into action, it's important to think through how these changes will be received. Whether it's an office move or an upgrade, any change in the work environment will affect people in a variety of ways. They will need to adopt new work practices, and get used to working in a space that looks, feels and functions differently from what they are used to.

It's a common mistake to create a shiny new space packed with 'brilliant' innovative solutions and then to expect people to adopt new habits straight away. Even if the changes are well thought-through and are intended to benefit workers, the workers themselves may have a different perspective.

Many seemingly well-designed workplaces fail to function the way they were planned to because people don't receive sufficient support in getting accustomed to changes, nor any incentive to do so.

What will work best for your organisation?

Naturally, with different personalities and priorities, everyone responds to change differently. Some people thrive on it; they are constantly looking out for opportunities to experience new things, and if it was possible, they would jump into new experiences or rearrange their workspace every few days. Others prefer 'sameness'. These are the people who may stay in the same job for decades, and if it was possible, they would never move a thing in their office.

Just like individuals, organisations also have their own distinct approach towards change. Before any plan goes ahead for workplace design, it's worthwhile to take a look at your culture around change, and consider questions like:

- How is work in your business and in your industry changing?
- What changes do you need to implement in your business in order to remain competitive?
- What is the extent and type of change your people should be able to deal with or initiate?
- What sort of people do you really want to work with? What's their attitude towards change?

Being clear about these questions will help you not only to create a workplace that will work for your teams and your business in the long term, but also to identify the implementation strategies that will give you a smooth ride. Also, your workplace will attract people on a similar wavelength, and support a culture in which implementing change is a relatively straightforward process. Unfortunately, many businesses that see themselves as fast-changing and innovative are stuck in inflexible, static workplaces. No wonder their people are confused about what is expected from them, and have disagreements about how to implement changes.

Resistance to change

Resistance to change is a natural human response. While we all appreciate good news and seeing things evolve around us, we also need, to a greater or lesser extent, certainty and stability in our lives. Change involves facing the unknown, using time and energy to learn new skills and develop new habits, and letting go of things that might be precious to us.

You might also face **skepticism** when initiating changes, which is not surprising in an era when we are constantly sold on great ideas that are supposedly designed to make our lives easier and more enjoyable, but that often fail to live up to their promise.

When people are already exhausted from regular transformations, any new proposal that requires them to learn new skills or adapt their work patterns may be greeted with eye rolling, due to **change fatigue**. This is especially likely when people feel that the changes are imposed on them, and cannot see how they themselves will benefit.

Workers often tend to **'nest'**, putting their personal mark on and protecting their immediate work area. To some extent, this is natural behaviour and has some practical benefits. (For example, it improves wellbeing, helps people get mentally prepared to work, and helps them save time.) However, sometimes people become quite **territorial** and claim ownership over their work area. This is a common response to working in unpleasant conditions, especially in workplaces that do not offer people sufficient privacy, personal space and control. Paradoxically, the worse the conditions are, the more people resist change. In such environments, rolling out any changes that impose upon people's 'territory' can be especially challenging.

Pushing through vs getting buy-in

What happens when people are thrown into a new environment and are forced to make changes they don't want to make? They become frustrated and disengaged, or develop elaborate strategies to get around the new constraints and maintain their old habits in the new space wherever possible. In some cases, they may even choose to sabotage the changes or leave. Either way, the new design fails to achieve its objectives, and possibly causes more damage than good.

On the other hand, when people appreciate the proposed changes, they not only put up with them, but often take an active role in making the most out of them. It is therefore always worthwhile to ensure that people have buy-in to the changes you are planning to implement. Having clear, honest conversations with your people about why the changes are useful, educating them about how to use the new space, and involving them in decision making (discussed in Principle 5: Caring) are just a few strategies that can make the transition smooth and efficient.

Managing change through design

The design of the workplace can assist with this process, and provide opportunities for people to gradually adapt to change. Here are a few strategies:

- Ensure that the new space **can be used in different ways** – both the old way and the new way. For example, a large table could be initially used as a meeting or dining table, and then gradually transformed into a collaborative work area (by changing the activities, not the design). Or an enclosed meeting room could be transformed into a quiet room or project room.

- Provide a **point of stability** (some people call such place a 'nest', a 'base', or a 'home') – an inviting area that doesn't change much, so that when people need to take a break from change, they have a place they can go to find familiarity and a sense of feeling settled. This could be, for example, a library or a breakout space.

- Make the new ways of working **more attractive** than the old ways. Provide people with benefits they didn't have before, such as freedom of choice and/or a higher quality environment.

- Use fitout items that are **easy to manipulate**, such as movable furniture and sliding partitions. This will allow you to implement the changes in phases, but without dragging on with messy fitout works. (To learn about creating a flexible and adaptable environment see Strategy 2 below.) Here is an example:

> ## 💡 Try it out safely
>
> When the directors of Socom, an Australian PR company, asked me to develop a design concept for their new Melbourne office, they were interested in transitioning into a more flexible and collaborative way of working. But they were not sure about the best approach, and their team also had mixed opinions about how far to go with the changes. Some were enthusiastic about working around one large table like a family, others not so much.
>
> The initial floor layout had a lot in common with the old office, for example everyone had an allocated desk. But we also created a collaborative area, with a large table located in the most attractive part of the office, near the windows.
>
> The layout was designed to be easy to reconfigure – to reduce the number of allocated desks and to increase the size of the collaborative area – in anticipation that more and more people would choose to work in the collaborative area full time and become ready to give up their allocated desks. This solution gave everyone the chance to try out a new way of working 'safely', and to decide when they were ready to make a shift.

Let me make it clear that it's not always necessary, or even useful, to make changes in baby steps, and to avoid upsetting anyone at all costs. Here is an example:

Case study: Wealth Enhancers

(Part 2, continued from Principle 6: Engaging)

Previously we looked at how Wealth Enhancers, a nimble financial advisory practice with a youthful attitude, created an empowering office for its employees. In my conversation with co-founder Sarah Riegelhuth, she also gave me insights into the culture of change in her business, and how they use and constantly recreate their workplace:

> 'We're all about innovation, continually pushing the boundaries, seeing how we can become more productive, more efficient. If you're moving forward, all the time, there will be financial benefits.'

Wealth Enhancers has created a fast-paced environment with a culture of constant change. They don't view change as something that needs to be analysed and managed; their team anticipates and creates change all the time.

> 'Everyone's KPI is that they have to innovate something in the business every week.'

> 'When I was a child, I used to change my bedroom around every few months. When you do that, or you move house, you feel renewed, you have a sense of freshness. I get driven mad bad if I don't change things all the time. It's probably the reason why my business ended up this way.'

Sarah's team wanted to create an office that always feels new. They constantly change the space, setting up a lounge in one corner, then swapping the lounge furniture to little tables and chairs, adding more desks when more people come on board, and so on. Being a paperless practice gives them a lot of flexibility. They also change what's stuck up on the wall, adding things to track how they are travelling.

> 'They don't sit in the same place ever; they actually have to change. If I notice someone has been sitting in that corner, I come in early the next day and sit there to make sure that they change. We all do that to each other. I think by changing where you sit each day, or every couple of days, you never have that feeling of staleness.'

The whole team loves working this way. They are all on the same wavelength, being the sort of people who thrive on change.

> 'They're so happy, and they feel they're at home when they are working.'

> 'In our recruitment process we ask candidates how they feel about change. In the past, we have had employees who came along and couldn't cope with all this change; they moved on and found a job more suited to them. We're not saying our way is the right way, it's just how we are doing it.'

> 'You need to be drastic sometimes and just go into it in order to change a culture. I see a lot of people trying to move forward slowly

and meeting a lot of resistance. If you drag it over a six-month transition period, the whole time they are torn. Whereas, if you just go, "I'm taking this away from you, this is what you are doing from now", they might crumble for a little while, but when you ask them next week how they are going, generally they say, **"It's pretty good actually, I'm fine"**. They will get it, provided you've thought through why you're doing it. I never had anyone wanting to go back to the old way after two weeks.'

'That's how we approach change: "OK everyone, today is gone, tomorrow we'll start again." And it really works.'

Strategy 2:
Create spaces that are easy to change

A single office table for 125 employees

A New York-based internet advertising company recently implemented the most unusual interior design concept: a single office table capable of seating all of its employees. This desk with laser-cut structural elements and a jointless glossy white table top (made from resin, a material like a surfboard top) looks spectacular, as it undulates throughout the office and slopes upwards at some points, forming the roof of semi-enclosed meeting and social spaces underneath. The design – giving a flowing atmosphere to the workplace – received international attention.

This table might do great service in promoting collaboration and in attracting young talent excited by the free-thinking, courageous culture of this office which clearly manifests in the design. But to be the devil's advocate, my concern is for the total lack of flexibility: How will the space work for them in a few years' time? What will they do when they need, for example, more workshop space and less desk space, or when they need to do more quiet work? How will they keep the space fresh and energising once the initial high wears off?

> Some argue that in certain organisations, creating a space that reflects the brand and culture is more important than long-lasting functionality. However, I don't believe we need to settle for such a trade-off. For me, the most inspiring part to the design process is to find innovative solutions that achieve it all.

There's no such thing as a 'finished workplace'. After building works are complete, furniture is installed and the space is open, there should still be opportunities to adapt the design to immediate and future changes, including unforeseeable conditions.

It should be possible to alter some elements of the workplace regularly – for example, to change the furniture layout of a meeting room between different types of meetings. And the workplace should also support long-term change, allowing workers, for example, to create new types of work areas and to install new technology, all without causing major disruption to operations or having to invest a fortune.

'Chameleon' spaces

Flexible, multifunctional spaces offer workers the opportunity to change their environment – or the way they use it – at will.[1]

Remember the 'twenty second rule' (from Principle 3: Productive)? When people are able to adapt the space to their needs in less than twenty seconds, it's more likely that they will make the effort.

---

[1] This requires a radically new approach to interior design. Traditionally, the main role of workplace designers has been to develop a functional floor layout. However, to create a highly flexible environment, more attention needs to be given to furniture types and interior systems. When most things can move, the traditional floor plan becomes meaningless, as it can only show one possible configuration.

Design suggestions

For changing **the layout and the use** of the space:

- Install mobile partitions for dividing work areas (e.g. operable walls, sliding doors, curtains and screens).

- Provide furniture and props that are easy to move around (e.g. desks, cabinets and whiteboards on wheels), and that are easy to store (e.g. stackable chairs and flip-top tables).

- Provide furniture that is adjustable for different activities (e.g. desks with adjustable height that can be used as sitting or standing desks), or that can be used in different combinations (e.g. small desks that can be used individually or pushed together to form larger tables).

- Provide versatile and multi-functional building elements and props that can be used in several different ways (e.g. 'walls' that can be used as partitions or whiteboards or display boards; 'building blocks' that can be used as seats or tables or partitions). The case study about Stanford d.school, under Strategy 5, includes some great examples.

For changing **the quality and ambience** of the space:

- Install lamps that can emit light in different colours, so that the colour and ambience of the space can be changed with a switch.

- Install walls that can be either see-through or non-see-through (e.g. glass partitions in combination with curtains or blinds), instead of building solid walls.

- Have some interesting items available that can be quickly brought out of storage to bring new life into the space (e.g. artefacts, cushions and toys).

- Use wall displays that are easy to update (e.g. magnetic boards or electronic screens).

Benefits of regular change

Creating a dynamically changing work environment has many benefits beyond supporting new activities and work styles.

By creating flexible multipurpose work areas, you **can use the space more efficiently**; you can establish a diverse environment that meets your functional requirements on a smaller floor area than what you would need for achieving the same functionality through static design.

When we move into a brand new workplace, we might feel highly inspired and energised on day one, but only mildly so on day one hundred and one if nothing changes in the meantime, as the impact fades over time. Regular changes **keep the space new and fresh**.

In a changing environment we are less likely to sink into a stale routine and get too set in our ways. By facing new conditions every few days, we are encouraged to constantly **think about how we could work better**, and to try out new strategies.

An environment where it's easy to make changes **empowers us to be proactive**, and to adapt the space to our needs. The features built into the design suggest to us what changes we are allowed to make. (However, this message needs to be consistent with the culture of the organisation. Creating a highly flexible environment without encouraging people to move things around can only confuse them.)

Spaces that are in constant motion usually feel somewhat unfinished. While this may not sound very appealing at first, such spaces in fact provide a **great setting for creative work**. In an 'unfinished' environment we are more likely to take risks and experiment with untested ideas, while in finished spaces we usually gravitate towards 'safe' solutions.

💡 An 'unfinished' space

Swinburne Design Factory (Melbourne, Prahran Campus[2]) has been designed to serve as a platform for students and researchers to do innovative work in interdisciplinary teams. They are there to solve real-life problems, and while doing this, to also experience new ways of learning and working, and to get better at what they do.

Swinburne Design Factory is a refurbished, single open space in a university building, with a striking visual appeal. Most of the walls and features are bright fluorescent green. Diagonally positioned sliding walls with whiteboard surfaces separate the work areas of different groups, while providing the means for capturing ideas. There are no isolated desks; the environment tells you that you are there to work with others. And the whole room looks somewhat messy and unfinished.

Päivi Oinonen (SDF Coach) and Dr Agustin Chevez (Lecturer and Researcher in Interior Design) say that the space was intentionally designed to feel unfinished. They explained that when a space is polished and feels finished, it distances people and hinders their creativity. They not only feel that they cannot create mess, which is part of the creative process, but it also gives them the sense that it is not acceptable to have their projects or ideas unfinished. So they are less likely to venture into unexplored directions, take risks and experiment.

On the other hand, in an unpolished space students can become more engaged with their projects, feel liberated to move things, test things out that may not work, and also use humour – which, by the way, also helps them to do what they do better.

The design of this new collaborative space took all of this into consideration, and has turned out to be really successful: it allows students to work in a way they couldn't work elsewhere, and helps them produce outstanding results.

---

2 Since the time of writing this book, Swinburne Design Factory has moved into a new location (Hawthorn Campus). The design team faced the challenge of creating a similar, unrefined aesthetic in a brand new, high quality building, but they certainly had the creative resources to tackle this issue!

Too much flexibility

Flexible design features, while offering great benefits, might also have drawbacks:

- Many of the flexible design solutions (e.g. adjustable furniture, sliding or operable walls) **come at a premium**. Creating an overly flexible design that is hardly ever used to its capacity is a waste of money.

- Working in a space that is 'too flexible' can be **exhausting and disorienting**. We all need balance between change and stability. In a workplace where everything is in motion, it can be very challenging to establish a productive work routine.

- Too many options may **limit people's creativity**. In some circumstances, dealing with constraints can provide a great boost to creative thinking, as shown by research.

You may need to provide **training and clear guidelines** about how to use the space, and what is acceptable. Without set rules, the use of shared work areas might become a source of friction.

Future-proofing the workplace

There are construction techniques that make it possible to undertake major transformations to office interiors – for example, changing the room layout or upgrading the building services – without causing too much disruption, damage or waste. These include modular partitions and joinery units, modular flooring and ceiling systems (such as carpet tiles and grid ceilings)[3], lighting and air-conditioning systems with plug-in features, and prefabricated building elements such as meeting rooms.

By installing such building systems, you ensure that in future upgrades, the construction works can be completed within a shorter timeframe, and at a relatively low cost.

---

3   Unfortunately, many of these systems have a rather institutional look, but a good designer should be able to find a solution that is both functional and appealing.

Strategy 3:
Test, evaluate and refine the design as you go

'Uncertainty guaranteed'

You may have the most diligent approach to planning your workplace – doing in-depth research, exploring many possible scenarios, and learning about workplace design from the best sources (which is obviously the case ☺). Unfortunately, none of these guarantee that the new workplace will become a perfect fit for your business. You're working with humans, after all. And given that there are no workplaces out there that do exactly what you do – employ the same people, have the same culture, provide the same services – it is difficult to find workplace models to copy.

So how do you know which design solutions will help your people excel? Creating a flexible design will give your people the opportunity to fine-tune the workspace once it's already in use, but the core design concept of the space will need to be right from the start. Chances are that the only way to find out what works for your teams is through trying out your design ideas experimentally first, before implementing them in a more permanent format.

In the usual rush of completing a workplace, testing out design concepts might seem like a waste of time, money and effort. (And if it's not done thoughtfully, it probably is.) But how much more wasteful is it to build a workplace that turns out to be the wrong fit, hindering work rather than supporting it? Testing out new workplace solutions and refining the design based on the learnings takes the guesswork out of the design process, provides valuable experience for all involved, and most importantly, leads to a better workplace than just making educated guesses. (And after all, this process is not that different from developing a new product or service in a business, is it?)

Here are four ways of doing this:

1. Testing a design concept before an office move

Before moving into a new workplace, consider testing out new design concepts (e.g. collaborative spaces, quiet rooms, hot-desking) in your existing space. This also provides opportunities for space users to provide feedback, and to get accustomed to the changes that will be imposed by the office move. An example:

> I once worked with a land development consultancy with a staff of around 30. When I met the managers, they were reviewing the changing work dynamics of the business, and were planning to do a light upgrade of their office to support a more collaborative way of working. Since the company was going to move into a new building the following year, they saw the upgrade as an opportunity to test out how a new semi-open informal meeting space would work for them, how workers would cope with a smaller desk space, and how fewer partitions and a new floor layout would impact on acoustic issues. This experience yielded useful insights which fed into the design of the new building.

2. Upgrading only part of the space

Before upgrading a workplace (or creating a new space to move into), you may want to implement the proposed changes only in part of the space to start with. This strategy, beyond giving you insights into how the new solution works, can also make the transition smoother; it enables 'early adopters' to jump into a new way of working immediately while giving skeptics time to see the results before they get fully involved. An example:

> In Principle 2: Smart we looked at how Arup, a global engineering firm, experimented with Activitiy-Based Working in one of their offices. Here is a quick recap:
>
> Until late 2012, Arup had its Melbourne group located in two separate buildings, making interaction between departments difficult. Testing out Activity-Based Work in the smaller office space for a six-month period – with voluntary participation

> – allowed management to assess the success of the venture at low risk, and to work out the problems before moving everyone into one large office and adopting Activity-Based Work throughout. This experience made the transition easier for all, and helped tailor the new space to better support productive work.

3. Prototyping and temporary fitout

It's possible to build a prototype interior out of crafting materials such as paper, cardboard, foam, fabric and wire. The space 'prototype' doesn't need to look expensive and be fully functional to help with the design. Mock-up building elements are useful for creating the settings for role-playing exercises at design workshops, but some may also be suitable for creating a real, functional office space.

'Temporary' furniture and building elements, while they are not suitable for all businesses, often have a certain charm, and can create a playful yet grounded atmosphere. An example:

> As mentioned earlier, Huddle, a service design company, once invited me to help them design their new Sydney premises, an innovation facility where Australia's service organisations (including themselves) could develop services for their customers. They loved the design I prepared for the interiors, meeting the brief. But since it was an untested concept, they weren't sure who the people using the space would be, and how the plan would work out. So before implementing the full plan in detail, they decided to create a temporary fitout – using cardboard, labels and sticky tape for defining the space – to test out the design in practice. This was a natural progression for them; prototyping services for clients was part of their business. They were going to upgrade the design in three stages over a period of six months, building on the experience of how the temporary fitout worked. Already early on, the plans significantly changed, as the exercise revealed a lot about which of their ideas were viable and which weren't. However, they were able to learn about their 'mistakes' without getting locked into major investments.

4. Testing and adapting

The ultimate in experiential design is bringing all these strategies together, and giving the design process a life of its own – in other words, seeing design more as a culture, and less as a project with a deadline. In this process, the different phases of design follow each other in cycles – identifying areas for improvement, designing solutions, implementing them, and testing them – without a clear end point. The 'outcome' is a constantly evolving space which not only helps people work better in any circumstances, but also teaches them a powerful approach to problem solving.

Here is an example, one of my favourite design projects:

A non-traditional workplace: Stanford d.school

Stanford d.school is an educational institute that teaches 'design thinking', a step-by-step process for producing creative solutions to loosely defined problems. The school's mission is to prepare its students to tackle today's complex innovation challenges, giving them not only the skills, but also the outlook they need to succeed.

The design process

The school's new home is a pioneering example of optimising a space for enhanced teamwork and problem solving. The design of the space has been refined through six years of exploration and testing. Every single part of the space – every wall, screen, desk, seat, cabinet, booth and gadget – has been developed to serve the project's grand vision: creating the most conducive environment for collaboration, learning and innovation.

Having their own project served as an opportunity for the school to practise what it teaches in the context of building design. The design process was the application of 'design thinking', which involves: gathering data, prototyping, identifying what works, and starting it all over again until the best solution is found. So d.school is not only a facility for the rapid prototyping of ideas, but is itself a prototype. It constantly evolves as the needs of students and faculty change, and as they learn more about how to engage with the space.

Design philosophy

The main purpose of the facility is not to create beautiful objects, but to solve 'big, hairy, audacious problems'. Accordingly, the aesthetics of the space is not what you might find in design magazines. 'The space isn't precious,' says d.school founder David Kelley. 'The whole culture of the place says "we're looking for better ideas," not "keep your feet off the furniture."'

The space, which is designed to be reworked daily or even hourly, sends an important message to students: their work and ideas are not the end point, but the start of something new. It also reminds them that beyond being mindful of the process and the team, engaging with the environment is also a critical aspect of successful work.

The space

The spaces at d.school can be used in a huge variety of ways; everything can be moved and rearranged. Sliding partitions, furniture on wheels, and pushed-together tables make it possible to reconfigure the space at will.

Most items are designed to serve multiple purposes. Big foam cubes and timber boxes can be used as seats or footrests, or as building blocks for creating makeshift walls and work surfaces. Each area suggests ways that the space could be used, but there is plenty of opportunity for improvisation. Nothing resembles traditional, standardised university classrooms.

An abundance of surfaces are provided to help capture and showcase unrefined ideas. The 'White Room', for example, has all walls and floor covered with whiteboard paint; in this room, students' scribbles are the only 'decoration'. Walls covered in sticky notes and sketches of early ideas – while leaving a messy sight – contribute to an exchange of ideas, and help students learn from each other.

What we can learn

Optimising each temporary space became a valuable learning experience about how the place itself can drive the culture of innovation and promote behaviours critical to problem solving such as empathy and experimentation. Subsequently, d.school has been attracting attention not only from other educational institutes, but also corporations ready to explore new ways of using their space.

While d.school's approach may be a bit too radical for many organisations, there's plenty we can learn from it to apply in more traditional settings. These are just a few ideas:

- Create a flexible design which enables your team to change their environment, and encourage them to experiment with different ways of configuring the space to find out what works best.

- Encourage your people to show their work in progress. Create areas where they can display their ideas in a large format so that others can see it and contribute.

- Where creative activities happen, keep the space informal and non-precious (including the sketches and artefacts used for communicating ideas).

- Observe the behaviour of your people. Take note of what works and what doesn't, and make changes as needed.

Strategy 4:
Consider people working remotely

In our increasingly mobile world, location is no longer an obstacle to forming partnerships and to delivering information-based services. We can *almost* as easily communicate and collaborate with team members from other continents as we do with people in the same room.

The advancement of communication technology has removed most barriers to mobile working. A myriad of technological advances allow our experience of web-based communication to be free of friction, and as close to face-to-face meetings as possible.

A new way of working is emerging, where team members do not commute to a central workplace every day (or ever), but work from home, public places such as coffee shops and libraries, or other workplaces. This way of working is called many things, including: teleworking, remote working, mobile working, anywhere working, workshifting, telecommuting, and alternative workplace arrangement. (Did I miss something out?) More and more organisations and workers are adopting this new way of working, full time or part time.

Teleworking is fundamentally changing the way business is done, and along the way also changing the perceptions of what's considered a professional work setting. For example, not so long ago, business meetings were 'supposed' to be held in formal environments such as glossy meeting rooms. But this has loosened up a lot recently, and today meetings can happen virtually anywhere.

Especially with new generations reaching the workforce, there is an increasing pressure on business owners to adopt flexible work arrangements. A 2014 Cisco study that surveyed over 2,900 professionals in 15 countries has revealed some interesting findings: 26% of Gen X and 29% of Gen Y professionals said, 'Yes, I would be willing to accept a pay cut in return for greater work flexibility'.

Benefits

Teleworking presents enormous opportunities for all involved: the business, the workers, the customers and the planet – **when implemented well**.[4] Creating a workplace that is ready to support mobile working will enable your business to enjoy the following benefits:

- Teleworkers (typically) work faster and more effectively. This is partly due to their ability to avoid interruptions and to work at the time of the day when they are most productive. Teleworkers also usually have higher spirits, improved attitude towards work, and the empowering feeling of being trusted by their managers. (According

---

[4] While teleworking is a growing trend, it's a highly debated topic. Teleworking is not for everyone – neither people nor businesses. Even those organisations that are well-suited to it may face challenges. Adopting an alternative workplace program requires thorough preparation and careful implementation; you can't just tell people, 'off you go!'. Companies need to offer education and support to people to help them overcome ingrained habits and practical hurdles as they adjust to their new work arrangements. This shift needs to take place on many levels: communication and data management systems may need to be upgraded, and in addition, leaders will need to manage cultural change, and most importantly, shift from the practice of monitoring people's working time to assessing their performance. This may require setting new performance targets.

to the Telework Research Network, workers' productivity increases by 27% on days when they are working remotely. Other studies show even higher figures for work practices where teleworking is combined with cutting-edge communication technology.)

- Teleworking reduces real-estate and commuting costs, enables the business to outsource more efficiently, and reduces the environmental impact of business activities.

- It can increase customer satisfaction, since customers prefer to deal with workers who have a positive attitude and the habit of quickly responding to their needs; teleworkers are more likely to be these sorts of people.

- Teleworking also brings new players into the game of business, experts who in the past didn't have the chance to participate. Furthermore, it brings knowledge exchange and collaboration to a whole new level, enabling people from different industries and locations to work together in a way that would have been unimaginable before the mobile era. This creates the most fertile ground for innovation.

The changing function of the workplace

You may wonder: how can the workplace support work that is done elsewhere? How does the 'absence' of people influence the design?

Workplaces that employ mobile workers (should!) function very differently from offices where everyone is present full time. For example, the traditional workplace needs to cater for all individual and team activities that ever need to be done at work. On the other hand, in a workplace where much of the work is done remotely, the types and number of activities that the space needs to support are naturally different.

Workplaces that support mobile working typically have fewer workstations dedicated to individual work than the number of people employed, and often adopt Activity-Based Work (see Principle 2: Smart). On the other hand, they have more facilities for collaborative work, workshops, events and experiential work, since participating in these activities is among the main reasons why mobile workers come to the office.

To know exactly what sort of environment you need to create to facilitate teleworking, take the time to consider the following questions:

- What activities are (or should be) done remotely? For what reasons?
- What activities are (or should be) done in the workplace? For what reasons?
- What are mobile workers' challenges? What are their mental and emotional needs?
- What do mobile workers come to the office for?

The challenges of teleworking

Having choices about where (and when) to work is certainly an attractive option for many people. It not only offers the promise of an improved lifestyle, but also makes it possible to work in greater comfort, and with less stress. However, the 'ultimate dream' of a virtual workplace – which is often portrayed as a peaceful home office, a beautiful hilltop, a tropical beach or a grassy meadow – where work is always productive and easy, is a heavily distorted version of reality.

Working from home, away from the team, has many traps that can take a toll on our productivity and wellbeing if we jump into it unprepared, or if the workplace is not set up for complementing the work we do from remote locations. It takes effort to remain disciplined, focused and accountable. It's very easy to fall into bad habits or get distracted or procrastinate. Also, it's a common mistake to blur the boundaries between work and home demands, not achieving much in either of them, while getting exhausted by living and working without a routine.[5]

Feelings of isolation are another common problem. While it's easy to communicate via technology (some of which allows us to engage many of our senses and convey emotions), this cannot replace the experience of

---

5   Blurring boundaries between work-life and home-life is a natural phenomenon today, especially among younger generations. According to a survey by Microsoft and Ipsos, 39% of Australian workers (in the age group of 18-35) are happy to be contacted 24/7; 53% play or do personal tasks at work; and 44% do work activities after the normal working hours at home. However, maintaining productivity when our normal working structure is taken away is a skill most of us need to develop.

face-to-face meetings. A lack of regular social interaction can drain our energy and inspiration, and diminish our social skills as well as our professional skills, which is not the point at all.

What teleworkers seek in the workplace is what the home environment cannot offer them:

- Being in an environment that boosts their energy and motivation
- Support in maintaining a productive work routine
- Opportunities for social interaction and face-to-face collaborative work
- Being around people who are on the same wavelength and share a common purpose
- Being in a space where they are able to fully immerse themselves in their work

Educating people about working from 'home'

The quality of teleworkers' 'virtual office' is also very important; their choices about where and how to work naturally have a great influence on their experience of work and on their results.

To make the most of remote working, people need to learn some 'virtual office' tips:

- For home-based work, allocate a space or room dedicated to work only. Using the same space for work as well as leisure or home activities will diminish your performance and wellbeing. You need clear boundaries for having head space for work, and head space for non-work.
- Choose your spot wisely. Explore what sorts of spaces support you best in various tasks. There are many different places you can choose to work from: your home office, third places such as cafés and libraries, and coworking places (discussed in the next section). And even within these spaces, be mindful about where you sit (or stand!).

- Understand when it is the right time to go to the workplace. Get into the habit of scheduling 'office time' (for example, time for collaborative and social activities); set boundaries and stick to them.

Strategy 5:
Get ready for coworking

Coworking is a style of work in which independent professionals and/or organisations share the same workplace. The coworking movement started when some bright sparks set up collaborative workplaces for young independent freelancers to share. The first dedicated coworking space in the world only opened in 2006 (Citizen Space in San Francisco), and in Australia in 2011 (Hub Melbourne).

According to the Global Coworking Census, conducted by Deskwanted, in February 2013 there were 2,948 shared coworking spaces in 80 countries around the globe, including 65 in Australia. This reveals an 89% rise in the number of collaborative workspaces in the world over the previous twelve months, and an increase of over 300% since 2010. It appears that this number will grow steadily as more and more workers and business leaders discover the benefits of coworking.

During its short history, this style of working has already expanded beyond dedicated coworking places. It has been adopted in a wide variety of settings, and has become attractive for people from different industries, with different work arrangements, and across all generations. Today, more and more organisations are sharing their own space with coworkers, who might be clients, project team members, or independent workers. At the same time, many businesses are encouraging their staff to spend some of their working time in collaborative workplaces, knowing that they will come back with fresh ideas, knowledge and opportunities.

New standards of workplace quality

The idea of coworking emerged as a promising response to the challenges entrepreneurs and businesses had been facing in the changing landscape of work. Freelancers and mobile workers were seeking opportunities to get out of the house, be around passionate people and share resources and knowledge with each other. Companies became aware that the key to their growth was innovation. They wanted to create exceptional performance gains, and found that the answer to this problem lay in networking, collaboration and education across disciplines. Organisations found that fluctuations in staff numbers were inevitable, and were searching for a solution to better utilise their space.

Coworking has been proven to provide unprecedented benefits, including:

- **Community:** Bringing passionate people together who are deeply committed to their own performance and success at work
- **Empowerment:** Promoting a culture of sharing and openness; encouraging people to be proactive and follow what they believe in
- **Attractiveness:** Attracting talent by creating casual, social, flexible environments that operate without traditional hierarchies
- **Motivation:** Helping people stay motivated (it's uplifting to mix with people who are there by choice, and there is always someone around having a great day)
- **Efficiency:** Supporting the efficient use of space and resources, by optimising occupancy of spaces
- **Productivity:** Helping people be more productive and waste less time than in standard offices (coworkers tend to hold each other to higher standards, and are happy to help each other out)
- **Collaboration:** Promoting interaction and teamwork, and providing opportunities for testing ideas and building relationships across disciplines
- **Innovation:** Assisting individuals and teams to generate creative solutions to complex problems
- **Education:** Teaching people new skills and work practices
- **Connections:** Supporting the formulation of business partnerships and alliances

> **Who would have thought ...**
>
> The Indy Hall in Philadelphia is one of the world's most respected coworking communities. At the Coworking Conference Australia 2013, Alex Hillman, cofounder, has repeated the astounded comment he heard from a member: **'I had no idea that work could be done that well.'**

Objectives to address

The design of a collaborative workspace needs to address a set of unique objectives:

- Coworkers can have vastly **diverse work styles**, needs and cultures. The design needs to support and appeal to everyone using the space, and help minimise conflicts that may arise due to these differences.

- It can be hard to predict what sort of people will use the space. The design needs to be either very flexible, or universal enough to serve all potential users, even though **we don't yet know who they are**.

- Several organisations with different brands might be sharing the space. Still, in order to provide a home for them all, it needs to have a **distinct character**, and reflect the shared purpose and values of the users. Creating a bland space without a personality with the intention of pleasing everyone will probably end up pleasing no-one.

- **Rapid growth** in the number of users is not uncommon in collaborative workplaces. The space needs to be able to accommodate this growth.

- Large numbers of people may walk in and out of the space each day, and users can change quickly. The design needs to ensure that people's data and belongings are **safe and secure**, while maintaining the casual nature of the space.

- When people adopt coworking or join a coworking space, often leaving their corporate background behind, they go through a **cultural transition**. It can take months to adapt to the new culture, and the space needs to assist with this transition.

- Most coworking organisations have a flat structure, which can make decision making quite a challenge. There needs to be a solid strategy for **decision making** during design.

Design strategies

Learning from successful examples

There is no shortage of successful coworking spaces we can learn from about effective design. These can serve as great references even for more traditional workplaces, since all spaces are at a basic level about one thing: maximising human potential.

While coworking spaces are refreshingly diverse, they have many common attributes. They are:

- Authentic, real, comfortable and welcoming (you rarely see ceiling tiles, carpet tiles or institutional-looking workstations)
- Diversified, interesting and fun to be in
- Supporting intense activity and dynamic teamwork
- Making it easy for people to build connections and difficult to work in isolation
- Providing access to a range of technologies
- Enabling people to organise the space to suit their needs

(The design strategies for achieving these qualities have been discussed in previous chapters.)

Codesign

Codesign is a collaborative process where the design is largely developed by the users. Design professionals are still involved, but their role is primarily to facilitate this process and to provide expert advice and guidance to the team, rather than to dictate a plan cooked up behind closed doors.

The vast majority of coworking spaces are designed using this approach. Codesign not only engages the users in the process and uncovers their needs, but it also capitalises on their experiences and insights. At the same time, it builds on the designers' knowledge and skills. Interiors resulting from this collaboration are usually both well-planned and engaging.

The key to the success of this process is to know when to leave decisions to the community, and when to take the lead.

Case study: Hub Melbourne

Hub Melbourne is Melbourne's first dedicated coworking space, part of the world's first global network of coworking organisations, 'The HUB'. It is located in the iconic Donkey Wheel House, a 120-year-old building of historical significance.

Hub Melbourne was launched in early 2011 to bring together a diverse community that drives innovation through collaboration. The founders' goal was to create an environment which provides the best resources for its independent members to tackle complex challenges and excel in business.

Less than a year after its opening, the space needed to be redesigned and extended[6] due to the rapid expansion of the Hub's membership, and it is now a highly popular, vibrant coworking space which fully lives up to its name.

Design objectives

Brad Krauskopf, CEO and founder of Hub Melbourne, told me about the creation of the space, and its role in the life of the community.

> 'We don't look at the place as a cost centre; we think of is as a value generator. At the Hub we're trying to capitalise connections across sectors, disciplines and generations, and a tool that we use in order to create those connections is this space.'

---

6 Since my interview with Brad, a second extension has been completed, carrying through the design principles that made the first extension successful.

The space needed to be welcoming to a wide range of sectors, including people from banks, universities, government bodies and community organisations, as well as small businesses and freelancers (most of whom are working there by choice). It also needed to be authentic and to foster trust between people.

All these needed to be achieved in a very intense environment used by hundreds of members, more or less round the clock. The fact that the building is heritage listed so no walls could be built, and that the budget was very small, further added to the challenges.

Design solutions

These challenges, which couldn't have been solved by conventional design methods, called for unique solutions, and led to an exceptionally flexible, dynamic and engaging work environment.

The focus of the design was not about deciding where the walls and workstations should go, but about creating a system that enables maximum flexibility while maintaining a distinct character.

Most furniture is on wheels, so the space can be easily reconfigured or transformed into an event space. Making things easy to move around is not only functional, but also gives people permission to adapt the space to their needs – the design itself tells them what is it that they can or cannot do. 'Hubbers' believe that it takes about six months before the design settles, and it's never completely finished, since moving things around is the nature of work.

The space is airy and light-filled, with plenty of indoor plants, playful decoration, meaningful messages, and a mix of office, domestic style and outdoor furniture. The kitchen is a main centrepiece; members go there for considered conversations and to form relationships, not just to get a coffee. The library and the 'vault' provide space for quiet activities and yoga sessions.

The physical space complements very well the technology used by the members, such as Yammer, the Hub's own social media channel. While members typically go online to share quick ideas, they go to one of the various types of meeting spaces to catch up in person.

Results and feedback

When you enter the space, even for the first time, you immediately feel a certain buzz – the energy of a productive, collaborative hub. The space has a distinct character, resonating with the community it attracts, because everything there has been designed to support people's connection with each other and to remind them of their shared values and purpose.

> 'It's an expansive environment, expressing the message that "things are possible here". The whiteboards are big whiteboards, and they are everywhere. The roof is like 30 foot high and there's a tree painted here. There's an outdoor area over there that's indoor. We made statements, that this is what's possible when you're in a heritage listed building, where you "can't do anything".'

At the Hub, you often hear stories about connections which created business for somebody or solved a big challenge. The founders see this as an excellent measure of success.

Since the Hub's first extension, the Hub Melbourne membership has significantly diversified; they have started to attract people from a wider range of industries and business types. Today, entrepreneurs, academics, non-profit organisations and corporate employees are happily working side-by-side, or rather, in collaboration.

Design process

The design was the collaborative effort of the community, expert advisors, and architects at Hassell[7], an international design practice.

 100 members making decisions?

> The space was designed in two stages, through codesign. Brad explains what he has learnt from these experiences, especially about effective decision making:

---

7 At the time of the upgrade, it was still an unusual situation for a leading architectural firm to be involved in codesign with an entrepreneur community. However, architects at Hassell were really interested in coworking and the future of work, and were prepared to adapt their work style to suit this new arrangement.

'Learning from past experience, we were able to work out what the meaningful opportunities were to get input from the community, and when it wasn't really effective. Last time we wouldn't even pick a chair without leaving it to the members to find consensus about it. That was incredibly expensive, took a huge amount of time, and at the end of the day it didn't produce commercially sustainable results.'

'In round two, we provided key points along the design process for our members to provide input. At the very start, they were part of the formulation of the brief; we had an open place-making process in which we discussed what we needed for our business model to work. This brief then went to the architect. Later we had three other key events where members fed in.'

'We also provided opportunity for expert input from our membership. I had one-on-one meetings with people who had genuine experience to offer.'

'Don't ask 100 members for an expert opinion, when only two of them are experts. Ask 100 members a general question: "What do we want to achieve?", and then ask a couple of experts for their opinion. That worked. That was a lot more cost-effective, and ultimately, we've got a result where people are connected to the space, and it's a sustainable model.'

The future of the Hub

The Hub has been expanding to other cities in Australia, learning from the experiences of creating Hub Melbourne. Brad has a grand vision for the Hub in Australia:

'At the moment we are building a trusting community with more talent under the one roof than any organisation could ever hope to employ. In the future we will actually act as a collaborative agency, but without the hierarchy and bureaucracy of traditional structures. This will hopefully make us incredibly agile, and incredibly resourced to tackle wicked problems and awesome opportunities.'

Putting things into practice

❓ Questions to consider

- What industry-wide trends are influencing the way your business operates?
- What future challenges and opportunities do you anticipate?
- What needs to change in your business so that it can continue to flourish?
- What will work look like in your organisation in, say, three or in ten years' time?
- How do you and your people feel about the future? What are your concerns? What are you excited about?
- What is your organisation's culture like towards change?
- What is your ideal team member's attitude towards change? How adaptable are they?
- Which attributes of your workplace can you not decide about yet?
- What level of flexibility would best support work in your organisation?
- How much effort are your team members willing to put into setting up the space for their needs on a daily basis?
- What opportunities do you have to test and experiment with different design options, either in your current workplace or in the new one?
- Do any of your team members work remotely (or are they likely to in future)?
- If yes, where do they work from? What are their needs and challenges? What do they come to the office for?

- Would you like to be able to invite clients and external team members to work with you in your workplace?
- What places and facilities outside the workplace could become extensions of your work environment?

PUTTING THE PIECES TOGETHER

By now you'll be familiar with a range of design solutions that could elevate the performance of your people and your business. But there are so many options – how can you be sure which ones will work best for you?

Working like an orchestra

As you might have already realised, the seven principles and associated design strategies discussed in this book are all closely interlinked. (I've grouped the strategies into those seven principles only for the purpose of clarity.) A single strategy can benefit many different areas of the business simultaneously, and at the same time, the different strategies and principles can work together towards the same goal. So when applied together skillfully, the different strategies can enhance each other's power, like instruments in an orchestra.

For example, we've looked at how an 'Engaging' workspace supports the formation of trusting relationships. Actually, the other principles also contribute to this goal in some ways. A 'Visionary' space invites people to focus on their common ground and a shared purpose, helping them connect. A 'Smart' space makes it easier for them to form groups and to communicate. A 'Diversified' space highlights the value in people's differences and thus promotes empathy and respect. A 'Caring' space inspires people to better care about each other. And so on.

As another example, let's look at your clients' experience. A 'Visionary' space will strengthen your client's confidence in your brand and your offer. A 'Productive' space will support an efficient and timely delivery of your services. A 'Diversified' space will assist your team to develop a customised, unique solution for them. Your clients will enjoy meeting with your team more in a 'Caring' space. Your team members will work with more passion and enthusiasm in an 'Engaging' environment, and will deal with your clients in the same spirit.

Give and take

At times you will need to navigate between conflicting interests and make sensible trade-offs, since a design solution that positively influences one aspect of performance may have adverse consequences on another. For instance, an open and transparent workspace is beneficial for collaboration and trust, but can create distractions and make it difficult for people to find privacy. An Activity-Based Workspace offers people freedom and choice, but at the same time, working there can be disorienting and exhausting. What works as a solution for one person might be a problem for another. For example, extroverts thrive in dynamic social environments where introverts tend to struggle.

To find the right combination of design solutions, you will need to understand the benefits and the costs of the different options, and balance pros and cons. Sometimes you need to be creative about finding the best solution.

Constraints should not stop you

It is inevitable that your workplace design project will have constraints; every project does. But there are also always many opportunities – some of which might not be immediately apparent – and you can always enhance the quality of your workspace by making the most of these.

Sometimes small changes can have substantial results. Arup's case study (discussed in Chapter 2: Smart) is proof that you can transform your workspace even without moving desks, just by using the space more smartly. Many spectacularly successful workspaces have been established in old refurbished buildings that imposed major design constraints, such as regulations prohibiting building new walls or changing existing ones.

You have many resources

You can count on many different types of information sources to help you make well-informed, effective decisions. I often see design professionals throwing their arms up in the air saying, 'We don't have enough evidence', which is clearly not the case. You just need to know where to look and how to combine the different pieces of information to create a complete picture.

The power and limitation of science

Psychology, place science, biophilia and anthropology are just a few of the different scientific fields that can provide us with valuable insights. A number of institutes all over the world specialise in researching the influence of the physical environment on human psyche and behaviour, and work on spreading the message.

Evidence-Based Design – the method of using credible scientific evidence to create buildings that support specific human and organisational outcomes – has been successfully practised for decades, especially in the design of healthcare facilities, and also, to some extent, educational buildings. In these types of buildings, measuring performance outcomes (whether health recovery rates or maths test results) is relatively straightforward and also common practice, and so an abundance of data is available for scientists to analyse. The fruit of their efforts is a solid and ever-growing knowledge base of effective design solutions designers can draw on to create better facilities.

On the other hand, what science knows about high-performance workspaces is more patchy. Some of the most important aspects of work performance, such as trust or innovative thinking, are difficult to quantify. Furthermore, business cannot take place in laboratory conditions; when the workplace changes, several attributes of the space change all at once, and there are also other shifts in the organisation that influence work performance, such as adopting new technologies or pursuing new business strategies. For these reasons, it's often impossible to accurately estimate or measure how a specific attribute of the physical space affects performance.

Therefore, in workplace design we can get much further with a holistic approach rather than confining ourselves to quantitative analysis alone.[1]

This doesn't mean that we can't learn from science when designing a workspace; it is in fact a potent resource, and whenever possible, we should choose design solutions that are supported by evidence and deliver predictable results. Nevertheless, the limitations of science doesn't need to limit our ability to create thriving work environments. Where science stops, we can carry on using other information sources, such as case studies, building modelling, experiments, user input (conversations with your team members, clients and partners), as well as common sense and intuition. There is an appropriate place for using all of these.

Bridging the gap

Bridging the gap between workspace design and performance (for example, working out how the colour of the break space will improve staff retention) is a real challenge when you try doing this in one step.

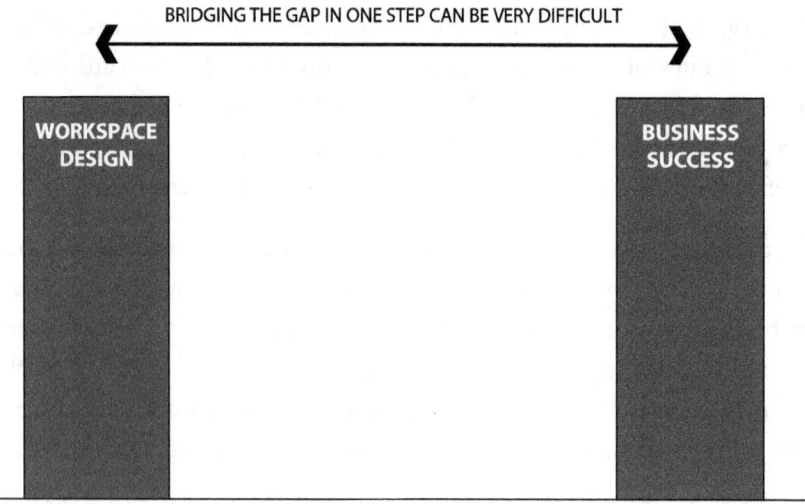

---

[1] The way I see it, workspace design is similar to what we call 'wicked problems'. A wicked problem is a unique and complex issue presenting many uncertainties and conflicting interests. There is no agreed path towards its resolution, and the ideal outcome is often debated. This kind of problem usually cannot be solved with a purely analytical approach – which is how science operates, expecting practitioners to research, plan, measure and evaluate every step. The solution will more likely arise from guided conversations with all involved, exploring all facets of the issue.

You're more likely to succeed if you break it down into smaller chunks, and then work backwards, starting with the end in mind.

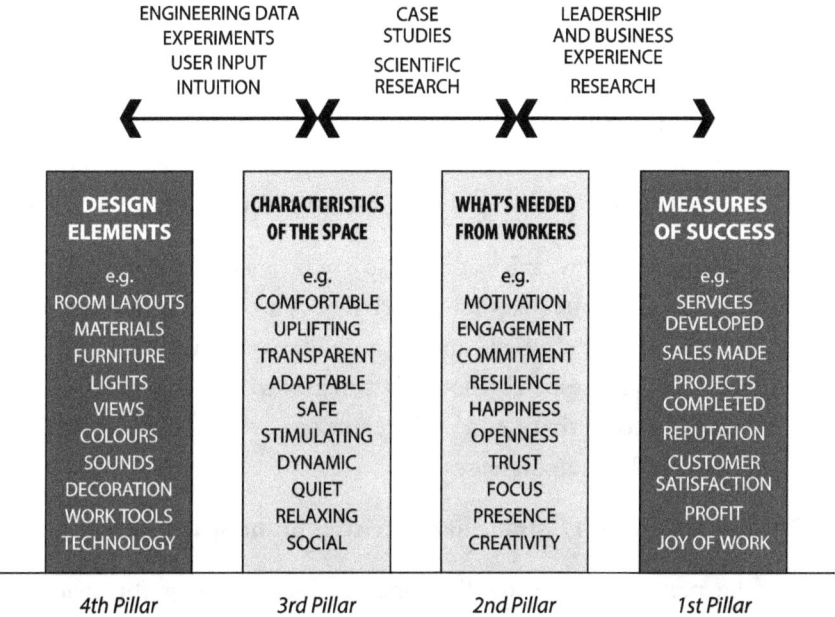

Here is how to apply this model in practice:

1. **The 1st pillar: Your goals and measures of success**

    First, you need to be clear about what success means to your organisation. What are your main priorities? Which of the core principles discussed in this book are the most important to your business? What are the key performance objectives? (These could be, for example, the number and quality of ideas generated by your team, services developed, sales made, projects completed, and team members or clients retained. Also, the reputation of your business and brand, customer satisfaction, profit generated, and the amount of joy people find in their work.)

    Information sources: **You and your leadership team** are probably the most qualified to answer these questions.

2. **The 2nd pillar: What is needed from your people**

   Then you need to work out what your team members will need to do, and what skills, behaviours and attitudes they will need to demonstrate in order to produce the results your business is after. (Think about motivation, engagement, commitment, resilience, intelligence, adaptability, happiness, openness, trust and work ethic. Some of the preferred qualities will vary depending on the work activity; for example, at times people may need to be focused, present and independent, and at other times more creative, contemplative or social.)

   Information sources: Most of these can be answered in-house, based on **your and your people's experience** of working in the organisation. **Research studies** can also provide you with useful insights. (For example, research shows that increased engagement and trust improve productivity and staff retention, or that happiness in the workplace leads to higher sales.)

3. **The 3rd pillar: Desired characteristics of the space**

   The next step is to identify what characteristics of the space can support the different work activities and promote skills, behaviours and attitudes you would like to see. To do this well, you need to think through what difficulties your people will need to overcome, and what qualities need to be embraced by the design. Ask yourself, for example: what in the workplace distracts your people, and what are their sources of stress? What are the sources of motivation and inspiration, and what are the foundations of trust? (Some of the desired characteristics might be: comfortable, uplifting, playful, transparent, adaptable, serene and safe. Some areas may need to be stimulating or low-key, dynamic or quiet, energising or relaxing, social or private, formal or casual, and so on.)

   Information sources: **Case studies** and **research studies** are great resources to identify what sort of environment can best support your people. (For example, research suggests that moderate background noise can boost creative thinking. And case studies show that workers tend to be more empowered in environments characterised by equality and transparency.)

4. The 4th pillar: Design elements and features

Following the first three steps will leave you with a set of clear and relevant design targets, and with this knowledge you will be able to make well-informed decisions about the specific elements of the design. These include: room layouts, materials, furniture and fittings, lights, views, colours, sounds, decoration and props, work tools and technology.

Information sources: For these decisions, you can use **engineering data, tests and experiments** as well as **user input**. (For example, computer daylight modelling can help you optimise your floor layout to provide natural light where it's needed most. Tests and experiments can reveal which furniture configuration is the most effective in a particular space. And your team members can tell you what sort of decoration and furniture style they prefer.)

You can use your common sense and intuition[2] throughout this process, but especially in Step 4, there's no point in overthinking things. You really don't need a manual to work out what makes a space feel playful, relaxing, or socially engaging, for example.

Feel free to engage your creativity! The purpose of following a design framework is not to come up with the ultimate design solution, but to make informed decisions with confidence. There is plenty of scope to be inventive.

Remember, developing your workspace is a journey; it doesn't end when you have 'crossed the bridge', i.e. when the space is ready for you to work in. There's a chance that you will take a few wrong turns along the way. But by creating a flexible space that allows for adjustments during operation, you will have the opportunity to smooth out many of the issues later on that you couldn't address beforehand. Furthermore, you will be able to fit the space to your organisation's changing needs as you go.

---

2 The most successful business owners I know are all comfortable making decisions based on gut feel. They do their best to ensure that they get a good return on investment, but when analysing the benefits is difficult, they just make decisions that resonate with the spirit of their business and that feel right. They know their organisation inside out, and recognise that their innate intelligence is worth trusting.

Talking to the right people

Though workplace design is a huge job, many people can offer you help.

A project team typically involves building professionals such as architects and/or interior designers and engineers. You may choose to engage specialist consultants, for example IT specialists, art consultants, or signage and wayfinding specialists. If your office move or upgrade is triggered by some sort of a transformation within your business, you might already be in contact with innovation, brand, management, or business systems consultants, who can also provide valuable advice about the design of your workspace. Furthermore, it might also be worthwhile to consult with experts from the property sector, such as real estate agents, tenant representatives and facility managers.

And don't underestimate the advice of non-experts.[3] Your team members, clients and partners know your business better than any external consultants, and might be able to offer you insights you haven't considered before. They could bring in a fresh perspective, leading to original ideas and breakthroughs. It might also be worth talking to business owners who have recently relocated or gone through an upgrade. There is a lot you can learn from their experiences, how they handled the process, and what their results were.

Workplace strategists (such as myself) can assist you to pull it all together, as their role is to help you create a workplace that aligns with your business strategy and maximises people's potential. They can assist you with establishing a strategic design brief, guide you through the design and implementation of your fitout, and oversee every step to ensure that your initial objectives are met and properly executed.

Keep in mind that for successful teamwork, members need to pursue a shared vision and maintain focus on the big picture objectives of the project. Whoever you work with, make sure that they are truly on your side – willing to work on your terms and support your priorities.

---

[3] People trained in design tend to have different perceptions of spaces than those who aren't. For example, designers tend to prefer different colours and design styles compared to the general public. So it is important that your workers' preferences are considered; no-one's preference is right or wrong, just different.

Your investment

Creating a thriving work environment involves an investment of significant amounts of time and money, and of course a lot of energy and emotion. Some design strategies take more time to research, decide upon and implement than others, and the costs also vary, so it makes sense to choose those that are best suited to your schedule and resources.

Remember that you don't need a huge budget to create a great quality space. To keep costs low, the key is to ask the right questions, use your resources wisely, explore your options carefully, and make crucial decisions early in the design process. As the design progresses, the costs of making fundamental changes increase exponentially![4]

Nevertheless, always keep things in perspective, and never lose sight of the big picture. Instead of thinking of the space as a cost, think of it as an investment. How long are you going to use the space? What are the anticipated business expenses during this period, such as rent, maintenance costs and wages? What could be the impact of a thriving work environment on your people's performance and experience of work, your company's culture and brand, and the success of your business? And what is at stake if you end up with second-best results?

Benefits

Get the design right, and you will notice improvements in every area of your business. In a nutshell, your team members will work significantly better and with more enthusiasm, and your clients will receive a higher quality service as well as a better experience. Your workplace will attract greater talent and more exciting opportunities, and you will notice improved relationships and collaboration between anyone who comes into contact with

---

[4] Here is a theoretical illustration: The schematic design phase is the best time to make decisions about what type of air-conditioning system to install. Changing this decision during the design development phase might cost you $10 thousand, as parts of the building might need to be redesigned. Changing this decision during construction might cost you $100 thousand, as existing product orders might need to be cancelled, the design and construction teams might need to work around constraints imposed by building elements that cannot be changed, and the construction might be delayed. And once everything has been built, if some building elements need to be ripped out and replaced, it might cost you an additional $1 million.

your organisation. Your space will help increase profits, reduce costs, and elevate the market position of your business.

Your own personal experience will also transform. Not only you will have a more pleasant physical space to work in; you will become surrounded by loyal and caring team members who can't wait to make a difference. You will hear more breakthrough ideas, experience more support, and find work more enjoyable for many years to come.

The future

Nobody really knows what the workplace of the future looks like. Some believe that the whole concept of the workplace will soon disappear altogether, but this seems to be an extremely unlikely scenario. While there is a strong shift in how workplaces function today, their importance is not diminishing.

Workplaces, in general, are becoming more about interaction, collaboration, learning and community support, and less about individual work. As more and more work is done remotely, especially solo work, people have a growing need to be able to come together regularly and connect face-to-face. So I'm convinced that the workspace where team members can meet in person, exchange ideas, nurture relationships and get inspired is here to stay for a long time.

Workplace design strategies are changing fast. The solutions that will help you stay at the top of your game will inevitably be different in a few years' time, but not the core questions you will need to ask that will guide you to the best results. The seven principles discussed in this book will help you to keep these questions in mind, and to focus on what's important: keeping your workplace current, and providing the best environment for your people and your business to thrive even as times change.

Related Readings

Let's Begin

Anthes, E. (2009), *Building around the mind*, Scientific American Mind, 20(2), pp. 52–59, Available from: http://www.scientificamerican.com/article/building-around-the-mind/

At the bottom of the top, Australia and the 2013 Global Innovation Index (2013), The Conversation, Available from: http://theconversation.com/at-the-bottom-of-the-top-australia-and-the-2013-global-innovation-index-16246

Spira, J.B. & Feintuch, J.B. (2005), *The Cost of Not Paying Attention: How Interruptions Impact Knowledge Worker Productivity*, Basex, New York, US.

Steve Vamos speaks at Creative Innovation 2011 (Ci2011), Creative Innovation conference talk, Video available from: https://www.youtube.com/watch?v=iziquAnsPEM

Heerwagen, J. (2008), *Psychosocial Value of Space,* Whole Building Design Guide, Available from: http://www.wbdg.org/resources/psychspace_value.php

Fordred, C. (2007), *Tenant productivity at 500 Collins Street through the roof,* Ecolibrium, November 2007 issue, Available from: http://mail.airah.org.au/downloads/2007-11-F01.pdf

Principle 1: Visionary

Strategy 1: Invite people on an exciting journey

Branson, R. (2013), *Screw Business as Usual,* Virgin Books, London, UK.

Michael Rennie at Ci2012 - "Love, Fear and High Performance" (2012), Creative Innovation conference talk, Video available from: https://www.youtube.com/watch?v=NjBQ3Q4_fwA

Your Fast Start Marketing Report. Prepared for the motivated small business owner By Timbo Reid & Lukeee Moulton – Hosts of Australia's #1 small business marketing show, Available from: http://smallbusinessbigmarketing.com/wp-content/uploads/2011/06/FAST-START-MARKETING-REPORT.pdf

Strategy 4: Stay in harmony with the environment

The Business Case for Green Building (2013), World Green Building Council, Available from: http://www.worldgbc.org/files/1513/6608/0674/Business_Case_For_Green_Building_Report_WEB_2013-04-11.pdf

The Road to 'Green Property' (2011), Davis Langdon, Available from: http://issuu.com/nosetotail/docs/davis_langdon_sustainability_handbook

Hayes, D. (2012), *Green Is Naturally Beautiful*, Arcade, Available from: http://arcadenw.org/article/green-is-naturally-beautiful

Principle 2: Smart

Technology and workplace design

Ryall, J. (2014), *The Australian Workplace of The Future Is Here and It's a Bit Blurry*, Mashable, Available from: http://mashable.com/2014/08/25/the-australian-workplace-of-the-future-is-here-and-its-a-bit-blurry/?utm_medium=feed&utm_source=rss

Life on Demand: How technology is transforming daily life (2014), Ipsos & Microsoft, Australia, Available from: http://az370354.vo.msecnd.net/whitepapers/Life%20On%20Demand%202014.pdf

Design for knowledge management

Chevez, A. & Aznavoorian, L. (2014), *Space as a knowledge management tool*, Work & Place, Published by Occupiers Journal, September 2014 issue, pp. 11-14.

Waber, B., Magnolfi, J., Lindsay, G. (2014), *Workspaces That Move People*, Harvard Business Review: Why We Hate Our Offices, October 2014 issue, pp. 68-77.

Dishman, L. (2014), *Forget what you think you know about the office of the future*, FastCompany, Available from: http://www.fastcompany.com/3035569/the-future-of-work/forget-what-you-think-you-know-about-the-office-of-the-future

Gladwell, M. (2000), *Designs for Working*, The New Yorker, 11 December 2000 issue, pp. 60-70, Available from: http://gladwell.com/designs-for-working/

Allen, T. J. (1977), *Managing the flow of technology: Technology transfer and the dissemination of technological information within the R&D organization*, MIT Press, Cambridge, MA.

Allen Curve, Wikipedia, The Free Encyclopedia, Available from: http://en.wikipedia.org/wiki/Allen_curve

Allen, T. J., Henn, G. W. (2006), *The Organization and Architecture of Innovation: Managing the Flow of Technology*, Butterworth-Heinemann.

Strategy 1: Promote the use of the right work tools

Kim, P., Lee, D., Lee, Y., Huang, C. & Makany, T. (2011), *Collective intelligence ratio: Measurement of real-time multimodal interactions in team projects*, Team Performance Management, Vol. 17, Iss: 1/2, pp. 41-62.

Strategy 3: Create a well-functioning floor layout

2008 Workplace Survey United States – A Design + Performance Report, Gensler, US, Available from: http://www.gensler.com/uploads/documents/2008_Gensler_Workplace_Survey_US_09_30_2009.pdf

2013 U.S. Workplace Survey – Key Findings, Gensler, US, Available from: http://www.gensler.com/uploads/documents/2013_US_Workplace_Survey_07_15_2013.pdf

Strategy 4: Support flexible ways of working

Stewart E. (2011), *Activity based working pushes into Australia*, broadcast by ABC Lateline Business on 25 July 2011, Transcript available from: http://www.abc.net.au/lateline/business/items/201107/s3277714.htm

Strategy 5: Make the most of Activity-Based Working

Shave, M. (2014), *Building's flexibility breaks the office mould*, The Australian, 18 June 2011 issue, Available from: http://www.theaustralian.com.au/business/buildings-flexibility-breaks-the-office-mould/story-fn71714s-1226076698534

Marsden, M. (2011), *Perspective – Corporate Strategy Driving Workplace Design: The changing face of property*, Smith Madden.

The rise of activity based working (2014), Konekt, Available from: www.konekt.com.au/news/newsletters/issue-4/the-rise-of-activity-based-working/

Blundell, L. (2012), *GPT: The business of workplace transformation*, The Fifth Estate, Australia, Available from: http://www.gbca.org.au/uploads/194/34242/5th-Estate-GPT.pdf

Strategy 6: Create 'neighbourhoods'

Dunbar's number, Wikipedia, The Free Encyclopedia, Available from: http://en.wikipedia.org/wiki/Dunbar's_number

A non-traditional workplace: Falkenburg Road Prison

Auriemma, A. (2014), *Why the Best Offices Are Like Jails*, The Wall Street Journal, Available from: http://blogs.wsj.com/atwork/2014/03/28/why-the-best-offices-are-like-jails/

Principle 3: Productive

What productivity is and isn't

Scott Hanselman's Complete List of Productivity Tips (2014), Scott Hanselman, Available from: http://www.hanselman.com/blog/scotthanselmanscompletelistofproductivitytips.aspx

New challenges

Heerwagen, J. (1998), *Design, Productivity and Well Being: What are the Links?*, J.H. Heerwagen & Associates, Seattle, US.

Casey, L. (2013), *Stress and wellbeing in Australia survey 2013*, Australian Psychological Society, Available from: http://www.psychology.org.au/Assets/Files/Stress%20and%20wellbeing%20in%20Australia%20survey%202013.pdf

Smith, F. (2013), *Stress: the new workplace epidemic*, Australian Financial Review, Available from: http://www.afr.com/p/national/stress_the_new_workplace_epidemic_E5MDtPWbXsVuIgxil07CiN

Attention Span Statistics, Statistic Brain, Available from: http://www.statisticbrain.com/attention-span-statistics/

Schumpeter (2011), *Too much information*, The Economist, Available from: http://www.economist.com/node/18895468

Heerwagen, J. (2010), *The Changing Nature of Organizations, Work, and Workplace*, Whole Building Design Guide, Available from: http://www.wbdg.org/resources/chngorgwork.php

Kirsh, D. (2000), *A Few Thoughts on Cognitive Overload*, Intellectica, Vol. 1(30), pp. 19-51, Available from: http://adrenaline.ucsd.edu/kirsh/Articles/Overload/published.html

Some office designs don't help

Open Plan Office Space, The Pros And Cons (2011), Movehut, Available from: http://www.movehut.co.uk/news/open-plan-office-space-the-pros-and-cons-329/

Strategy 2: Make people feel comfortable – not too hot, not too cold

Understanding the stress response (2011), Harvard Health Publications, Available from: http://www.health.harvard.edu/staying-healthy/understanding-the-stress-response

Stress (biology), Wikipedia, The Free Encyclopedia, Available from: http://en.wikipedia.org/wiki/Stress_(biology)

Lang, S. S. (2004), *Study links warm offices to fewer typing errors and higher productivity*, Cornell Chronicle, Available from: http://www.news.cornell.edu/stories/2004/10/warm-offices-linked-fewer-typing-errors-higher-productivity

Thermal comfort, Wikipedia, The Free Encyclopedia, Available from: http://en.wikipedia.org/wiki/Thermal_comfort

Langevin, J., Wen, J & Gurian, P. L. (2012), *Relating occupant perceived control and thermal comfort: Statistical analysis on the ASHRAE RP-884 database*, HVAC&R Research, 18:1-2, pp. 179-194.

Roberts, T. (2011), *When designing for comfort, remember perception*, Building Green, Available from: http://www2.buildinggreen.com/blogs/when-designing-comfort-remember-perception

Augustin, S. (2009), 'Seeing: Vital, Focal and Influential', In: *Place Advantage: Applied Psychology for Interior Architecture*, John Wiley & Sons, Hoboken, NJ, US.

Brager, G. S., Paliaga, G. & de Dear, R. (2004), *Operable Windows, Personal Control, and Occupant Comfort*, ASHRAE Transactions, Vol. 110, Part 2, pp. 17-35.

Strategy 3: Provide good quality lighting

Augustin, S. (2009), 'Seeing: Vital, Focal and Influential', In: *Place Advantage: Applied Psychology for Interior Architecture*, John Wiley & Sons, Hoboken, NJ, US.

Hobsetter, D. (2007), *Daylighting and Productivity: A study of the effects of the indoor environment on human function*, The Space Place, Available from: http://www.thespaceplace.net/articles/hobstetter200703.php

Bergland, C. (2013), *Exposure to Natural Light Improves Workplace Performance*, Psychology Today, Available from: https://www.psychologytoday.com/blog/the-athletes-way/201306/exposure-natural-light-improves-workplace-performance

Walerczyk, S. (2012), *Human Centric Lighting*, Architectural SSL (June 2012), pp. 20-26, Available from: http://humancentriclighting.com/wp-content/uploads/2012/07/Stan-Article-SSL1.pdf

Light and Health, Natural Spectrum Lighting, Available from: http://www.nasli.net/en-healthy-lighting

Strategy 4: Minimise distractions and interruptions

Konnikova, M. (2014), *The Open-Office Trap,* The New Yorker, Available from: http://www.newyorker.com/business/currency/the-open-office-trap

Is there such a thing as a "too quiet" office? (2012), Workplace Solutions, Available from: http://workspacesolutions.com/blog/is-there-such-a-thing-as-a-too-quiet-office/

Shellenbarger, S. (2013), *The Biggest Office Interruptions Are...,* The Wall Street Journal, Available from: http://online.wsj.com/articles/SB10001424127887324123004579057212505053076

Strategy 5: Reduce the sources of negative thoughts and emotions

Lee, D., *Employee Stress and Performance,* Human Nature at Work, Available from: http://www.humannatureatwork.com/Workplace-Stress-2.htm

Coward, S. (2007), *The Catch-22 of Open Plan: Social facilitation in the workplace,* Woods Bagot, Australia.

ReClaire, J. (2013), *What Shrinking Offices Mean For Your Business Center,* Officing Today, Available from: http://www.officingtoday.com/2013/08/what-shrinking-offices-mean-for-your-business-center/

Augustin, S. (2009), 'Crowding', In: *Place Advantage: Applied Psychology for Interior Architecture,* John Wiley & Sons, Hoboken, NJ, US.

Strategy 6: Promote good posture, movement and exercise

Robbins, A. (1992), 'Physiology: The Power of Movement', In: *Awaken the Giant Within,* Free Press, New York, US.

Scutti, S. (2014), *Change Your Posture To Improve Your Mood, Memory, And 5 Other Aspects Of Your Life,* Medical Daily, Available from: http://www.medicaldaily.com/change-your-posture-improve-your-mood-memory-and-5-other-aspects-your-life-289724

Giang, V. (2015), *The Surprising and Powerful Links Between Posture and Mood,* FastCompany, Available from: http://www.fastcompany.com/3041688/body-week/the-surprising-and-powerful-links-between-posture-and-mood

Bennett, D. (2012), *Kill Your Desk Chair – and Start Standing,* Bloomberg Business, Available from: http://www.bloomberg.com/bw/articles/2012-06-28/kill-your-desk-chair-and-start-standing

Dishman, L. (2013), *The Truth About Treadmill Desks, Increasing Productivity, and Decreasing Waistlines,* FastCompany, Available from: http://www.fastcompany.com/3020193/work-smart/the-truth-about-treadmill-desks-increasing-productivity-and-decreasing-waistlines

Godshaw, R. (2014), *Hamster Wheel Standing Desk,* Instructables, Available from: http://www.instructables.com/id/Hamster-Wheel-Standing-Desk/

Strategy 7: Encourage productive habits

Konnikova, M. (2014), *The Open-Office Trap,* The New Yorker, Available from: http://www.newyorker.com/business/currency/the-open-office-trap

Achor, S. (2010), 'Principle #6: The 20-Second Rule', In: *The Happiness Advantage: The Seven Principles that Fuel Success and Performance at Work,* Crown Business, New York, US.

Strategy 8: Provide opportunities for quality breaks

Tierney, J. (2011), *Do You Suffer From Decision Fatigue?,* The New York Times, Available from: http://www.nytimes.com/2011/08/21/magazine/do-you-suffer-from-decision-fatigue.html?_r=0

Attention span, Wikipedia, The Free Encyclopedia, Available from: http://en.wikipedia.org/wiki/Attention_span

Augustin, S. (2009), 'Comforting', In: *Place Advantage: Applied Psychology for Interior Architecture,* John Wiley & Sons, Hoboken, NJ, US.

Principle 4: Diversified

Bourke, J., Smith, C., Stockton, H. & Wakefield, N. (2014), *From diversity to inclusion: Move from compliance to diversity as a business strategy,* Global Human Capital Trends 2014: Engaging the 21st century workforce, Deloitte, University Press, pp. 87-93.

Diversity is everywhere

Augustin, S. (2009), 'Applying Place Science', In: *Place Advantage: Applied Psychology for Interior Architecture,* John Wiley & Sons, Hoboken, NJ, US.

Comaford, C. (2012), *Got Inner Peace? 5 Ways To Get It NOW,* Forbes, Available from: http://www.forbes.com/sites/christinecomaford/2012/04/04/got-inner-peace-5-ways-to-get-it-now/

Strategy 1: Press people's 'genius' button

Gladwell, M. (2000), *Designs for Working,* The New Yorker, 11 December 2000 issue, pp. 60-70.

McCoy, J. M. & Evans, G. W. (2002), *The Potential Role of the Physical Environment in Fostering Creativity,* Creativity Research Journal, 14, pp. 409-426.

Reynolds, G. (2011), *How Exercise Benefits the Brain,* The New York Times, Available from: http://well.blogs.nytimes.com/2011/11/30/how-exercise-benefits-the-brain/

Reilly, L. (2013), *Why Do Our Best Ideas Come to Us in the Shower?,* Mental Floss, Available from: http://mentalfloss.com/article/52586/why-do-our-best-ideas-come-us-shower

Kaplan, M. (2012), *Why great ideas come when you aren't trying,* Nature, Available from: http://www.nature.com/news/why-great-ideas-come-when-you-aren-t-trying-1.10678

Science of Daydreaming (2011), Dartmouth Undergraduate Journal of Science, Available from: http://dujs.dartmouth.edu/fall-2010/science-of-daydreaming#.VHGY-GSOHiJ

Bellock, S. (2012), *Why Your Best Ideas Come When You Least Expect It,* Psychology Today, Available from: www.psychologytoday.com/blog/choke/201202/why-your-best-ideas-come-when-you-least-expect-it

English, J. (2013), *The Positive Health Benefits of Negative Ions,* Nutrition Review, Available from: http://nutritionreview.org/2013/04/positive-health-benefits-negative-ions/

Strategy 2: Allow people get into the right 'work mode'

Cleese, J. (1991), *A lecture on Creativity,* Video Arts lecture, Transcript available from: http://genius.com/John-cleese-lecture-on-creativity-annotated

Gasper, K. (2004), *Permission to seek freely? The effect of happy and sad moods on generating old and new ideas,* Creativity Research Journal, 16, pp. 215–29.

How to increase the volume and diversity of your ideas (2014), Inventium, Available from: http://www.inventium.com.au/how-to-increase-the-volume-and-diversity-of-your-ideas/

Strategy 3: Promote the right sort of thinking

Augustin, S. (2009), 'Emotional and Cognitive Responses to Sensory Information', In: *Place Advantage: Applied Psychology for Interior Architecture,* John Wiley & Sons, Hoboken, NJ, US.

Psychological Properties Of Colours, Colour Affects, Available from: http://www.colour-affects.co.uk/psychological-properties-of-colours

Shahid, U. (2014), *6 ways to use colour psychology to your benefit,* The Express Tribune, Available from: http://tribune.com.pk/story/803160/6-ways-to-use-colour-psychology-to-your-benefit/

Jalil, N. A., Yunus, R. M. & Said, N.S. (2012), *Environmental Colour Impact upon Human Behaviour: A Review,* Procedia - Social and Behavioral Sciences, 35, pp. 54-62.

Best 5 Colors That Increase Productivity, Moredays, Available from: http://moredays.com/blog/best-5-colors-that-increase-productivity/

Cannell, M. (2009), *This is Your Brain on Architecture,* FastCompany, Available from: http://www.fastcompany.com/1278814/your-brain-architecture

Research: Too much, too little noise turns off consumers' creativity (2012), News Bureau, University of Illinois, Available from: http://news.illinois.edu/news/12/0514NoiseCreativity_RaviMehta.html

Got a tricky problem to solve? This is where you need to go (2013), Inventium, Available from: http://www.inventium.com.au/got-a-tricky-problem-to-solve-this-is-where-you-need-to-go./

Blue light may fight fatigue around the clock (2014), Science Daily, Available from: http://www.sciencedaily.com/releases/2014/02/140203191841.htm

Strategy 4: Support different types of interaction

Augustin, S. (2009), 'Seat Placement', In: *Place Advantage: Applied Psychology for Interior Architecture,* John Wiley & Sons, Hoboken, NJ, US.

Lehman, S. (2014), *Standing meetings may improve group productivity,* Reuters, Available from: http://www.reuters.com/article/2014/06/20/us-psychology-group-meetings-productivit-idUSKBN0EV29V20140620

Knight, A. P. & Baer, M. (2014), *Get Up, Stand Up: The Effects of a Non-Sedentary Workspace on Information Elaboration and Group Performance,* Social Psychological and Personality Science, Available from: http://spp.sagepub.com/content/5/8/910

Strategy 5: Accommodate different personalities

Oseland, N. A. (2013), *Personality and Preferences for Interaction,* WPU-OP-03, Workplace Unlimited, London, Available from: http://www.workplaceunlimited.com/Personality%20and%20Interaction%20v1.1.pdf

Big Five personality traits, Wikipedia, The Free Encyclopedia, Available from: en.wikipedia.org/wiki/Big_Five_personality_traits

Cain, S. (2013), *Quiet: The power of introverts in a world that can't stop talking*, Broadway Books, New York.

Susan Cain: The power of introverts (2012), TED video, Available from: http://www.ted.com/talks/susan_cain_the_power_of_introverts?language=en

Principle 5: Caring

Living in an era when caring matters

2008 Workplace Survey United States – A Design + Performance Report, Gensler, US, Available from: http://www.gensler.com/uploads/documents/2008_Gensler_Workplace_Survey_US_09_30_2009.pdf

Caring and work performance

Achor, S. (2010), 'The Happiness Advantage at Work', In: *The Happiness Advantage: The Seven Principles that Fuel Success and Performance at Work*, Crown Business, New York, US.

Achor, S. (2011), *The Happiness Dividend*, HBR Blog Network, Available from: https://hbr.org/2011/06/the-happiness-dividend

Spreitzer, G., & Porath C. (2012), *Creating sustainable performance*, Harvard Business Review: The Happiness Factor, January-February 2012 issue, pp. 92-99.

Strategy 1: Create a healthy workplace

Bijlsma, N. (2009), *Sick Building Syndrome Manual*, Australian College of Environmental Studies, Victoria.

Healy et al. (2012), *Reducing prolonged sitting in the workplace – An evidence review: full report*, VicHealth, Victoria.

Strategy 2: Create a pleasant and harmonious space

Augustin, S. (2009), 'Designing with Nature', In: *Place Advantage: Applied Psychology for Interior Architecture*, John Wiley & Sons, Hoboken, NJ, US.

Knight, C. & Haslam, A. (2010), *The Relative Merits of Lean, Enriched, and Empowered Offices: An Experimental Examination of the Impact of Workspace Management – Strategies on Well-Being and Productivity*, University of Exeter, UK.

Unit 10 Neurobiology: Expert Interview Transcripts – Fred Gage, PhD, Annenberg Learner, Available from: http://www.learner.org/courses/biology/units/neuro/experts/gage.html

Strategy 3: Boost positive emotions and happiness

Achor, S. 2010, 'Principle #1: The Happiness Advantage', In: *The Happiness Advantage: The Seven Principles that Fuel Success and Performance at Work*, Crown Business, New York, US.

Strategy 4: Help people to connect with the space

Knight, C. & Haslam, A. (2010), *The Relative Merits of Lean, Enriched, and Empowered Offices: An Experimental Examination of the Impact of Workspace Management – Strategies on Well-Being and Productivity*, University of Exeter, UK.

Strategy 5: Promote caring relationships

Michael Rennie at Ci2012 – "Love, Fear and High Performance" (2012), Creative Innovation conference talk, Video available from, Available from: https://www.youtube.com/watch?v=NjBQ3Q4_fwA

Wu, L. et al. (2009), *Value of Social Network – A Large-Scale Analysis on Network Structure Impact to Financial Revenue of Information Technology Consultants*, MIT Solan School of Management, IBM Research & NYU Stern, US.

Harter, J. K., Schmidt, F. L. & Keyes, C. L. M. (2003), *Well-being In the Workplace and its Relationship to Business Outcomes – A Review of the Gallup Studies*, Flourishing: The Positive Person and the Good Life, Chapter 9, pp. 205-224, American Psychological Association, US.

A non-traditional workplace: ORA Dental Studio

ORA Oral Surgery & Implant Studio – ORA Dental Studio, Clinic Design, The Center for Health Design, Available from: https://www.healthdesign.org/clinic-design/clinic-examples/ora-oral-surgery-implant-studio-ora-dental-studio

Principle 6: Engaging

Why is culture important?

Goffee, R. & Gareth, J. (2013), *Creating the Best Workplace on Earth*, Harvard Business Review, May 2013 issue, Available from: https://hbr.org/2013/05/creating-the-best-workplace-on-earth

Giving everyone the chance to shine – How leading organizations use engagement to drive performance cost-effectively (2010), Hay Group.

The Best Places to Work

The Best Place to Work survey (2013), BRW, Available from: http://www.brw.com.au/p/leadership/the_best_place_to_work_survey_IEjzxUwhPf1SRTaS2DuLxL

Smith, F. (2013), *Best Places to Work list shows software dudes are the 'rock stars' of the job market*, BRW, Available from: http://www.brw.com.au/p/leadership/best_places_rock_work_list_shows_O8aELwWWkvPHRygQsB8bUJ

Hoskins, D. (2014), *Employees Perform Better When They Can Control Their Space*, HBR Blog Network, Available from: https://hbr.org/2014/01/employees-perform-better-when-they-can-control-their-space

Lovrencic, Z. (2011), *What Makes a Great Workplace, Great Place to Work*, Available from: http://www.greatplacetowork.com.au/publications-and-events/blogs-and-news/105-what-makes-a-great-workplace

Strategy 1: Set the foundations for a strong community

Woolsey, K. (2014), *4.5 Minute Wait for Coffee*, +CULTURE, Available from: http://kristinewoolsey.com/wait-for-coffee/

Trust Me! – Exploring the impact of trust in the workplace (2013), a Geyer, Swinburne, University of Technology & Great Place to Work research collaboration, Fertilizer #4, Australia.

Harter, J. K., Schmidt, F. L. & Keyes, C. L. M. (2003), *Well-being In the Workplace and its Relationship to Business Outcomes – A Review of the Gallup Studies*, Flourishing: The Positive Person and the Good Life, American Psychological Association, US, Chapter 9, pp. 205-224.

Strategy 2: Make the workplace open and transparent

Berens, M. J. (2014), *Supportive workplaces: The gift that keeps on giving*, MultiBriefs Exclusive, Available from: http://exclusive.multibriefs.com/content/supportive-workplaces-the-gift-that-keeps-on-giving

Bodin Danielsson, C., Wulff, C. & Westerlund, H. (2013), *Is Perception of Leadership Influenced by Office Environment?*, Journal of Corporate Real Estate, Vol. 15, No. 3/4, pp. 194-212.

Australia's best place to work 2013 – Optiver, the new face of finance (2013), BRW, Available from: http://www.brw.com.au/p/leadership/australia_best_place_finance_work_FoPT7uRhPaTjWNz57JZklM

Strategy 3: Provide a sense of ownership and influence

Lee, D. (2008), *Want More Motivated Employees? Think Autonomy,* HumanNature@Work, Avaiable from: http://www.humannatureatwork.com/articles/management_development/Autonomy.htm

Hoskins, D. (2014), *Employees Perform Better When They Can Control Their Space,* HBR Blog Network, Available from: https://hbr.org/2014/01/employees-perform-better-when-they-can-control-their-space

Pink, D. (2009), *Drive: The Surprising Truth About What Motivates Us,* Riverhead Books, New York, NY, US.

Kaufman, T., Chapman, T. & Allen, J. (2013), *The Effect of Performance Recognition on Employee Engagement,* Cicero, US.

Strategy 4: Let your team play and have fun

Scott, V. (2008), *Corporations that Changed the World; Google,* Google ebook.

Brendan Boyle speaks at Ci2011 – "Design Thinking and the Power of Play" (2011), Creative Innovation conference talk, Video available from: https://www.youtube.com/watch?v=FPkuwQNG93w

Cook, J. (2011), *IDEO: Big Innovation Lives Right on the Edge of Ridiculous Ideas,* 99U, Available from: http://99u.com/articles/7080/IDEO-Big-Innovation-Lives-Right-on-the-Edge-of-Ridiculous-Ideas

Strategy 5: Integrate work and life

Johnson, C. (2014), *Coworking is Awesome, Let's Keep It That Way,* Shareable, Available from: http://www.shareable.net/blog/coworking-is-awesome-lets-keep-it-that-way

Levy, S. (2011), *In the Plex: How Google Thinks, Works and Shapes our Lives,* Simon and Schuster, New York, NY, US.

Wojcicki, S. (2011), *The Eight Pillars of Innovation, Think with Google,* Available from: http://www.thinkwithgoogle.com/articles/8-pillars-of-innovation.html

Tate, R. (2013), *Google Couldn't Kill 20 Percent Time Even if It Wanted To,* Wired, Available from: http://www.wired.com/2013/08/20-percent-time-will-never-die/

A non-traditional workplace: Circus Oz

Fitzsimmons, C. (2014), *Nine tricks business can learn from Circus Oz,* BRW, Available from: http://www.brw.com.au/p/brw-lounge/nine_tricks_business_can_learn_from_Yap97zE1jXqwlAheKHc9dL

Principle 7: Evolving

Pushing the edges: the d.school, Steelcase 360° Magazine, Issue 60, pp. 14-15.

Strategy 1: Bring your people on board

Humphry, J. (2011), *Mess or nest: Do clean desk policies really help us work better?*, SmartCompany, Available from: http://www.smartcompany.com.au/leadership/management/36187-20110927-mess-or-nest-do-clean-desk-policies-really-help-us-work-better.html#

Strategy 2: Create spaces that are easy to change

Tan, D. (2014), *An Office With Just One Table That Is Long Enough To Seat All 125 Employees,* TAXI, Available from: http://designtaxi.com/news/363763/An-Office-With-Just-One-Table-That-Is-Long-Enough-To-Seat-All-125-Employees/

May, M. E. (2013), *How Intelligent Constraints Drive Creativity,* HBR, Available from: hbr.org/2013/01/how-intelligent-constraints-dr/

Strategy 3: Test, evaluate and refine the design as you go

Doorley, S., Witthoft, S. & Hasso Plattner Institute of Design at Stanford University (2012), *Make Space: How to Set the Stage for Creative Collaboration,* John Wiley & Sons, Hoboken, NJ, US.

Strategy 4: Consider people working remotely

2014 Connected World Technology Report, Cisco, Available from: http://www.cisco.com/c/dam/en/us/solutions/collateral/enterprise/connected-world-technology-report/cisco-2014-connected-world-technology-report.pdf

Lister, K. (2010), *Workshifting Benefits: The Bottom Line,* Telework Research Network, Available from: http://www.workshifting.com/downloads/downloads/Workshifting%20Benefits-The%20Bottom%20Line.pdf

Life on Demand: How technology is transforming daily life (2014), Ipsos & Microsoft, Australia, Available from: http://az370354.vo.msecnd.net/whitepapers/Life%20On%20Demand%202014.pdf

Strategy 5: Get ready for coworking

Global Coworking Census: 2013, Deskwanted.

Noble, G. & Krauskopf, B. (2013), *Breaking the Productivity Impasse*, Third Spaces Group, Australia, Available from: http://www.hubaustralia.com/wp-content/uploads/2015/03/FINAL_Breaking-the-Productivity-Impasse-1.pdf

Putting the Pieces Together

You have many resources

Dalmau, T. and Tidemann, J. (2012), *Solving Wicked Problems in the Workplace*, Dalmau Consulting

Wicked Problem, Wikipedia, The Free Encyclopedia, Available from: http://en.wikipedia.org/wiki/Wicked_problem

Note

This list of 'Related Readings' has been developed to provide you with a comprehensive range of reference materials along with additional background information for this book. This list includes a variety of resources, including academic research papers, reports, books, and formal as well as informal articles. Many of these readings can be accessed online. All URLs were retrieved on 9 April 2015; however, it's inevitable that some of these links will stop working over time. Although every effort has been made to select well-founded and credible information sources, the validity of online content, including those that on Wikipedia, cannot be guaranteed. Should you wish to discuss any of the materials referenced here, or seek additional information, please feel free to contact the author.

Acknowledgements

Amantha Imber, Angela Ferguson, Dan Atkins, Inge van der Poel, Maxine Bazeley, Peter Ho, Steve Coster –
thank you for generously sharing your knowledge and inspiring me through your words and your brilliant work.

Andrew Griffiths, Daniel Priestley, Glen Carlson –
thank you for valuable guidance and amazing insights; I couldn't have written this book without you.

Kath Walters –
thank you for showing me how to write better and with more confidence; what I learned from you was transformative.

Bronwyn Reid, Dallas McMillan, Ian Rankine, Kirsty Ognen, Lee Young, Robert Buhrke –
thank you for helping me stay motivated and focused, and for your wonderful support.

Erik Teichmann, Gabor Toth, Mike Lowe, Tamara Protassow –
thank you for helping me formulate my message and refine the manuscript, and for your patience and support.

Bo and Jelena Acimovic –
it's been a pleasure working with you on my book design; you have contagious passion, great taste, brilliant ideas and high standards.

Dr. Jim Skivalidas, Maurice Kiely, Rik Schnabel, Tide Huesser –
you had crucial roles in my journey to become the person and professional I am today, for which I'm most grateful.

All the staff of the Port Elliot Beach House –
thank you for making me feel welcome, and for looking after this beautiful and peaceful place where writing was a breeze.

Finally, I would like to thank everyone who contributed to this book with their insights, knowledge and case studies, and have their names mentioned throughout. This book would not be what it is now without you.

About Anetta Pizag

Through a love of travel and architecture, and noticing her own response to different environments, Anetta has developed a deep interest in how our surroundings affect who we are and what we do. As a design consultant, she is dedicated to harnessing the power of the physical environment: to create workspaces where people can perform to their full potential without work feeling like *work*.

Anetta has wide experience and training in architecture, building engineering, and environmental sustainability. She has achieved formal accreditation in Evidence-Based Design (EBD), the scientific method for designing spaces that support specific human and organisational outcomes. She is a Master of Neuro-Linguistic Programming (NLP), which helps her understand how the environment influences people's emotions, thoughts and actions. She has studied the areas of healthy buildings and effective learning environments, and she is also trained in business leadership and marketing.

With this unique combination of skills and expertise, Anetta knows how to implement design strategies that support the best results for individuals and businesses. Simply put, she understands people, places and performance.

Before specialising in workplace strategy, Anetta worked as an architect and environmental consultant in Europe, New Zealand and Australia for over a decade. She has seen hundreds of different workplaces, some of which were brilliantly designed. However, she realised that the majority of workplaces are disengaging and unpleasant, and conform to an old idea of an 'office' that is no longer relevant today as business and technology evolve.

While researching workspace design, Anetta was astounded to find what a huge difference even a small design feature can make in people's work experience and performance, and how often even the simplest opportunities to enhance a workspace are overlooked. This motivated her to grow and share her knowledge about this subject, and to found her workplace strategy and design consultancy, PIZAG – www.pizag.com.au.

PIZAG services clients from a wide range of industries, but what unifies them is their commitment to industry leadership, their passion for making a positive impact through their businesses, and their genuine appreciation and care for their people. In her practice, Anetta works in close collaboration with business owners, managers and space users towards the mission of creating thriving workspaces where businesses and work communities flourish.

Keep in touch

www.createathrivingworkspace.com
info@createathrivingworkspace.com
www.pizag.com.au
anetta@pizag.com.au
+61 414 085 405
LinkedIn: Anetta Pizag
Twitter: @Anetta_Pizag

www.ingramcontent.com/pod-product-compliance
Lightning Source LLC
Chambersburg PA
CBHW052306300426
44110CB00035B/1973